THIS NEARLY WAS MINE
A Journey Through Carlton Country

by
Dr. Barbara Castleberry Carlton

with
Barbara Harding Oehlbeck

The late John Groth, long time friend of Albert and Barbara Carlton, sketched this illustration for one of the family's celebrations.

John Groth was equal parts globetrotter, ladies man, and spinner of fantastic tales. But, above all, he was an artist.

THIS NEARLY WAS MINE
A Journey Through Carlton Country

By John Groth

The Little White House

Kate Reichart 2005

This is in special recognition to John Groth, Artist (deceased); Kate Reichart, Artist and also to: Edward Fox and Wes Marston, Photographers; Dale Conyers, Typesetter/Graphic Designer; Spessard Stone, Historian; Victor Milt, Artist; Joyce Hunter, Secretary/Girl Friday, computer guru, chef, professional shopper, dining/party designer, seamstress, handy person perfecto! And Merilyn Albritton Strickland, proof reader.

Last and not least, my dear, gracious new-found friend and co-author, Barbara Oehlbeck.

THIS NEARLY WAS MINE

A Journey Through Carlton Country

by

Dr. Barbara Castleberry Carlton

with

Barbara Oehlbeck

I have held many things in my hands, and have lost them all.
But whatever I have placed in God's hands, that I still possess.

- Martin Luther/Corrie Ten Boome

ISBN: 978-0-8200-0000-8

Published by:
Carlton Bar A Ranch
3587 W. Main Street
PO Box 1088
Wauchula, Florida 33873
Phone: (863) 773-6341
spelham@4cpartners.com

In Collaboration with:
Great Outdoors Publishing Company
An Imprint of Finney Company
8075 215th Street West
Lakeville, Minnesota 55044
Phone: (800) 869-6609
www.floridabooks.com

A̅ A̅ A̅

Be anxious for nothing,
but in everything by prayer
and supplication with thanksgiving,
let your requests be made known to God.
-Philippians 4:6

1 3 5 7 9 10 8 6 4 2
Printed in the United States of America

CONTENTS

PART ONE

PART TWO

PART THREE

PART SEVEN CONTINUED

PART EIGHT

PART NINE
Epilogue

$$\overline{A}\ \overline{A}\ \overline{A}$$

There are inevitably some duplications of events in this book which serve to corroborate the authenticity of the various stories.

THE CARLTONS

An historical biography can be that of many contributing voices that paint the picture – the kin of family and friends, employees or even some whose paths have crossed if only briefly. These voices see and hear and understand differently, variously adding shades of color and detail to the overall image from the outside, or views from the sidelines and insides. Some of these views are expressed by those who have worked for the Carltons and lived in Hardee County, Florida and surrounding areas for more than half their lives. There are those who have come, and gone, and eventually, some who have found their way back again.

This Nearly Was Mine is truly an historical biography – not of just one person but rather the Carltons whose lives have spanned several generations, as well as the vast land that provided the inspiration and resulting drive and determination for all that has come about since the beginning of the early years when the first Carlton came to this land over a century and half ago. These lives of these generations, their unrelenting activities and the land cannot be separated or held apart one from the other. They are bonded together inexplicably, much as a closely knit family that lives in harmony with each other through good times and bad times, successes and failure, through agonizing storms of change and traumatic challenges never imagined or dreamed of from one generation to the next.

The thoughts, opinions, and observations of those who have "spoken" on these pages have not been taken from, added to, or enhanced. The "voices" span the range of beliefs and philosophy, some fluent and educated, even poetic, some self-taught while others have "spoken" with language as wild and rough as the land and woods once were.

Some are quiet and unassuming while other voices are eloquently articulate. These many "voices" variously speak of devotion for the land, for creatures of forest and field, stream and slough, for cattle and crops, for clouds and rain, wind and spaceless sky. They speak of abiding love and dedication for those who have claimed the hallowed acres of Hardee County, Florida and environs which once upon a time was Manatee County, Florida and then DeSoto County, Florida until it was divided into now Hardee, Highlands, Glades, Charlotte and DeSoto, back in 1921.

This book had not progressed far down the writing road when it became apparent that no amount of third-person writing could realistically paint the pictures of the Carltons and their years of endeavors with the land as vividly as those who are now living it, and some who personally knew those who have passed on.

Oral history is the spoken word. The only way we can preserve the soul of oral history for those who will come after us, is by preserving in writing the spoken word of those who have lived the times and the events.

It is not for the writer to enhance or diminish these voices, but rather to faithfully uphold the authenticity and straightforwardness of the speaker who has voiced and lived these experiences of his life.

Some who have contributed to this work are highly educated, others are somewhat less and still others are without any formal book-learning.

Nevertheless, the latter have acquired an extensive knowledge on their own without benefit of schools and teachers and are extremely well self-educated people.

In each case a broad effort is sustained throughout to learn and respect their language, the dialect, as he or she has spoken... "scars and all." Had these pieces been rewritten to grammatical, punctuation and pronunciation perfection, not only the personality but the essence of the person would have been lost, as well as an integral part of the Carlton Country story.

An unrelenting determination has been made to honor the flavor and personal character of each contributor regardless of status. Otherwise, this book would simply be another colorless journal.

Barbara Oehlbeck

LINEAGE
THE CARLTONS

An historical biographical
narrative covering some 200 years...

Until a few years ago history books were generally thought of as those pertaining to wars, discoveries of new lands, and outer space as well as men and women who have become well known for multitudes of reasons... politicians, educators, physicians, scientists, entertainers, authors, explorers and some because they were simply born into prominent families.

There is however, that vast world of family and personal documentary histories which –unlike traditional histories – often reveal the innermost passions and true grit that not only enabled the first settlers to survive but ploughed fields for future generations.

These stories are about the land from which Carlton descendants forged a living – staking their very lives and dreams in the warm earth of early Florida, bringing to light the successes, trials and tribulations of the descendants of those courageous pioneers.

Through the years they became large cattle ranchers and citrus growers, bankers, merchants, doctors, lawyers, artists and a governor. Among those descendants are living examples of some of their tragedies and sheer struggles to survive, continuing travail, accomplishments, and powerful revelations of love and devotion for the legacy of the land.

An anatomical dissection of the Carlton Family would be so revealing you would see the guts and heart, and at the same time appreciate the fervor and spirit that literally flows through the land by hand of the man.

IN THE BEGINNING

This story of the Carlton Family begins with Thomas Carleton, Revolutionary Soldier, and his wife, Martha. They had a son named John Carlton (it was John who dropped the "e" from the name Carleton) who was born April 20, 1775, in Duplin County, North Carolina. John married Nancy Ann Alderman also from Duplin County. They had nine children. Alderman, the third child, was killed in the Indian Wars in 1856. He had married Martha Maria Alderman. John and Martha had 14 children. The first child was Daniel Wilson Carlton who married Sallie Ann Murphy. Daniel and Sallie had 12 children. The third son, Albert, married Martha McEwen and the sixth son, Lewis, married Martha's sister, Mary Ann, daughter of the Rev. William Penn McEwen and Rutha McEwen. Albert (Grandfather Albert) had 10 children, one of which was Carl who had three children. One of these three was Albert, who married Barbara Castleberry. Albert and Barbara had four children. The offspring of these four totals 11.

The direct lineage of Thomas has produced nine generations for a total of 64 descendants.

Dr. Barbara Carlton: *How the Carltons, Hendrys, and Wilsons sorted out their relationships is a medical puzzle because there was so much intermarriage among these three families.*

At the time Grandfather Albert moved his family from the Vandolah house to Azalea Hill on East Bay Street in Wauchula, the ages of his 10 children were:

Ella 34		Carl 23	
Charles 32		Gettis 21	
Thomas 31		Doyle 18	
Albert 28		Leland 15	
Alton 26		Leffie 6	

PROLOGUE

Dr. Barbara Castleberry Carlton:

Born in the heart and soul of Dr. Barbara Castleberry Carlton (Mrs. Albert Carlton) this book covers the lives and loves, the struggles and heartbreaks, achievements and failures and the very living of generations of Carltons as well as some few others whose lives have become entwined with theirs.

"Carlton Country" had its Florida beginnings in Hardee County when Carl S. Carlton married Daisy Platt and began their lives together in the Carlton Homeplace.

Carl and Daisy lived in the original homeplace, The Little White House, built in 1905. Their two daughters, Mattie Mae and Matred, were born there.

Extending for over a century, The Little White House has endured births and deaths, drenching rain and droughts as well as hurricanes.

This book also captures the beauty of life, the seasons including the fragrance of spring citrus blossoms, summer rains, the striking leaves of fall, warm fireside winters.

Through these pages there is also the story of a ranch that supports the roping of calves, shipping of hogs, milking cows, feeding chicks, grinding cane, grubbing orange trees... and playing in the creek. People have lived here and died here and yet they have left an indelible mark for future generations.

I could not help but think of everyday things that these people did not have and wondered how many of them had survived. I kept thinking that the stories of these people who had lived through dire times "making do" just to live, should be preserved for future generations.

Thus the idea of this book to try to capture some of their spirits and courage in the hope that we can more fully appreciate what they did and how they lived, and perhaps even glean an idea or two from them.

Carlton

Castleberry

This book is written, in part, to look back into the intricate and life-threatening struggles of these pioneer families.

They were embedded in Seminole Indian country and faced the frontier trials of mosquitoes, alligators, diseases of all sorts, searing heat and cold, as well as weeks and months of droughts and flooding rains. Yet their will to survive, regardless of conditions, never waned nor wavered. Their dogged determination was to make a better life for their families than the one they had come from.

On these pages you will see how they lived in an extraordinary and personal way from the living testimonies of those who narrated to us in their own words their personal stories.

In documenting the history and capturing the spirits and courage of these people, the story (stories) are handed down to the present and to generations yet to come.

We hope the events told here and shown in pictures will awaken and inspire the interest of those who treasure our heritage and our legacy.

It is not unusual for books, particularly those dealing with many years of history, to be overlapping concerning minor details of certain events. When such overlapping does occur it is due to the fact that characters who are telling the stories or who have lived the stories see and feel events of their times differently, which does not alter the accuracy of the history itself. It simply means that some see events differently in different lights of the times.

The widow of Albert Carlton, Dr. Barbara Castleberry Carlton, has been and continues to be the driving force behind these accomplishments today. Her love for the land, the Carlton land, is unquestioned. Yet she does not lay "claim" to it.

She says, "Through the years the Carltons have acquired acres and acres of these grassy flat lands and hollows, enough for us and the generations to come... that is, if we are careful, if we are diligent and tenacious in caring for and preserving that which has been entrusted to us."

> I have held many things
> in my hands, and have
> lost them all. But
> whatever I have placed in
> God's hands, that
> I still possess.
> - Martin Luther
> Corrie Ten Boome

INTRODUCTION
by
Tom McEwen

Tom McEwen

I am ingrained in a very distant and special way to the Carltons. My great grandfather was the Rev. William Penn McEwen, a Methodist circuit rider in the early 1800s. He married Ruth Sheppard. One issue of this marriage was Martha McEwen who became the bride of Albert Carlton in 1868. This mighty union of Albert and Martha produced 10 children - one daughter and nine sons. This is their life's story as well as their descendants.

In the world of history books, maybe especially in Florida, the list is endless. No one book or even a dozen will tell all you want to know about a given place, people, or events of times gone by, events that formed the culture of this chosen part of Florida. This book is about the people who came here more than 150 years ago, who loved the land, the climate, the location and whose faith in their dreams was steadfast and relentless.

The Land... The Land...

Everything traces to the land, everything begins with the land, everything ends with the land. The water that flows on it and the water that flows beneath it and is supplier of the water of the marvelous aquifer.

Its rivers, its streams and its springs, marshes and beach fronts, everything grows from the land... its palms, the great oaks, the pines, the scrub oaks and the small trees and giant trees, the eucalyptus, its citrus, its mangoes, its banyans.

Everything comes out of the precious land. First, the pioneers came to it and sought to make themselves a complete people from everything that grew in Florida. They ran cattle on it, the cowboys tended them, the wild horses, and wildlife, the Florida panther, great boars, snakes of all kinds, moccasins, rattlers, alligators, birds of beauty, birds of prey and of the food chain and fish of the rivers, lakes, mangroves and the sea on all sides of this grand peninsula called Florida. Flor-i-da, The Land of Flowers.

The Carltons are among the great families of Florida. They were pioneers and are here today; they became very modern people. They did it all. They farmed, fished, hunted, grew citrus and vegetables and pine trees for turpentine. Daniel and Albert Carlton penned the name Carlton on twenty sons. They were very prolific, and boys seemed to be in the Carlton genes.

The result being that the Carltons are related to just about everybody in the Wauchula area of Florida, while other Carltons and Carlton relatives are scattered here and yon throughout the state. However, if you can't claim a kinship of some sort with the Carltons in Hardee County and environs, you're a newcomer.

So, here is the story of the land that became known as Florida and it is the story so very much like other great families who settled the land for themselves and contributed to its future development. For today this versatile territory has come into its own prominence as a Gator Nation.

This story of our Great State and the land is told by two extraordinary women, Dr. Barbara Carlton, my cousin, and Barbara Oehlbeck, who I wish were.

THIS NEARLY WAS MINE

A Journey Through Carlton Country

While this is a history book that delves deeply into the lives of the Carltons in the heartland of Florida, it is also a history of the land and its native inhabitants. Conjointly this is a biographical memoir of the life of Dr. Barbara Castleberry Carlton who borned the idea of the project and tenaciously dug out every historical fact regarding the lives of those who settled this land with love, devotion and determination, and whose descendants have continued to do so for some two hundred years.

PRELUDE

This is the story of a journey through the land that has come to be known as Carlton Country, beginning in the 1800s in the heartland of Central Florida, now Hardee, DeSoto and Manatee Counties.

Dr. Barbara Castleberry Carlton: Although I was born a Castleberry, I became a faithful and dedicated Carlton. Oddly enough, a significant part of this journey begins the year I was born in 1932, the same year that Carl Carlton (father of my future husband) was accidentally killed.

Dr. Barbara Carlton sitting in a comfortable rocker on the porch of the original Carlton-Vandolah home relocated to Cracker Country at Tampa Fairgrounds, reflects on her beginnings as a Carlton.

My life took on an entirely new direction when, in 1958, a telephone call came from Wauchula, Florida, a place I knew little or nothing about. I was asked to go to this small central Florida town to cover for Dr. Miles Collier who was ill. Dr. Collier had a small general hospital doing everything from pediatrics, OB, and general surgery to and including a full time family practice.

At that time I was in my second year of internal medicine at Eugene Talmadge Hospital in Augusta, Georgia. Of course, I responded to the call, traveled south into a land I had been in only once, and actually began my life where I would spend the rest of my days.

And now as I think back, I don't believe I would still be here had it not been for Jeanne Archambault (Dr. Collier's "Girl Friday") who arranged a blind date for me with Albert Carlton the second night I was there. I was told that he was 'the most eligible bachelor in Florida, a cattleman and citrus grower' and that he had women 'falling at his feet' all over Florida and the Southeast and that he was very reluctant to date this woman doctor who had rolled into town.

However, he finally agreed. As for me, I was so tired after staying up all night treating emergencies at the hospital, that I fell asleep on his shoulder while Jeanne and the others who were with us talked. I was told later that this did it for him. He fell madly in love with me, and I found myself falling in love with him.

We were married on June 24, 1959.

Barbara and Albert's wedding reception at the C. J. Carlton home, Bay Street, Wauchula, Florida, 1959.

THIS NEARLY WAS MINE

This title is "borrowed" with respect and admiration for Richard Rodgers and Oscar Hammerstein II, whose *South Pacific*, adapted from *Tales of the South Pacific* by James Michener, opened on Broadway in 1949.

> *One dream in my heart,*
> *One love to be livin' for,*
> *One love to be livin' for*
> *This nearly was mine.*
>
> $\overline{A}$ $\overline{A}$ $\overline{A}$
>
> *Now, now I'm alone,*
> *Still a-dreamin' of paradise,*
> *Still sayin' that paradise,*
> *Once nearly was mine!*

This was the most requested number for my husband, Albert, to play. He was a gifted pianist, playing almost entirely by ear since early childhood. If there was a piano wherever we were, he was at the keyboard.

This was our song. Albert frequently played it on very special evenings in our guest house when there were just the two of us. We had both seen the original Broadway production of *South Pacific* in New York starring Robert Goulet as the soloist in the show on Broadway circa 1960.

DEDICATION

To all my children - Will, Pat, Julie, and Charlie - and to my grandchildren with this note: For each of you, this is required reading.

This is an historical treatise linking the Carlton Family to the beginnings of the rich heritage in our beloved State of Florida.

This book is also dedicated to Lawton Chiles, former Florida Governor and Senator and my Turkey Hunting Friend.

Lawton's Gate at Horse Creek

Dr. Barbara Carlton and the late Governor of Florida, Lawton Chiles (1930-1998).

SPESSARD STONE

And to Spessard Stone who was a true inspiration, contributing to this book in an immensely significant way in his quiet, humble manner. Spessard is an honored, long-time historian of Hardee County who shared his research and his knowledge of the area and its people. He meticulously documented his information of the Carlton Family for this effort. He is the son of Annie Stone who had an intimate relationship with Albert and Martha Carlton and their ten children. His contributions to this book are invaluable and deeply appreciated.

Spessard has authored over 300 articles published in various publications, the last including *South Florida Pioneers*, the *Polk County Historical Quarterly*, the *Sunland Tribune*, and *The Herald-Advocate* of Wauchula. He is the author of *John and Willam Sons of Robert Hendry, Lineage of John Carlton*, and his latest, *Hardee County: Its Heritage and People*, 2007.

Everyone reading this book may find reason(s) to pause in his own life in order to reflect on his family's past history which could energize and inspire their lives today through the stories of yesterday in all sorts of documents... diaries, family notes, newspapers, magazines, letters, even old books in which various notes are often made.

This book injects life into this long lineage of descendants from Thomas Carleton in the 1700s to the now vibrant residual eleven grandchildren who live in the 21st century.

The Carlton journey is woven intricately into a homespun tapestry on life with a continuous thread spanning nine generations. They indeed were surrounded by a rich heritage that was endowed from "On High."

As a mother and grand-mother there is great joy reflected by the lives of the children and grandchildren. A sense of place and duty is the reward of a life lived until it "nearly was mine."

It is my hope and prayer that others will be inspired to write similar books of their own families.

Photo by Victor Milt

Dr. Barbara Carlton

THIS IS HISTORY...
THIS NEARLY WAS MINE
A JOURNEY THROUGH
CARLTON COUNTRY

This is a history book, yet it is much more than just history. It is a lively documentary on the lives of the people who came to Florida seeking a better life... what they did, how they lived, how they worked and played. And importantly, how they fell in love with and became devoted to the land that is Florida. They did not find utopia on a platter, but they did recognize and find opportunity and they fought magnanimously to keep it, enhance it, and preserve it not only for themselves but for their children, and their children and all the generations that would follow. They did not entertain the idea of "going back." While they did not know what the future would hold, they knew what the past held and Florida represented everything they needed to forge ahead, to find a better life than they had left behind. They found beauty and joy in their homes, their work and the land. They helped each other in good times and bad times, sharing work and dreams as they went about their daily lives which included the Indian Wars, wild animals, intense heat and bitter cold as well as disease and hunger.

Yet, they built their houses, forts, churches, schools, roads... whatever they needed to keep going, some of which are still standing today. There being no central government in those first years, there was no such thing as asking for a "hand out" from "on high."

For the most part, these early pioneer settlers were hard-working, thankful people, doing what they had to do to survive, to make their future fruitful and to assure their families that Florida was their promised land,

A number of Carltons in this book are past ninety years old and they, without exception, have extraordinary recall of their lives and what it took not only to survive but to find fulfillment and happiness in so doing. They did not fret over food. They were thankful to have rich soil, water, and a warm climate in which to grow vegetables, fruits and berries as well as woods and forests where they could hunt for meat for their tables. Ponds, lakes, rivers and creeks afforded an abundance of fish the year round. Preserving food was a way of life – canning, sunning, drying, salting and smoking all played a part in assuring these settlers that starvation never knocked on their doors.

And war was no stranger to these early settlers. Since the first Carltons set foot in Florida in the 1800s, they fought and lived through the Third Seminole War. Some of the forts built to protect the families are still in existence.

The language of these first Floridians has been respected – has not been changed.

Herewith are various writings that more or less introduce the historic periods that make up this book for the best part of two centuries.

PART ONE

JOHN CARLTON

John Carlton, son of Thomas and Martha Carleton, was born April 20, 1775, in Duplin County, North Carolina.

It was John who changed the spelling of his surname from Carleton to Carlton, leaving out the "e."

On Nov. 17, 1797 John married Nancy Ann Alderman, daughter of David Alderman, a Revolutionary War soldier, and Jemima (Hall) Alderman in Duplin County. John and Nancy lived in Duplin County until around 1800, at which time they moved to Sampson County, North Carolina.

John Carlton was a farmer. On April 7, 1821, he appointed Alfred Ward of Duplin County as his attorney to collect seven hundred pounds from creditors in both Sampson and Duplin Counties. Thereafter, the family migrated to Bulloch County, Georgia, and then, about 1825, they settled in Thomas County, Georgia. In 1826, John became a member of the first grand jury ever to be appointed in that county with the Superior Court having convened for the first time in June 1826.

The next year, in 1827, John was a member of the grand jury that indicted five Indians for robbery, arson, and murder. It is said that he was one of the first judges of the Inferior Court of Thomas County.

Living on the Ochlockonee River, John owned and operated a sawmill and gristmill, yet he remained a farmer. Living with John and Nancy Ann were the minor orphan children of the Rev. Thomas Carlton... John, Elizabeth Ann, and Thomas A. Carlton. John and Nancy Ann's own nine children were Thomas, Mary, Alderman, Stephen, William, Elizabeth, Lydia, John Wright and Martha Ann.

In 1852 John Carlton sold his property to Robert M. Hendry, his son-in-law, and then relocated in Madison County, Florida. Living with them were the families of John W. and Susan L. Carlton as well as Thomas A. and Elizabeth Carlton.

Nancy Ann Carlton died June 4, 1867, in Madison County. Less than a year later, John Carlton died February 26, 1868, in the same county. They are both buried in Friendship Cemetery near Moseley Hall in the southern part of Madison County. Their funerals were preached by the Rev. John M. Hendry whose text was, "Well done good and faithful servant, enter thou into the joy of the Lord."

The tombstones of John and Nancy Ann Carlton in the Friendship Cemetery near Moseley Hall in southern Madison County.

T. MABRY (JACK) CARLTON

T. Mabry (Jack) Carlton (1901-1991), grandson of Albert Carlton as well as the family historian, relates the following events about the Carlton family. This special commentary is from a personal taping by him at Cracker Country in the 1980s. The following excerpts are from the video. This story begins with Alderman Carlton who migrated to Florida from Georgia and settled in Central Florida in the 1840s.

People don't believe it, but Fort Meade was named for General George Meade. He was highly respected.

Alderman Carlton's homestead was just north of where Fort Meade is now where that Ford place is. His captain was Captain Durrance. Alderman Carlton was killed at the Tillis Farm that's referred to in history so much. He was leading the charge and was killed there. Alderman's son, Daniel Wilson, killed the Indian who killed his father.

Going back to a point that I think has been overlooked, and that was the pioneer woman. Pioneer women were strong components of the developing frontiers in Florida.

One of the early groups, a sister, married John Simmons. We have a Simmons family here in Hillsborough County. And then two of Nana Wilson's sons married two of the Simmons girls. Quite a few of that family are here.

Jack Carlton, local historian, tells about his acquaintance with Billy Osceola, who died a few years ago with a malignancy and was one of the few Indians that accepted Christianity. Most of them went for the Great Spirit and Happy Hunting Ground, but he became a Christian and a minister. He was the great-grandson of the old chief. Of course, he's dead.

I think there should have been more negotiations regarding the Indian wars… plus all of that cruelty that happened at the homesteads… Well, as I understand, there was a movement for Osceola, who was a genius when it comes to jungle warfare. He's the one who planned the Dade massacre up here in Sumter County in 1835. He was to meet with the official for the purpose of discussion. So, he showed up, and they took him into custody and carried him to South Carolina… to Charleston where he died.

I still wonder if war has settled any questions.

My grandfather, Albert Carlton, was Daniel Wilson Carlton's son. He and his brother went to what is known as Fort Hartsuff… in what is now Hardee County. Fort Hartsuff is south of what is now Wauchula. That is what was known as the Hartsuff community with eight homesteaders. He and his brother were one of them but one of the outstanding people at that time was William Penn McEwen who was a Methodist circuit rider. He moved into that fort when the war was over and it was in that fort that Albert Carlton and his wife were married in 1868. She was a McEwen, the daughter of the old circuit rider. The preacher circuit rider would leave his family in the fort. Of course the Indian War was over but they were still in and out. He would go on his route horseback all out and west over in Manatee County from one homestead to another. He died at Nocatee.

Daniel Wilson Carlton took Rev. McEwen over to this old Joshua Creek Cemetery in Arcadia where he's buried. But his wife is buried at Wauchula; her grave is marked.

He was one of the outstanding men in the field of religion. And the closest partner of the Rev. McEwen was the famous Baptist preacher, John Hendry. They worked together, had meetings together. One would accept members for the other and refer them back and that's how close they were. Parson John Hendry is buried at New Zion. He organized the Wauchula church in 1876. My father, Thomas, was born in 1872 during the Reconstruction period. He was Thomas N.

Carlton, son of Albert and Martha McEwen Carlton. He was born on the Vandolah homestead before they built the Azalea Hill house.

See that wooden tub, Albert carved a wooden wash tub for Martha to wash clothes in, that was in 1869, and there was a center to it to begin with. The neighboring women

Rev. William Penn McEwen and his wife Rutha.

The Carlton Vandolah home with Albert, Martha and some of their children. Circa 1890s.

said Martha could wash her clothes here and dry them there and never change the water.

They built a platform about three foot high and filled it with dirt on the side of the log house, that's where she did her cooking. She could cook there and not have to bend over.

Bottom row from left to right: Gettis, Albert, Leland, Martha, Doyle and baby Leffie. Back row from left to right: Alton, Charles, Ab W., Ella, Thomas and Carl. (Picture of Leffie added later.)

It's said that she delivered about fifty percent of the babies because there was no doctor. People said we'd starve to death at the little log cabin but we didn't. We had ample provisions... plenty of sugar cane, plenty of sweet potatoes and corn and all kinds of game on that old homestead.

That spring the Indians would come and camp around it; it had good water and they would trade with my grandfather and grandmother... deer skins and venison for sweet potatoes and syrup. They were friendly; there were no problems.

This is a picture of Albert and Martha Carlton, they had one son born after that picture was made in late 1880s or 1890s. That small boy to the right is Doyle Carlton, Sr., and the small boy on his mother's left is Leland, a surgeon in Tampa for years. He was buried in Tampa. (See photo on page 6)

The rest of the family is buried "down there" at Wauchula.

The tall one there is my father, Tom. He was born in 1872. Tom's sister, Ella Southerland, was born in 1869.

If you notice the house here, there was a room upstairs, a private stairway

The restored Vandolah home built in 1885, as it is today at Cracker Country.

7

they fixed for her (Ella). The boys stayed in the big dormitory room and they went up to their room by stairs on the front porch. There was only one girl, the rest of them were boys. The baby at the bottom is Leffie.

Daniel Wilson Carlton and his wife are buried at Joshua Creek in Arcadia, Florida, Albert's father, my great-grandfather, and this is a generation back. This is Alderman Carlton, the one that was killed at Fort Meade in 1856. He was Daniel Wilson's father and he's the one buried in the city of Fort Meade.

My grandfather Albert was born in 1845 here in Florida. He married Martha McEwen in 1868. They went directly with an ox team to the land they had homesteaded and built a log house near Troublesome Creek. Then in 1884-1885 they built this old house on Vandolah land but by that time most of the children were grown and gone.

It was there that the original seedless orange was developed by accident. Albert Carlton had the first one. It was a tree in the grove from which the boys would start eating the oranges early in the fall... he wondered and went down there and checked on it and found it was seedless. And that's where the seedless oranges came from and they still have some in the grove.

And in that grove we have a grapefruit tree, a huge seedling tree that's over 105 years old. One of my sons found it when he was five years old, and it's there today in perfect condition... right here where the old house was.

GOVERNORSHIP OF DOYLE CARLTON
Florida's Governor from 1929 - 1933

I was in Stetson University when Doyle Elam Carlton was in the race and became governor. Coming from a small town people didn't think he'd stand much of a chance of being governor. I don't like to brag about it, but I think the greatest asset in the world is a man's reputation. If a man's word is no good he is no good.

He, Governor Doyle Carlton, Sr., had a good reputation.

There was an interest that was promoting gambling. They were trying to influence him to endorse gambling, with which he could not agree, saying it would lead to horse racing and legalized gambling and prostitution and he was strongly opposed to those things.

He refused to sign "that" bill. He was offered a tremendous amount of money at that time to sign it. His answer was "if my signature is worth that to you it's worth that to me." That was his answer to the lobbyists that were lobbying. Of course they overruled it and legalized horse racing and that type gambling. It became law after he was out of office. He was opposed to any type of legalized gambling.

I personally don't believe you can build any type of a society on that type of money.

The governor and his wife, Nell, had a wonderful religious background and I think today, with all the trouble we're in, if people would go back to faith in God that our founding fathers had we'd find an answer.

The first thing my father told me when I was about eight years old was: "Son, if you put your knees under my table you're gonna work." And we had a home life there that had a Christian background. Now I think the biggest part of our trouble in America today is the degeneration of the home. We don't have the home life. The mother and the father both work and the children left alone. I think I was fortunate to come along at a time when they would have prayer and Bible reading in the home and not only that we had to work. When I was seventeen years old I was riding what was known as the rough string on the open range. Rough string was a horse that was green or not broke. We were taught to work and to respect our elders and our home life, but since then it has degenerated.

I'm afraid it could lead to many things, that's where all your crime and dope and all that come from. The church and the schools can't do it. It's got to

June 16, 1964. Left, Doyle E. Carlton, Sr. and Albert Carlton

start in the home. Give the child proper teaching in the home, then you've got a foundation.

It should be noted that Florida's 25th governor, Doyle E. Carlton, Sr., of Tampa (1929-1933) served in a most critical peace time period of the state. There were four major disasters: the collapse of the state's four land booms, a violent hurricane, the Mediterrean fruit fly pest, and the National Depression.

ALDERMAN CARLTON

Lt. Alderman Carlton, killed by Indians in 1856

The rich heritage of the Carlton Family began when Alderman Carlton migrated to Florida from Georgia in 1843. At that time Florida was frontier territory. He had married his first cousin, Martha Maria Alderman, and moved to land probably in Alachua County where he was a planter. Later he moved to the Alafia Settlement in Hillsborough County where he volunteered in 1849 to fight with the Florida Mounted Volunteers serving as a fourth sergeant.

A detailed account of Lt. Alderman Carlton's military years is documented by Spessard Stone, historian, who has written an historical perspective titled "A Goodly Heritage" which follows:

The Carltons, in diverse fields from the cattle ranges to governor, have exerted a prominent influence in Florida for over 150 years. This is an overlay of the family.

When Alderman Carlton settled in Florida in January 1843, Florida was a frontier territory. He and his contemporaries would be astonished at how Florida has evolved in the interval into a modern state with its accompanying infrastructure, technology, and tourism. Probably only on the cattle ranches would they readily feel at home.

Alderman Carlton was the scion of a colonial family. Thomas Carleton, his grandfather, was born May 10, 1747. He and his wife, Martha (1751-1797), lived in Duplin County, North Carolina where he rendered service as a private during the Revolutionary War. Thomas died October 3, 1795, in Duplin County. In his will Thomas made mention of prior modest bequests to his daughters, Rachel, Anna, Elizabeth, Lydia, and son, John, with his "dearly beloved wife Martha, all the rest of any property both and stocks of all kinds and negroes her lifetime," except after her death, his sons, Stephen and Thomas, to inherit separate lands.

John Carleton, the third of seven children of Thomas and Martha was born April 20, 1775, in Duplin County, North Carolina, John, as others of the family changed the spelling of his surname to Carlton. In Duplin County on November 17, 1797, John married Nancy Ann Alderman, born November 17, 1775, in Duplin County, daughter of David Alderman, a Revolutionary War soldier and Jemima (Hall) Alderman. John and Nancy lived in Duplin County until about 1800 when they moved to Sampson County, North Carolina. In the early 1820s the family migrated to Bulloch County, Georgia, and then, about 1825 to Thomas County, Georgia. They lived on the Ochlockonee River, where John owned and operated a sawmill and gristmill and farmed. In 1852 John sold his property and relocated to Madison County, Florida. There Nancy Ann Carlton died June 4, 1867, and John Carlton died February 26, 1868. Sales from Carlton's estate which included 120 acres of land and 40 head of stock cattle, realized a modest $1011.30.

George W. Hendry remembered his grandfather for his spiritual, not material, walk in life: "John Carlton resembled greatly old Abraham. I never read of old Abraham, but in my mind's eye I behold my grandfather. He had his family worship mornings and evenings as regularly as the days came and went. I can recall vividly the verbiage of many of his prayers, and can sing many of the songs that I learned when but eight years old at my grandfather's hearthstone as though it was but yesterday... The whole family, from grandfather down, were exemplary Christians, their piety proverbial..."

John and Nancy Ann Carlton had nine children. Alderman Carlton, their third child, was born January 4, 1803, in Sampson County, North Carolina on September 27, 1822, he married his first cousin Martha Maria Alderman, born March 3, 1806, Duplin County, North Carolina, daughter of Daniel and Mary Wilson Alderman. About 1825, Alderman and family moved to Thomas County, Georgia. During the Second Seminole War, Alderman was a member of the companies commanded by Capt. Tucker and Capt. Browning, these companies were raised in August and September 1836; he participated in the Battle of Brushy Creek in Lowndes County, Georgia.

Alderman, under provisions of the Armed Occupation Act of 1842, received 160 acres on May 10, 1843, at Newmansville, Florida permit # 414 for the land, which was probably in Alachua County. Alderman later removed to the Alafia Settlement in Hillsborough County where he was a planter. During the Indian trouble in 1849, he served as fourth sergeant in Capt. John Parker's company, organized July 1849. In 1851 city commissioners of Tampa deeded to L. G. Lesley, Dr. F. Branch, W. B. Hooker, Alderman Carlton and C. A. Ramsey, trustees for the First Methodist Church of Tampa, Lot 3 of Block 14 of the survey of 1847. On July 3, 1852, he registered the following mark & brand: "undersquare and underbit in one ear and undersquare in the other brand."

Alderman, about 1854, moved his family near the Campground Branch on the Fort Meade and Fort Frazier Road. During the Third Seminole War on December 29, 1855, he was mustered into service as a second lieutenant in Capt. Francis M. Dur-

IN MEMORY OF
LT. ALDERMAN CARLTON
LOTT WHIDDEN
WILLIAM PARKER
KILLED
JUNE 14, 1856
AND
ROBERT E. PRINE
GEORGE HOWELL
KILLED
JUNE 16, 1856
AND OTHERS WHO WERE WOUNDED

rance's Company. In the spring of 1856 he was commander of the garrison at Fort Meade and on June 14, 1856 led six men to the defense of the Indian-besieged Willoughby Tillis family. In so doing, he was slain, as were two of his men, William Parker and Lott Whidden, while his son, Daniel W. Carlton, John C. Oats, and John Henry Hollingsworth were wounded. Although wounded, Daniel killed the Indian who had killed his father.

Rev. J. M. Hayman was the administrator of the estate of Alderman Carlton. A partial inventory included in part: 32-year-old Negro woman named Charity, 4-year-old Negro boy named Joe, several houses at Fort Meade, corn mill, crop of corn in the field, 140 head of cattle, 30 head of hogs, 5 head of sheep, 2 yoke of oxen, 1 gray mare, 1 colt, 1 single horse buggy, saddle and bridle, large wagon, lots of books. *The Florida Peninsular of Tampa* dated October 4, 1856, published this notice by J. M. Hayman: "Will be sold to the highest bidder before courthouse in Tampa, on 15th of November next, one negro woman age about 35 years, good house or field hand – also with her, a boy about 5 years old – very smart healthy child—will be sold together, as boy is her child and part of the Estate of Alderman Carlton for benefit of heirs." In July 1859, Hayman gave notice that he was to sell of the estate 161.5 acres in the Alafia area and 160 acres near Fort Meade.

After Alderman's death, Martha Carlton lived in Tampa with her daughter and son-in-law, Martha Jane and J. M. Hayman. On September 1, 1857, she registered her mark and brand: crop half crop in one ear, undersquare & underbit in other-brand "Z." In the fall of 1858 yellow fever broke out in Tampa, and Martha Carlton died from it on December 13, 1858.

Alderman and Martha Carlton had 14 children, Daniel Wilson (1823-91 of Hardee County); (2) Mary Ann (1825-93), Mrs. Timothy Alderman of Ga.); (3) William Thomas (1827-91 of Alachua Co.); (4) Martha Jane (1829-95, Mrs. J. M. Hayman of Bartow); (5) Elizabeth (1831-31); (6) Manerva (1833-42); (7)

Isaac (1835-97 of Hillsborough Co.); (8) Priscilla (1837-1919, Mrs. Eli English of Wauchula); (9) Susannah (1839-78, who married G. H. Johnson and Rev. Robert N. Pylant of Bartow); (10) Missouri (1841-43); (11) Sarah (1844-87, who married Stephen P. Hooker and William C. Hayman of Owens); (12) Georgia Ann (1846-1931), Mrs. Robert A. Carson of Immokalee); (13) Thomas C. (1850-50); (14) Nancy (1851-51).

PIONEER SPIRIT LIVES ON

If the Carlton name denominates the Wauchula area, one reason may be that Great-grandfather Daniel Carlton and his son, Albert, pinned the Carlton name on 20 sons. The result is that the Carltons are related to just about everybody in the Hardee area, while other Carlton relatives are scattered throughout the state. In Wauchula, if you aren't a cousin of the Carltons you're considered a newcomer.

In the Peace River Valley, the Carlton Family goes back to the 1850s when Alderman Carlton came to the Fort Meade. A lieutenant in the mounted volunteers, Lt. Carlton was killed in one of the last entanglements in the wars between the Seminoles and the whites.

Since the end of the Indian wars, the Carltons have prospered. Lt. Alderman Carlton's line has produced a governor of Florida, Doyle Carlton, Sr., and very nearly a second governor, Doyle Carlton, Jr., then a state senator, who ran for governor in 1960 but was defeated in the primaries by Farris Bryant.

Other Carltons have served the state legislature, among them Verle Pope of St. Augustine, a descendant of Alderman Carlton on his mother's side. Justice Vassar Carlton of the Florida Supreme Court also traces his line to Alderman Carlton.

Although wounded so badly in the same battle in which his father died that he eventually became paralyzed, Alderman's son, Daniel, lived to sire 11 sons and a daughter – all hard-working, deeply religious, confident, and possessing more than average intelligence.

When Albert Carlton married Martha McEwen in 1868, he could offer her no more than a log cabin in the woods four miles west of Wauchula. Albert went to work for an uncle who owned a herd of range cattle. As payment for his labor, Albert was permitted to put his own brand on every fifth calf he branded. Slowly he accumulated both cattle and land, which he homesteaded, and on the land he planted citrus. The cattle he ran on the open range.

In 1885 Albert built a two-story house of unusual design which still stands. With a growing family of nine boys and one girl, Albert sealed off an upstairs room that could be reached only by a stairway in the parent's bedroom. Here the daughter, Ella, slept behind a solid wall separating her room from the dormitory arrangement on the second floor for the boys. To reach their room, the boys had to use an outside stairway on the porch.

Albert Carlton, frugal, hard-working, shrewd and foresighted, continued to prosper, and in 1904, he had become affluent enough to open a bank – the Carlton National Bank – in Wauchula. He had also accumulated enough property to give each of his offspring 20 acres of citrus grove land as they married. The result was a family agricultural community dominated by Carlton families.

About 1903, with most of their children grown, Albert and Martha Carlton moved to "Azalea Hill." Which Albert had built after he opened the bank.

Martha McEwen was a unique pioneer woman in her own right. She was the daughter of a Methodist circuit rider preacher and her family was embedded in the center of Seminole Indian territory. She spent time living in the Indian fortress called Fort Hartsuff near Wauchula, Florida.

Martha met Albert Carlton and was married in the fort by the Rev. John W. Hendry. They moved four miles west of Wauchula and built a small log cabin on Troublesome Creek where eight of their 10 children were born by 1885.

Martha's life was that of a pioneer centered around caring for her many small children and washing in a dug-out wooden foot tub. A platform about three feet high was "planted" against the side of the log house where she did most of the cooking. It was well known that most of her babies were delivered by a midwife, there being no doctor available.

Martha Carlton was an accomplished seamstress and quilt maker, as well as one who kept up with the every day mending, a continuing chore.

The Indians were ever present around their log cabin but apparently they had made peace with the Carlton Family there on Troublesome Creek.

Sugarcane, sweet potatoes and corn were plentiful. In addition there was an abundance of wild game on this old homestead. And there were exchanges and trades with the Indians for deer skins and venison.

The family of Albert and Martha grew to 10 in number, thus creating a growing need for a larger home. Therefore, in 1885, a new home was built on Vandolah Road, but Martha's chores escalated from child-rearing into those turbulent teenage times with boys outnumbering nine to one!

Not only was she a mother and housekeeper but she was a pillar in the First Missionary Baptist Church where she was a member for more than sixty years.

She founded the Martha Sunday School Class along with her sister, Mary, who founded the Mary Sunday School Class. Later the two classes merged becoming the Mary-Martha Sunday School Class which still lives and thrives to this day in the First Baptist Church of Wauchula.

Dr. Barbara Carlton is an active member of this church and attends the Mary-Martha Sunday School Class.

Albert and Martha were devout Christians all their lives.

Martha Mary Sunday School Class, 2009. Taken at the Hoss Creek Camp. Front row l to r: Eleanor Hartley, Jo Thompson, Deloris Jo Smith, Jeanne Love, Maurice Albritton, Margaret Maddox (teacher), Betty Binson, Marjorie Harrison, Alberta Weidman, Fay Dickens, Pastor Ken Smith, Joanne Douglas. Back row l to r: Bess Stallings, Doris Lambert, Dr. Barbara Carlton and Shelia McClenithan

First Baptist Church of Wauchula, established 1876

Photo by Edward Fox

Present First Baptist Church of Wauchula, dedicated May 5, 1985

DANIEL WILSON CARLTON

Sallie Ann Murphy Carlton and Daniel Wilson Carlton

The lineage continues with Daniel Wilson Carlton, oldest of the 14 children of Alderman and Martha Carlton. He was born July 2, 1823, in Wilmington, North Carolina. Daniel married Sallie Ann Murphy of North Carolina. They had 12 children.

Their third child was Albert Carlton, born May 9, 1845.

Alderman Carlton, father of Daniel, received from the Armed Occupation Act of 1842 a considerable land grant.

During the third Seminole War, Daniel Wilson Carlton served as a private in Captain Francis M. Durrance's Company, Florida Mounted Volunteers. In the Willoughby Tillis battle June 14, 1856, his father, Alderman, was killed by the Indians and Daniel was wounded.

Captain William B. Hooker recounts the gory battle massacre between the Indians and the mounted volunteers. The best evidence shows that three Indians were killed and seven wounded.

Lt. Alderman Carlton died valiantly as well as Lott Whidden nad William Parker in that battle.

Daniel Carlton survived a wound to his arm, yet he tracked the Indian who had killed his father and killed him.

In September 1856, Daniel enlisted as a private in Captain Leroy G. Lesley's Independent Company, Florida Mounted Volunteers, and was honorably discharged on February 19, 1857, at Fort Brooke. At his enlistment he was later described as being 5 feet 8 inches, with grey eyes, light hair, light complexion, and a farmer by occupation.

In the late 1850s, Daniel Wilson and Sallie Ann and their family resettled in what is now called Troublesome Creek (between present day Wauchula and Ona) and were recorded in the Fort Hartsuff area in the 1860 Manatee County, Florida Census. In 1859 Enoch Daniel, John Parker, and Daniel Carlton were appointed trustees of Manatee County School District No. 3. Daniel was one of an unofficial group, who with a committee, met in April 1866, with the Manatee County commissioners, which voted to move the courthouse to what became Pine Level, the new county seat.

About this time Daniel resettled in Nocatee. A cattleman, he was taxed on 2,100 head of cattle in 1872. In 1873 he was taxed on 2000 cattle, 4 horses and 3 hogs.

Daniel and Sallie were both Baptists and members of the Mt. Moriah Baptist Church. He served as a delegate to the Manatee Baptist Association meeting.

Daniel Wilson Carlton died in Nocatee, April 2, 1891, and was buried in Joshua Creek Cemetery, Arcadia, Florida.

In January, 1902 Sallie Ann applied for a pension as the widow of Daniel, which was approved.

Sallie Ann died April 15, 1905 and was buried in Joshua Creek Cemetery, Arcadia, Florida.

GRANDFATHER
ALBERT CARLTON

The patriarch of the Carlton dynasty was Albert Carlton. He accumulated vast land holdings and pioneered in developing citrus varieties as well as being a devout Christian, banker, businessman and father of nine sons and one daughter.

Albert Carlton and Martha Winfield McEwen-Carlton

Albert Carlton, third child of Daniel Wilson and Sallie Ann (Murphy) Carlton, was born May 9, 1845. According to family sources, he was born in Marion County, Florida, but Albert was unsure of his birthplace. In October 1911, in his Civil War pension application, he cited, "Florida-Alachua or Marion County." With his parents he moved to Hillsborough County, Florida, prior to 1850 and in the late 1850s to Fort Meade, then to Troublesome Creek, DeSoto County, which is now Hardee.

During the Civil War, Albert enlisted at Fort Myers as a private on June 15, 1864 in Company B, Second Florida Cavalry, United States Army. He later stated he only participated in skirmishes. He was mustered out with his company on November 29, 1865 at Tallahassee.

In Manatee County on October 11, 1868, Albert was married to Martha Winfield McEwen by the Rev. John W. Hendry at Fort Hartsuff formerly DeSoto County now Hardee County. Martha was born February 10, 1851, in Washington

County, Georgia, the daughter of Rev. William Penn McEwen and Rutha (Sheppard) McEwen. Albert and Martha homesteaded about four miles west of the area that is now Wauchula on the road now known as Vandolah Road in the present-day Oak Grove community.

An industrious cattleman and early financier, Albert Carlton's mark and brand were "A. C." He originally had 120 acres which he increased to 340 acres with 80 acres being set in oranges. He grazed his cattle on the open range.

Albert and his son, C. J. Carlton, according to the *Florida Times-Union* of July 1902, stated that... "they (Albert and C. J.) have purchased the residence, store and merchandise of B. L. Mitchell and will conduct the business in the future."

Left to right: Seated W. W. Bateman, Carl S. Carlton, standing in front of the vault and Charles Jesse Carlton.

They then opened the Wauchula Hardware Company, corner Main Street and Fifth Avenue. Soon plans were laid for a bank. The *Florida Times-Union* carried notices of its progress, and on July 14, 1903, it reported, "J. Bruyiere architect of Avon Park, is consulting Carlton & Carlton regarding plans for the new bank building." On Jan. 29, 1904, it was noted that "The new bank building will soon be ready for occupation. The bank expects to be ready for business by February 15." On February 21, the paper stated, "Carlton & Carlton have received the vault for their new bank."

March 15, 1904, Wauchula and present-day Hardee County's first bank, Carlton & Carlton Bank, was established in the corner of the Wauchula Hardware Company. Albert Carlton was president, Charles J. Carlton was cashier and Charles A. Roe was assistant cashier.

In 1909 a proper building of sand block was constructed. In 1913, the bank relocated to the Carlton Building on the corner of 5th Avenue. The bank was incorporated as Carlton National Bank February 15, 1915, with Albert as president until his death. The bank failed during the Great Depression in February 1929 but had until then been the area's leading financial institution.

The bank building remained intact until Hurricane Charley destroyed it on August 13, 2004.

Carlton & Carlton Bank, circa 1909

Wauchula - Call of the sandhill crane

25

About 1874, the Fort Hartsuff section had become known as English, named after Eli English who had opened a store about a mile south of the area, and in 1886 was renamed Wauchula from the Mikasuki word meaning "the call of the sandhill crane."

On September 29, 1902, an election was held at the Carlton store, resulting in the incorporation of the Town of Wauchula. An election of town officers followed and those elected were: Thomas G. Wilkerson, mayor; A.G. Smith, William A. Southerland, A. B. Townsend, F. B. Rainey, J. M. Beeson, and Charles J. Carlton, town aldermen; George M. Goolsby, clerk; and A. L. Turner, marshal.

On January 24, 1903, Albert purchased for $1,900 the 31-acre homesite of Eli English at 302 East Bay Street, Wauchula, named "Azalea Hill."

A few details of Albert's plans were featured in the Wauchula column of the Jacksonville paper, the *Florida Times-Union*. On February 2, 1903, it stated, "Albert Carlton contemplates dividing the land he recently purchased from Eli English into small plats and building a number of substantial cottages. This tract of land contains some of the best land in this vicinity and will make desirable houses and profitable truck farms." On May 14, 1903, the paper updated: "Messrs. Albert Carlton and A. G. Smith have the material on the ground to erect a $3,000 residence."

The large two-story Princess Anne residence, built in 1903, was described in January 1990 by Elizabeth C. Underwood in the "Florida Nomination Proposal" for the National Register of Historic Places, which states in part:

"When completed in late 1903, the house stood on a slight hill, surrounded by a white picket fence, one block southeast of Main Street.

"A road led up the hill to the stately two-story home. With its clapboard siding painted glossy white, it stood out against the deep green of orange groves to the east and south. Cows grazed behind a fenced in area to the west.

"Large moss-draped live oaks formed a path from the west porch to the rail-

"Azalea Hill", Residence of Albert Carlton, Wauchula, Florida 1903

The house was constructed of native pine, with most of the material cut and sawed on the Albert Carlton farm at Troublesome Creek, west of Wauchula, and then hauled by ox-teams to the site on Bay Street. It is believed that J. Bruyiere of Avon Park was the architect, with the house being constructed by Joseph L. Bostick, a Wauchula carpenter.

road and across to the east corner of Main Street to the north where Albert Carlton's bank was located.

"A large barn to the south of the house held supplies for the groves and two horses, two stables, cribs, wagons, and a buggy. A garage between the house and barn provided shelter for Albert Carlton's Paige automobile. At a later date, three other houses were built on the property to house workers in the grove and for rental to town people.

"In October 1903, a seedless orange, commonly known as Carlton's Seedless, was found in a 75-year-old tree in Albert's grove of 950 others, west of Wauchula. The orange, classified commercially as "Fancy Golden Bright," was widely distributed by a nursery and became quite well known. The variety is no longer in commercial production."

Albert and family were early advocates of county division of DeSoto County. On March 13, 1907, Albert Carlton, Charles J. Carlton and five others were selected in a mass meeting held in the Wauchula Opera House to push county division before the coming legislative session. The committee, chaired by A. G. Smith, collected

Cattle grazing in ftont of "Azalea Hill" on East Bay Street, Wauchula, Florida.

data and presented it to the legislature. The candidate favoring county division, however, was defeated in the May 19, 1908, election. Not until April 23, 1921, was DeSoto County divided to form the counties of DeSoto, Hardee, Highlands, Glades, and Charlotte. Wauchula, which had been named the temporary county seat, was chosen the permanent county seat of the newly created Hardee County in an election held Dec. 30, 1921.

Ox team pulling a wagon of oranges. From left: Doyle E. Carlton, Sr., Carl S. Carlton, Mr. McLeod, Emory Welch and Albert Carlton, circa 1895.

Albert was a member of New Zion Baptist Church, the oldest Baptist Church in the Orange Blossom Association. The church was originally located (as Maple Branch Baptist Church) north of present-day Fort Green Baptist Church, but in 1873 was relocated by its pastor, Rev. John W. Hendry, to about seven miles west of (now) Ona.

In 1876 Fort Hartsuff Baptist Church was founded with the Rev. John W. Hendry as its first pastor. Its charter members were: Albert Carlton, Lewis Carlton,

Edward F. Bostick, Lodusky McEwen, Zachariah F. McEwen, and Mr. and Mrs. Dennis M. Cason. Martha Carlton was also an early member. As Rev. Hendry, a circuit rider, was often away, the pulpit was frequently filled by Rev. William Penn McEwen, a Methodist circuit rider and father of Martha Carlton. According to Tommy Underwood, church historian, the name of the church was changed in 1887

New Zion Chuch as it appears today.

to Harmony Baptist Church; however, minutes of the Fifth Annual Session of the Manatee Missionary Baptist Association, convened at Mt. Moriah Church (Joshua Creek) on Nov. 12, 1880, show that Harmony Baptist Church, Post Office Fort Green, sent a delegation which had as its church clerk Albert Carlton. In 1889 the church became the First Baptist Church of Wauchula. Albert and Martha were members until death.

On Feb. 25, 1908, Albert Carlton of Wauchula applied for a pension based on his service as a cavalry man in Company B, Second Florida Cavalry. The pension varied monthly and was paid until his death.

The *Tampa Tribune* of May 18, 1924 reported: "Albert Carlton was seventy-nine years young last Friday. On Saturday about one hundred of his relatives and friends gathered together at the old homeplace of the Carltons about four miles west of Wauchula on the Vandolah Road to do him honor and enjoy with him a big birthday dinner prepared by his children.

"Mr. Carlton came to this area during his early married life and spent many years on this place where most of his children were born and raised. Thus it is fitting that he should celebrate the milestones of his life at the old homeplace which holds so many tender associations and pleasant memories for him. All 10 of his children were present.

"Mr. Carlton is one of those of whom it can truly be said that he is seventy-nine years young, for he is as active as many years younger and looks not a day older than he did twenty years ago."

It is ironic that only one year later, Albert Carlton died on Sept. 1, 1925 at the home of his son, Dr. Leland Carlton, in Tampa, Florida. Burial was in the Wauchula Cemetery. Besides his widow, Martha, he was survived by his 10 children, 35 grandchildren, and six great-grandchildren.

Albert and Martha's frame home on Vandolah Road (their second home)

Albert and Martha Carlton's Vandolah Road Home before restoration and relocation to Cracker Country, circa 1970.

was erected in 1885 to replace their original log cabin and was donated in 1979 by the T. Mabry Carlton family to the Florida State Fair Authority, where it became part of Cracker Country.

Under the "Act of May 1, 1920," Martha McEwen Carlton on Aug. 3,1927, applied for a pension as the widow of Albert Carlton of Company B, Second Regiment Florida Cavalry. Under date of July 17, 1928, the widow was granted a pension in her own right at the rate of $30 per month from August 8, 1927 and $40 per month from June 4, 1928.

Martha McEwen Carlton died August 6, 1944 at Wauchula with burial beside Albert in Wauchula Cemetery.

Issue of Albert and Martha (McEwen) Carlton:

1. Ella Louise Carlton, born Sept. 15, 1869; died Feb. 17, 1958; married on June 26, 1894 William Asbury Southerland.

2. Charles Jesse Carlton, born May 10, 1871; died Nov. 14, 1963; married on March 8, 1905 Martha Ann Skipper.

3. Thomas Newton Carlton, born Dec. 27, 1872; died Dec. 8, 1948; married (1) Feb. 28, 1895 Ada Altman, div.; (2) Priscilla Sauls, div.; (3) Oct. 12, 1924 Alice Christiana Mobley Thornhill.

4. Albert William Carlton (known as Ab. W.), born Jan. 17, 1875; died Dec. 10, 1925; married (1) April 30, 1896 Cornelia Catherine Strickland, div.; (2) Louise Claire Barkley.

5. Alton Hudson Carlton, born Feb. 9, 1877; died Jan. 13, 1967; married on April 14, 1898 Mary Vashti Whidden.

6. Carl Simeon Carlton, born Sept. 3, 1880; died Dec. 21, 1932; married (1) Oct. 19, 1904 Daisy Platt; (2) Sept. 1920 Emma Edwards.

7. Gettis Stephen Carlton, born Sept. 2, 1882; died Feb. 18, 1971; married (1) June 28, 1905, Margaret Kate Rainey; (2) Mrs. Bertie M. Head.

8. Doyle Elam Carlton, born July 6, 1885; died Oct. 25, 1972; married on

July 30, 1912 Nell Ray.

     9. Leland Francis Carlton, born Jan. 23, 1888; died June 5, 1950; married on Nov. 23, 1921 Margaret Brown.

     10. Leffie Mahon Carlton, born Feb. 9, 1897; died March 8, 1983; married on May 27, 1917 Odell Imogene Ratliff.

     Great-Grandfather Albert Carlton was typical of the young, ambitious pioneers who homesteaded in the Heartland of Florida in the mid 1800s.

     He settled on 120 acres in the Fort Hartsuff area, about four miles west of what later became the village of Wauchula. Like most of the settlers he used a small portion of the land to build a log cabin with a lean-to cooking shed attached and to plant a garden and a few orange trees. But the majority of acreage he used to enter the major business of the Florida frontier – cattle raising. It was the business which brought prosperity to many of the pioneers but danger and violence, as well.

     Florida was perfect for raising cattle. Large acreage was needed and on the sparsely inhabited peninsula there was plenty of land.

     Cattle had a wilderness of woods and scrub palmettos through which to forage for the wire grass they ate. There was plenty of water. Strays from wild herds of those left by earlier cattlemen were available to the ambitious cowboy to start or add to his own herd.

     But with the wealth that came from the growing industry, came those that wanted to steal it. Joe Akerman, Jr., author of the book, "Florida Cowman," tells the story of cattle conflicts which began in the 1500s when the early Spanish explorers fought with Indian tribes over land and cattle. Violence continued through the Spanish mission ranch period of the 1600s and, following a brief period of calm, reappeared when attacked by British troops and Indian followers of the 1700s disrupted Florida's budding pioneer cattle industry.

In addition to extensive land holdings, Great-Grandfather Albert was deeply involved in the Wauchula Baptist Church taking an active part in the church affairs until his death in 1925.

The baptistry at the First Baptist Church was a gift from Albert Carlton and the Hardee plaque commemorating the gift was salvaged when the church was demolished in 1986-87. The plaque is now housed in the Carl Carlton Homeplace, The Little White House in Oak Grove.

Commerative marble inscription in the First Baptist Church Baptistry in Wauchula which was dismantled in 1987.

In the photo on the right - 1993 Carlton Family Reunion at "Azalea Hill" was attended by many of the descendants of Albert and Martha McEwen Carlton. Back row from the left Scott Saunders, Clay Saunders, Carl Saunders, Beth Saunders Wilson, Carol Carlton, Charlie Carlton and Pat Carlton. Next row from the left Cherise Christian, Mel Christian, Sharon Saunders, Carol Saunders, Lynn Saunders Callahan, Julie Carlton McClelland - holding Sam McClelland, Fletcher McClelland, Dr. Barbara C. Carlton and Will Carlton. Next row from the left Tammy Saunders, Carla Saunders Tinsley, kids Leslie Prescott and Ben Prescott, Kaleb Saunders, Jennifer Saunders, Catelyn Saunders Tinsley, Mattie Mae Carlton Saunders (wheelchair) holding Zack McClelland. To the right Loren Saunders Tinsley, Baylie Christian, Seth Carlton and Kate Carlton.

1933 Rolls Royce Roadster built by Carlton Carriage Co. Back row: L-R, Fletcher McCelland, Pat, Charlie and Will Carlton. Front row: L-R, Julie McClelland and sons, Zack and Sam, Grandma Barbara holding Seth and Katie, Carol Carlton at the 1993 Carlton Reunion.

THE CARLTON'S
VANDOLAH ROAD HOME

Originally located four miles west of Wauchula on Vandolah Road, the boyhood home of Florida's 25th governor, Doyle E. Carlton, as it stands now in Cracker Country Florida State Fairgrounds at Tampa. [1]

This is a village where cultural and architectural history have been preserved and are present in a living, interpretive atmosphere that represents life as it was before the turn of the century. The village is situated almost entirely in the shade of centurion live oaks. The buildings date from 1870 to 1912.

Albert and Martha Carlton's frame home on Vandolah Road (their second home) was erected in 1885 to replace their original log cabin on Troublesome Creek. This second home was donated in 1979 by the T. Mabry Carlton Family to the Florida State Fair Authority, where it became part of Cracker Country.

From the first step onto the porch it's as if time turns back more than a century.

The wide floor boards are solid but squeak with every step, reminiscent of the years of squeaks as the nine Carlton boys scampered back and forth in their growing up years. The entrance door hangs straight and strong from its wide, solid frame. Typical of boys of that age and time they jumped up and down the steps and climbed over the sturdy banisters that surround the porch. Porches were almost always built large and roomy to accommodate "living" as much as possible out of the house to take advantage of Florida's warm, balmy weather

There is an air of unwritten invitation for all those passing by to come in and sit a spell in the comfortable old well-worn rocking chairs.

(1) Much of the information regarding The Carlton Home at Cracker Country is from "Barefoot to Boots," the biography of the Charles William Flint Family and Southwest Florida itself... Like He Told it to Barbara Oehlbeck.

In those days, insulation was virtually unheard of; thus, houses were mostly uncomfortable except in wintertime. Throughout the rooms, there is the lingering spice-scent of heart pine, the ancient wood of which the house is constructed. The pungent fragrance of the old, all wood house is poignantly evident in every room.

Enormous live oaks shade the entire house and yard. Everything is aged and honored.

The Carlton sons were taught to do their share of tasks and chores in making a living for the family. They milked the cows, slopped the hogs, fed chickens, cleaned coops and cared for the horses, oxen and mules. As they grew older and big enough, they helped plough the fields and tend the cattle, crops and hoe the orange trees. It seems as though they were born with the knowledge of fishing and hunting which they never considered work but which added considerably to food for the family. And nearly every large ranch had a smokehouse where meat, poultry and fish were cured. Naturally, it was the Carlton boys who cut the wood and stoked the smoke house fires as well as keeping the wood box filled for the

cook stove, including a huge wood bin on the porch to feed the fireplaces in all the rooms. And always there had to be an adequate supply of kindling. It was a rule of the house that all the fireplaces had to be laid, ready to strike a match just in case of a sudden cold snap. Although sister, Ella, was the oldest, she was no match for the antics

Ella's bedroom at the Vandolah Road Home

of her nine brothers. As a little girl, who had no little girls
to play with, Ella spent most
of her time in the garden with
flowers and learning stitchery
from her mother and aunts
As she grew, she learned but-
ter-churning, baking and the
general art of cooking and
sewing for a large family.
Keeping up with mending
for ten children was a never-

The Parlor at the Vandolah Road Home

ending chore. Her mother, Martha, was an accomplished seamstress and quilt
maker.

Just inside the dog-trot of the Carlton house, the parlor is to the left. It's a
cozy small room with a fireplace opposite the door and windows on either side.
The wall above the fireplace is graced with a splendid formal portrait of Albert

and Martha McEwen Carl-
ton. Two small tables, two
chairs and several pictures
on the wall are the only furniture in the room.

The master bedroom is
across the dog-trot opposite
the living room. It, too, seems
too small for a growing family of that size. It's sparsely
furnished with a four-poster

The boys bedroom

The kitchen at the Vandolah Road Home with the old Raker's Best stove.

bed, a small, plain nightstand, table and a chair.

The kitchen, a medium size room, is off from the dining room. The large cast iron stove, the life-blood of rural country families, is situated on the south wall between two windows. The stove is Raker's Best and has a white enamel warming closet. On the stove top are a large water kettle, frying pans, and a larger stew kettle. Other kitchen furnishings include a cupboard, a coffee mill, butter churner, egg basket and a small marble top work table. On the table there's a pitcher of good, cool milk and buttermilk, just lifted from the well at the corner of the house. Also on the table is a jar of fresh cane syrup made from a recent cane grinding. Cooking for that large, 12-member family all took place in that small kitchen on one stove. The nostalgic fragrance of smoked country ham, hot biscuits and loaves of brown bread just from the oven, glistening with butter, stir up memories too good to miss.

The dining room is off the dog-trot in the back wing of the back of the house. This room is larger than others in the house. The dining table is narrow and will not seat a family of twelve! Other than the table and straight back chairs, the room is without other furnishings. The fireplace is on the north wall.

The boys' bedroom, for all nine of them, is upstairs and can only be reached by way of the narrow staircase on the front porch that leads to their room. The risers of the steps are only 9-10 inches wide making it difficult to go up and down.

The room is very small with hardly adequate space for three standard size beds to accommodate three brothers to a bed. In those days, it was customary to bed down three or even four to a bed. There is no accompanying furniture; however there is a cheery fireplace to warm the room in winter.

In the entire house there is only one closet, a very small one under a narrow, steep staircase leading up to Ella's bedroom. Ella's private access was served by this steep staircase that led directly from her parent's room to hers. Clothes were traditionally kept hanging on the back of a door or in a chiffonier, a high chest of drawers. Ella's room has a twin bed, a small washstand and a chair. Ella and the boys' room were the only rooms on the second floor of the house.

Naturally, there is no bathroom in the house. Night chores were taken care of with chamber pots, while day chores were attended to in the "little house at the end of the garden."

Traditionally, bath time was Saturday night which took place in the kitchen. Water was heated in big pots on the kitchen stove while the "bath tub" was the largest wash tub. The smallest children took turns bathing in the same water. In summer months it was not unusual for the mother of the house to send the children out in a summer shower to bathe with the "command" to... be sure to scrub behind your ears and between your toes! And there was always Troublesome Creek nearby to use for bathing.

There were times in those long-ago days that salt was difficult to come by. Thus it was not unusual for families to have a "salt vat." These vats (iron kettles with legs) were shaped like wash tubs and could hold up to 200 gallons of salt water which was boiled until all the water was gone, leaving dry salt around the edges of the water in the vat and in the bottom.

Keeping a family of 12 in clean clothes was a continuous, trying chore. "Wash" day could be difficult and usually took up a whole day. Early in the morning on wash day, it was the boys who drew the well water, filling the wash tubs near the "boil pot," an iron kettle suspended high enough that a good fire could be kept burning beneath it. Some of the wash pots had legs like the "salt vat," others did not and had to be hung by the handle over the fire.

Down through the generations it's been said that ironing boards were as much a part of the furnishings of the house as the dining table. Ironing clothes for a family of twelve could have taken more than one board! And to keep the ironing from being interrupted, at least two "flat irons" were kept on the stove, one being used while the other was heating. And it was not unusual for extra irons to be heated at the edge of the open fireplace. Often there'd be a small narrow iron that was used for hard-to-get-to places like collars, ruffled sleeves and pleats.

While the house looks quite large from the outside, its rooms are small. However, the porches in front and back are broad and long, and were used extensively taking advantage of Florida's outdoor-living weather.

Of the 10 Carlton children, eight were born in a small log cabin, their first home, on Troublesome Creek. These ten, one daughter and nine sons, were raised in their Vandolah home with only three small bedrooms before Albert Carlton built a spacious new home on East Bay Street in Wauchula. The home was later named "Azalea Hill."

ANNIE HENDRY STONE

Annie Stone with Dr. Barbara Carlton on the porch of the Carl Carlton Homeplace, The Little White House.

This is Annie Stone who is 97 years old – or young! She has lived in Hardee County all her life and she lived out in the New Zion area which was near the Carl Carlton Ranch when he was living and running cattle.

Miss Annie is the daughter of the late Rev. James Madison Hendry, one of his 17 children. She was the baby of all these children and yet her father lived until she was nine years old. She was born August 18th, 1912. She is also the mother of Spessard Stone, historian.

Miss Annie tells about her experiences with those Carlton cowboys and other stories.

Annie Hendry Stone: As a child we used to get in a buggy and go from our house all the way to all the churches back in there where Pa pastored, and Uncle John Hendry is the one that started the church here in Wauchula, the First Baptist Church and he was a preacher and Pa was a preacher, too. There were people who had come to the United States from other countries and they'd come with teams of horses all the way down into Hardee County (then DeSoto County)… some from Alabama, some from Georgia. They all come down and settled in there and then Pa married.

In the New Zion settlement we had services every other Sunday and there's a graveyard there and all of our people are buried there. I think part of Uncle John's bunch is buried at Fort Green cemetery about fifteen miles north of Wauchula. Fort Green is a village with a little store and all that kind of stuff, and they had big groves and big property owners. The Baptist Church is there and Uncle John and Pa both were pastors there.

Anyway, Pa preached there and in little churches all over. He started the church in New Zion, in Bethany and Dry Prairie and all these places around... it was Uncle John and my daddy that started these churches.

Rev. James M. "Boss" Hendry, 1839-1922, was Annie Stone's father. He was known as "Boss" because of his aggressive manner with almost everyone.

New Zion Church

He was a cattleman and merchant and in 1883 "Boss" was the one who gave Arcadia its name, in honor of Arcadia Albritton, a daughter of pioneer settlers who baked him a cake for his birthday. He appreciated it so much he named the city after her

Rev. James M. "Boss" Hendry

I always knew them, Carl Carlton and other Carltons, on account of where we lived we penned the cows. You see, they tromped the land, they'd put the cows in a certain area at night and the cows would put out their fertilizer and tromp it in. And the cows would have their calves and you see we kept the calves of a day and of a night we went all the way to Brushy Creek, us girls did, and run the cows back to the pens and mother would be out there loadin'. When the cows tromped the land a certain length of time they'd take the pens from one place and put 'em in another spot and fence 'em in there. And that's the way we fertilized all of our land. Us three girls penned the cows by foot.

One day, Gettis Carlton was on a horse and he went by a graveyard out from Ona. The gravedigger dug down and he come up there and had to beat that thing off with a whip when it tried to attack him. He'd done scratched

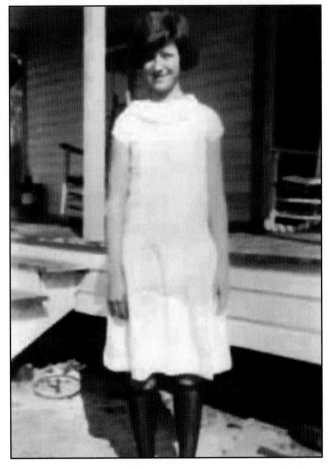

Annie Hendry Stone - circa 1921

through the coffin, we were so amused about it but we was afraid to go that far in so we got the boys to go with us to see. I guess it's still there unless the wind and water done washed over it. It was between Brushy and our place, back in there were Marion Roberts had lots of land. I don't know whether they still use that or not. We had all kinds of experiences. See we went all the way to Brushy and we drove the cows in and kept the calves, then drove the cows into the pens and you had to take up that part, put down posts and put a thing in between there and that's the way it was and you'd just take hold the panels and that would be the next place for tromping.

Pa ploughed and raised rice and done all that stuff right up to the time he died. He was 82 and he still went preachin' and he had a son, Sam, that was a postmaster in South Carolina and the other was in South Carolina that worked on a train from there to Jacksonville.

I went to Oak Grove Church. Ever'body at that time you'd load up on a truck and we'd go to Dry Prairie revivals and go to Oak Grove and just around ever'where. I had the most wonderful childhood you ever seen! I was a member of New Zion Church and was baptized in Horse Creek… on this side of the bridge, that was the baptizing place.

Pa and Uncle John give 50 or 60 acres o' land to the church and the school. And they built a church and they had on one side was like for beginners to the third grade and the other side was to the eighth grade. When I graduated the first time and I was so young me and Bonnie Roberts, we went back and taught a year but we didn't get paid nothin' for it. And then we taught school the second year to help Mr. Roberts. The superintendent was John Rooney and he was the one that was over ever'thing.

The only thing I remember about that awful thing in the Everglades where Carl Carlton was accidentally killed, was that ever'body took it so hard. At that time, ever'body was just like a big family. That family was just like it was my family. That's the way it was all over.

Mr. Marion Roberts, he just had girls, and in school and the Mamas and ever'body was just like family. You carried your dinner to church and you eat dinner at church and ever'thing that went on, ever'body loved ever'body.

I went to work for the Carltons at "Azalea Hill" and worked one summer. I had to fix 'leven dinners ever' day for all of her children. Sometimes we had doctors there, Dr. Leland and then Carl and different ones would come in and I canned stuff, oh, I done ever'thing but the laundry.

If you were a member of a church you weren't supposed to go to a movie, they were a hell-hole. As a preacher's daughter I wasn't allowed to go a movie, and if you did you were ruined.

I stayed with Aunt Martha one summer and when she paid me, I made 50 cents a day, and she took a quarter out for what I paid going to a movie and this was announced in church. So I was shamed! She took the quarter out of my wages for going to that movie.

We knew which calf belonged to which cow… us three girls. We went out and told which one belonged to which cow before it was branded. I had the most wonderful childhood in the world living in New Zion. Always had to work but I didn't mind.

I went through the eighth grade twice. The second year I taught, Bonnie Roberts and myself. Both rooms in the school was full of students. There was all them people there and he couldn't do the whole thing. Me and Bonnie took the examinations ever' term, and then we got through, Mr. Roberts insisted on us going in and taking a teacher's examination. And you know I passed ten of 'em! Then later on when I went back through high school I never even thought of doing that well.

I was going into nursing school in Miami when my mother died, and that was the end of my getting to go to nursing school... I think it was Jackson Memorial.

Doyle Carlton (Governor) bought our place out at New Zion. We had 90 acres and a new house. The house now looks just like it did then. We had all of the timber from the sawmill moved in by our house. They sawed all the timber and cut it up and what we got out of it was enough lumber to build the house. Well, before we got the whole house built and taken care of, the money give out and us kids planed by hand and planed enough for the living room. And that house today looks just like it did when I left it.

And they tell me now that a fence has been put around it... and there's a "For Sale" sign out front. Two different people have told me but I don't know about the "For Sale" sign. It must be that just the part that's fenced is gonna be sold, but we had 90 acres and a grove and a low barn and an old house and got $600 for it. By the time we paid $300 for Ma's funeral... that was it.

Governor Carlton bought it for $600. That was in the last part of 1937 or '36, one or the other I believe. One time Governor Carlton came to the door and asked about buying it. I almost had a nervous breakdown right there! He asked me to forgive him. It nearly scared me to death... I was there by myself... seeing a car coming up of a night and it was so far out in the country and I was by myself.

I loved New Zion and I still do, that was the most wonderful community anybody could ever be raised in. Fish fries, pound parties... you're supposed to take a pound of something to the party, baptizing in Horse Creek right by the bridge on that side. And there was an old fort there down a little ways... last time Jim went in there Pa had a mill in there for grinding rice and all that kind of stuff. He went in there and got some part that he needed a long time ago.

Spessard Stone: *I think it was called Fort Myakka, in fact I asked Canter Brown but he couldn't run it down for me. According to the Robert Roberts' book there was an account of when Robert Roberts married Mary Elizabeth Carlton. He had come down from Marion County after the Civil War. He'd brought his mother with him and she died in December 1877. They said that when they were digging the grave they came across skeletons which apparently had been buried from the time of the Third Seminole War. I've never heard anybody officially pinpoint where that old fort was. There's a little shed behind the church... it's gotta be nearby because that's where the grave was being dug to bury his mother.*

We had an outhouse back towards the McClellan's place. And the men, they just went out in the swamp.

They were running revivals all the time and the women spread blankets on long benches and they put down quilts for the babies to sleep during the service. And the Negroes, they came by the hundreds but they had to stay outside and they had to open the windows, winter or summer, spring or fall, so they could hear.

And Jill and Mrs. Ada Roberts used to shout a lot and we had carbide lights and I was scared to death she was gonna burn her fingers trying to light them while she was shouting. She was a b-i-g woman, she was my half-sister and she'd just shout and jump up and down. Mrs. Ada Roberts was a little bitty woman and she always shouted at ever'thing.

Spessard Stone: *You remember Colonel Moran? Jean Burton made a tape at Joshua Creek Cemetery, they went around to various cemeteries... Rev. McEwen actually died at the residence of Uncle Cab (Robert Calvin Hendry), husband of Nancy McEwen, daughter of Reverend McEwen.*

Alex's daughter lives with one of the Moye's bunch... she has all that stuff we had in our house... clocks and pictures of Uncle Cab and Uncle John and Pa. Alex was my brother and she's got 'em in New Zion. She married Ronnie Moye.

Alex was my brother and he died. He was a preacher. He was married first to Altha Duncan. Altha's age was 'tween me and Bidie. He lied about his age after Pa died and we didn't have nothing left and he went in service. After he'd been in there a certain length of time he turned his age in as seventeen. I mean he turned his age in as eighteen. Well, he finally run away from there, and I've never told nobody this. After he come home, he and Altha got married. He was too young and she was two years older than me. They got the pictures, the Alex bunch did and when Alex died and her mother died, then she has them. Alex and Altha buried a boy at New Zion Church.

I stayed with Aunt Martha McEwen Carlton one whole summer and there was always somebody coming in. And she had a fall… one day she slipped down on a dog that got on the porch and she was chasing him in the rain and the porch was wet and it liked to scared me to death. I called Mr. Charlie and he come. Her head kinda got busted up. She didn't like folks coming 'round in her stuff.

Gettis was upstairs and the whole time I was there I cooked for 12 people ever' day. Dinner. And nobody hardly come because they were all gone, all married but she had me cook just like they were all home. She had a big old wood range with a big old tank that'd hold water to do your dishes and had a table that'd seat that many children. She fixed for 11 whether there were 11 there or not. And I said that's the biggest waste I ever saw and she said no it's not. So we give it to the chickens so it wasn't no waste.

I never was upstairs. Gettis was up there by hisself I don't know about him… there was something wrong with him. He'd come down and eat meals once in a while but ever'body was cooked for. Dr. Leland and Doyle was there some. And I went to a movie one time and she took it out of my pay. I paid a quarter so that day I didn't make but fifty cents. It cost ten or fifteen cents to go to the movie. I saw some of the best westerns you ever saw... they were all like that… Gene Autry and Roy Rogers… Remember how he could talk… he was good. He had a special voice; he went right down to the nitty-gritty of everything.

I loved school. I was gonna be a teacher. I took teacher examinations when I was 14 years old, me and Bonnie Roberts. I passed 10 and failed two. One of 'em was geography and I never heard of the other subject whatever that was.

I say again, I had the most wonderful childhood of anybody in the world.

I took English and arithmetic and geography and physiology and I don't know what all it was, but anyway when I took it, they said it won't do you no good because you're too young to teach. After I finished high school and went back I didn't do nothing… in the sixties. You get out an arithmetic and you have other stuff you're seeing and all of a sudden you don't know arithmetic. And geography, you didn't have that in high school and all that stuff that you have... physiology. I taught but I didn't get paid. I lived on nearly nothing. There was plenty oranges, plenty to eat, plenty berries to pick, and the most wonderful thing was to go cut yourself a big swamp cabbage and at that time ever'body drank coffee. I've always loved coffee. We had a big ole pot and we'd put it on the wood stove and keep it going. And after we got that new house built, boy I was in clover! Then… had to give it away… $600 for the house and 90 acres. This was in the late '30s.

We always had everything growing… collards and cabbage, beans and peas and always Irish potatoes and anytime we could go out and get a swamp cabbage.

Aunt Martha never wanted those boys coming into the house with their dirty feet. So Ella stayed out on the steps of the porch and washed every one of those little boy's feet before they could go in the house. She was really set in her ways. Ever'day for one solid hour I'd have to stop and discuss what we were gonna do. It was unbelievable. It's a wonder she didn't live longer than she did. She was old when she died at 80-some but she was in good condition. She got real buxom and she was heavy at the time when she died.

She was real big on reading the Bible and I can still quote lots of the Bible that she read like this: *The heavens declare the glory of God; the firma-*

ment showeth his handiwork. Day unto day uttereth speech, and night unto night showeth knowledge. (Psalm 19:1-2) *There's no language where their voice is not heard.*

The boys would come at meal time but they didn't eat too much. She'd have everything fixed. This was when Carl and Charlie had the bank… that was a long time ago.

School had started and nobody had no money and the Carlton & Carlton Bank was on the corner and across from there was where you bought your books.

Sabal Palm - Commonly called Cabbage Palm is the State Tree of Florida.

I was standing there wanting a book and I didn't have no money to buy a book with, and at that time you had to furnish your own books. So Newell (her brother, Newell Hendry) come out and he give me a dollar for me to get my books.

While I was there, George Williams, he stopped there in front of the bank and went in with a corn sack. In a few minutes he come out of the bank dragging that sack and drug it up into his car and took off. My mother got a check and see, it was from that check that I thought I'd get some money for my books but the bank didn't give her any money for that check. The money was done gone.

That bank closing was a terrible thing. Ever'body just about starved. It was the first year I was in high school. You see I went through the eighth grade twice, I laid out a year, and then they wanted to run a bus service so Buck Hunt built a homemade bus and he picked up in Castalia and on around. So there all the money was taken up. Whatever it was, it was hard times. I never had a bite to eat from the time I left in the morning… I got up of a morning and lit up old Betsy – the wooden stove – and heated the water to bathe and cook breakfast and I never had a bite to eat during the day, from breakfast to supper, the whole four years I was in high school. Never had a nickel to spend ever. If I did get a nickel it was to buy paper.

It was a great depression. George Williams closed the bank when he got all that money out. The doors closed right then… The Carlton & Carlton Bank, right on the corner.

I lived in the best of times, and saw the worst of times when the banks failed which set off the Great Depression.

ALBERTA CARLTON ALBRITTON

Alberta Carlton Albritton in front of her home on W. Main St., Wauchula

I was born Nov. 1st, 1921, the same year that Hardee County was formed from the old DeSoto County.

I was born in this house at the corner of Vandolah and West 64-A, Wauchula, Floria. I've never lived anywhere else except for a short while when my husband was in the service.

This house is a frame structure built of the timber that stood on this land. It's very hard timber because it was never turpentined, it's real heart pine. It was built in 1900.

My father was Ab Carlton. Albert was his real name, but everyone knew him as Ab. He died in 1925. I have no memory of him as a person because I was so little at that time. He was one of nine boys and one sister of Albert and Martha Carlton.

Daisy Platt Carlton was married to their son, Carl.

All this land around here was Carlton land. As I understand it, my grandfather came out of the Civil War. And the U. S. government said if you would stay on the land for so many years and take care of it they would deed you a Homestead Certificate for it. And the land where this house sits right now is part of the original homestead, and I have the certificate to show that it was an original homestead. This certificate is signed by President Benjamin Harrison in June of 1891. (23rd president of the United States from 1889-1893)

My father, Ab, was born in 1875. He was quite a young man when this was

(4—404.)

THE UNITED STATES OF AMERICA,

To all to whom these presents shall come, Greeting:

Homestead Certificate No. _8694_

APPLICATION _1427_

Whereas There has been deposited in the General Land Office of the United States a Certificate of the Register of the Land Office at _Gainesville, Florida_, whereby it appears that, pursuant to the Act of Congress approved 20th May, 1862, _"To secure Homesteads to actual Settlers on the Public Domain," and the acts supplemental thereto_, the claim of _Willis B. Graves_ has been established and duly consummated, in conformity to law, for the _West half of the North East quarter & Section thirteen in Township Thirty two South of Range twenty two East of Tallahassee Meridian, and Florida containing eighty eight acres_

according to the Official Plat of the survey of the said Land, returned to the General Land Office by the Surveyor General.

Now know ye, That there is, therefore, granted by the United States unto the said _Willis B. Graves_ the tract of Land above described: TO HAVE AND TO HOLD the said tract of Land, with the appurtenances thereof, unto the said _Willis B. Graves_ and to _his_ heirs and assigns forever.

In testimony whereof, I, _Benjamin Harrison_, President of the United States of America, have caused these letters to be made Patent, and the Seal of the General Land Office to be hereunto affixed.

Given under my hand, at the City of Washington, the _twenty fourth_ day of _June_, in the year of our Lord one thousand eight hundred and _ninety two_, and of the Independence of the United States the one hundred and _sixteenth_.

BY THE PRESIDENT: _Benjamin Harrison_

By _M. McKean_, _Secretary._

A. Gibmore, _Recorder of the General Land Office._

Recorded, Vol. _17_, Page _317_

homesteaded. I don't recall how much land you had to homestead to qualify for this.

There's 80 acres in this plot right here where the house is, anyhow I have several first cousins who live right here around us because it was a large family and they all shared a portion of the property so we've just all stayed out here together. All of the ten children, the nine boys and one daughter, all qualified for a homestead plot (acreage under the U. S. Homestead Act).

Grandmother Martha said one time that they were clearing the land and it wasn't a very easy chore, and all that my Granddaddy Albert had in this world was in his wallet in his pocket. And I don't know how much it was, probably not very much money but anyhow he was out there working and he lost that wallet with the money in it and they never found it. That was a trying time.

I remember we lived three miles from town and you didn't go to town every morning just because you felt the urge to go. When you went to town you did all your errands because you wouldn't go back for a few days. The road here in front of the house was really just a wagon trail dirt road and then when Hardee County was made an independent county they paved this road. And that's the reason the road is so close to this house. It was here first long before the road came in.

Once my mother and daddy and we girls (I don't think my sister Peggy was born yet, and I was just a little thing) went to church – it may have been to an all-day sing. Those were really popular in this area a long time ago. My daddy loved to go to them – but my brother Freeman, whom we called Slim, and my cousin Maurice, Uncle Tom's son, stayed home. They were young teenage boys, and were getting their first taste of freedom from their parents' rules. That afternoon, the boys were sitting on the front porch, looking across the road where they could see Slim's little horse, Strawberry, grazing in the pasture. (It wasn't planted as an orange grove at that time.) Slim looked at Maurice and said, "I bet we could get Strawberry to go upstairs," and Maurice agreed. Why they hit upon this idea, I'll never know. Just boys! Well, if you know anything about horses, you know that you can lead one upstairs easily, and that's what they did. They got the horse into the upstairs south bedroom but then they had a problem. They soon found out that horses will go upstairs willingly, but they won't go down for anything. They spent hours coaxing and tugging, pulling and begging Strawberry to go downstairs. Well, Strawberry would not budge, and bless her heart, she was so nervous she made quite a mess in that bedroom. Before long, Maurice and Slim looked out the window and saw Daddy and Mother and the children in the buggy coming back from church! What they did not know, though, was that as he rounded the curve, Daddy looked up and saw Strawberry in the upstairs window. Just in the nick of time, they figured out that if they blindfolded the horse she'd go downstairs. They led her down and back out into the pasture while Daddy was unloading the buggy, putting his horses in the barn, and doing some chores. Then they slipped back upstairs to try to figure out how to clean up the terrible mess before anybody found out about it. Mother came into the house, took off her hat, and didn't say a word. The boys upstairs were quiet as mice then they heard Daddy come in, and they heard Daddy and Mother laughing in their downstairs bedroom. Then without moving from downstairs, Daddy called, "Boys you might want to get that mess up there cleaned up before supper!" They were so grateful not to be punished that they cleaned up that room in record time, and did a perfect job, too.

After my daddy was killed in an automobile accident, Mother was left to raise us children alone. Times were hard, but she managed to keep an immaculate house, and to manage her financial affairs well. She was known for sewing beautifully, and she was the best cook in the world. We were raised on home made yeast bread. She called store-bought bread "wasp nest bread." My daddy's brothers were wonderful to Mother, and they were a great help to her. Uncle Charlie and Aunt Mattie were like a brother and sister, and Uncle Doyle came often to see her. When Uncle Doyle was governor of Florida, he would come back to Wauchula to see his beloved "Ma," my grandmother, and when he came, he never failed to come to see us, too. We loved our uncles dearly.

I remember another thing… my Grandmother Martha who lived at "Azalea Hill"… I don't believe I ever sat at her dining room table that she did not have pickled beets on the table. It was her favorite food and I never remember having a meal at grandmother's without them. And she had a little kumquat tree in the yard and they'd make kumquat marmalade. She had a lady who was her cook and of course all of us little kids, like eight or ten years old, those kumquats were a real temptation to us. We'd go out there when we thought she wasn't looking and we'd snatch a few but then the housekeeper found us out there getting those kumquats and that's another thing you got called on the carpet about… taking those kumquats… they were keeping them for the marmalade.

Oh, I have to tell you this: Grandmother Martha would have her company in her bedroom. She had a formal living room but she didn't go in there. You went in her bedroom and she had a hump-back trunk. The adults would all sit in chairs but the children sat on the hump-back trunk. One day my aunt came in, Aunt Mattie, and Grandmother said to her, "I wish you'd go downtown and get me a new pair of slippers." They called shoes slippers. She said, "OK, I'll go get you some new slippers." So she went out and somebody said, "Well, how do you know how to go get her a pair of slippers? You don't know..." She said, "Well, she tells you she wears a Number Five but I buy her a seven and it fits her fine."

I thought about that the other night and how she always said, "Just get me a Number Five." All those years Aunt Mattie knew she'd never gotten her a size five, it was always a seven.

The house is still there in Wauchula, a big house on the hill which has always been called "Azalea Hill."

My Grandmother was Martha McEwen Carlton.

An interesting thing is my daddy Ab and Uncle Carl and all of them were double cousins because sisters married brothers so they were double first cousins.

In cool weather, Grandmother Martha entertained in her bedroom, but you were never allowed to sit on the bed which was a gold-plated brass bed. It was kept superbly shined. One time a member of the family said, "Grandmother, you just need some new furniture here in your bedroom. I think we need to get rid of that bed and get you some nice matching furniture. She gave the classic answer of all: *would that politicians could do it this well.* She said, "Well, Honey, I appreciate you thinking of me like that but your pa bought me that bed and if he hadn't wanted me to have it he wouldn't have bought it for me, and I will not be gettin' rid of it." End of sentence. Right there. Period. Wasn't that diplomatic!

Well, I tell you what, that lady never mentioned new furniture any more. But I don't know where the brass bed got off to. She had a feather mattress on it and you'd fluff that thing up and keep it smooth, you didn't lean on that bed, you didn't touch that bed because that feather mattress was fixed just right.

I remember Aunt Ella (oldest and only girl of the 10 children). She was raised in the Albert Carlton home on Vandolah Road which had two staircases. This is the old house that's now in Cracker Country. One of the staircases is on the front porch and goes directly up to the boys' room, and the only way you can get to that room is by that one staircase.

The staircase to Aunt Ella's room came directly into her parent's bedroom, the master bedroom.

Aunt Ella had two daughters, Ruth and Louise. Ruth was the principal of the grammar school in Wauchula for years and years. She was an accomplished musician. My middle name is Ruth… I'm named for her but I didn't get any of the music talent that she had. Aunt Ella had two sons. One son, Solon, worked for the *Lakeland Ledger* for years and years. Her other son, Edgar, was killed in

World War II in the Pacific theatre. Ever'body was so upset about his death and it took a long time to get him back home because it happened at the height of the bad fightin'.

Front row left to right: Doyle, Martha, Ella and Charlie. Back row left to right: Tom, Leland, Leffie, Carl and Alton. Photo taken at "Azalea Hill," Wauchula, Florida, Circa 1927.

Grandmother Martha's favorite thing was quilting. She made all kinds of quilts. They would sit on the porch and they'd quilt and talk, quilt and talk. I don't think I ever went there that she didn't have a quilt in the frame... getting ready to quilt it.

I think she spent her days cutting out those little pieces to sew together. It was a nice hobby for her.

I remember that when you went into the dining room, it seemed like a good sized room to me. Well, anyway, there was always a beautiful white cloth on the table. These are things that impress you when you're little...

They cooked on the old wood stove and you'd smell that good cooking when you hit the front door.

We had one department store in town... J. W. Earnest Department Store. And I tell you, if there was anything you wanted or needed and they didn't have it you didn't need it.

The furniture in The Little White House came from J. W. Earnest. It belonged to Polly Wood. They bought it new and were going to throw it away. It was completely refinished and now it's in The Little White House. If you could afford to buy furniture from J. W. Earnest you were pretty up in "G". (This means well-fixed, G. for grand.)

I'll have to talk a little bit about J. W. Earnest. It was a department store. It had a ladies department and there was the men's side. Back then ladies wore hats, ever'where they went they wore hats. And they'd have one whole window in the store decorated with all kinds of fine hats. That was the most fascinating thing you could ever imagine.

The two men who ran it were perfect for each other to be in business because they were so different. There was Mr. Cochrane, who was an older gentleman and quite conservative. He was the bean counter you might say, and then there was Mr. Albert Lane who was much younger, and he was kind of a flashy salesman.

I'll never forget, I was working in there one time at Christmas time wrapping presents, I think, some kind of a little menial job. Well, the clerk in there Miss Sadie Brown, waited on this lady who tried on a dress that was about three sizes too big for her. Sadie stood at her back and said, "Darling, this looks so pretty on you, I really think you need to get this." That lady looked around in that mirror and said, "Well, it does look good on me..." I've often wondered what she thought when she got home. Sadie, standing behind her, had gathered up the "excess" that was too big for her making the front and sides look as if it fit!

I'll tell you what: that lady could sell anything… anything.

The other thing I remember they had in that store was Buster Brown shoes. They had an x-ray machine that you put your foot in to see what your size was… to see if the shoe was correct for your foot. They had Florsheim shoes for men and you had to have a pretty good pocket book to get a pair of Florsheim shoes, and Buster Brown shoes for children.

Now isn't that funny… of all the things in that store these are the things I remember.

They carried nice name brand shoes like Walkover and I doubt many people remember about Walkovers for ladies. The fashion was for the heels to be high.

I'd go by there and think: *my land, how can those women wear those things spiked up under their feet like that*. I still think that today. But the shoes were really pretty.

And talking about that, Cousin Golda Carlton could have the prettiest shoes that you have ever seen. I think she got a new pair every week.

Ruth and Louise never married, neither one. Solon was the only one. Well, Edgar married but it broke up and he never did marry again. Solon had one child, a daughter, who was Aunt Ella's only grandchild. She was a beautiful child. They lived in Lakeland. It was the highlight of the month when Solon and his wife would bring the little girl down to see Aunt Ella.

I have some friends who had been on a big trip abroad. Oh, they'd been to London and they'd been to Paris and they'd been everywhere. They came to see me and I said, "Well, I know you've been here and there and a lot of places but I'm gonna take you to a place you will never forget. OK." So I took them down to "Rooster's" in Zolfo Springs and at "Rooster's" the cowboys come in at noon and their pickup trucks are covered in mud where they've been out cow hunting. They come in with their cowboy boots on and their spurs and their cowboy hats. They sit down and order their meal and they don't take off their cowboy hats. So these folks, they were so fascinated with that that they could not get over it. They just loved it. I said, "Now I know you've been a lot of places and seen a lot of things but this is the heartbeat of America. Now you're seeing what really honestly counts, this is down on the level like it oughta be." They said OK.

So now every time they come they say we don't care what else we do just take us back to "Roosters."

There's a picture on the wall, a framed picture of a big old rooster and in the front of it, instead of glass, there's a piece of chicken wire. "Roosters" closed in 2006. It is now Betsy Ross.

About Uncle Carl, I only remember the day they came to tell us when he had the accident. And I thought: *oh, I hope that's not right... I hope that's not right.* I remember so well standing at the front door and a man came up there, Buck Tillis, and he said, "I've come to bring you some bad news."

Carl Carlton was in the bank and I remember seeing him drive by in his car occasionally but I didn't know him as well as I knew Uncle Tom, his brother. . Uncle Tom was the closet in age to my daddy and I was just a little girl and Uncle Tom was one of those that would drive down the road and nobody would ever want to meet him on the road because he was counting cows and seeing everything along the sides and he never looked at the road. But he came by one day and said, "Let me take Shorty with me, I got to go in here for a little while." It being Uncle Tom, Daddy said, "Sure you can go, let her put on her better looking shoes." So I did and jumped in the car with him. It wouldn't have mattered if Uncle Tom had wanted to take me to Asia I'd a-gone with him. He said, "By the way, Shorty, we're going to this fella's funeral. Have you ever been to a funeral before?" I said, "I don't know that I have." And he replied, "Well, you're going with me and we're on our way."

So I went to that man's funeral and I came home and for years I didn't know who the man was, I honestly didn't and I had no more business at that funeral than nothing! I'd never laid eyes on him but I went to his funeral.

Another thing I remember about Uncle Tom. Now he was a real Florida Cracker. I'll tell you honestly. He come by here one day and told me, "Well, come on I'm going down to the rodeo in Arcadia." I said, "Oh, goody, yeah, uh-hum, yes…" We went down there and there was a lady that was really dressed up for the rodeo. She had on a big straw hat with a big red flower on the front and while we were there at the rodeo a big rain came up and that hat flopped down and that flower melted and it streaked down her face, and Uncle Tom said, "Shorty, looka there… she looks like an Indian."

And that was the day… Uncle Tom knew ever'body and he ran up to this man… all his friends at the rodeo and he'd say, "Oh, come on and have dinner with us. We're going over to Maurice Carlton (Tom Carlton's son) and Isabel and take dinner. You come on over there that's where we'll be." I don't know how many of his friends he invited. Poor Isabel didn't know anybody was comin' but him. She didn't even know I was coming or all of his friends.

All I can remember as we were driving over there was… *poor old Isabel, she doesn't know how many people she's gonna feed.*

Barbara Carlton: *I guess with ten children around and eventually their spouses that you cooked big… you had something cooking all the time. You didn't cook for just six people and let it go at that.*

There's a story that Doyle tells… J. D. Snell, he was a colored man, and he had a bad tooth, he worked for Uncle Alton. Well, let's go over here and check with Uncle Tom, he pulls teeth for horses and cows, maybe he can work on your tooth. So he took him over to Uncle Tom's and took him in the barn and he got out the little tool that he pulled teeth with on the horses. He dipped it down in the water of the horse trough, rinsed it off and said, "Awright, open your mouth." Snell opened his mouth and Uncle Tom pulled that tooth and gave it to him, then washed the tool off again and put it back on the shelf.

The Carlton "Azalea Hill" home as it looks today.

This painting of "Azalea Hill" was done by Elizabeth Cosey Underwood, circa 1980s. She was married to Tommy Underwood, grandson of Alton Carlton. After the death of his grandfather in 1967, the couple lived there for a number of years. The painting now graces the dining room of that home.

Well, I have to tell you how Uncle Alton got "Azalea Hill." Uncle Alton was not a very large man, most of the Carltons were large men but he was the smallest.

He's the one that accidentally shot his brother Carl, and he's the one that ended up with the house on "Azalea Hill." Uncle Alton was a very unassuming little person. The only thing he did was every year he bought a new Chevrolet automobile. I want you to know that they had a brand new Chevrolet automobile every year. He was the cutest little fellow and when Grandmother died they all met up at Grandmother Martha's, settling the estate and seeing what they wanted to do. And the person that would say the least of anything was Uncle Alton. They talked and talked and finally they set a price. And he said, "Well, boys, if it's just the same to you I'd like to have Ma's place and I can write you a check right now." They like to have fainted! And he got it and lived there until he died.

Uncle Alton's wife, Aunt Mary, rooted every one of those big azaleas that are there. And after they moved up there was when she rooted and planted those azaleas herself. And the big ones here under the oak tree, she rooted those, too. She really had a green thumb. She did not name the home, it was later on that it was named "Azalea Hill."

I remember they were setting the orange grove across there on Uncle Alton's place in Oak Grove. And somebody stopped by here and said, "Well, you oughta go over there and see Bruce Odum." I said, "What about Bruce Odum?" That was the man who worked for Uncle Alton. "They're out there settin' that grove and Bruce has put Mr. Alton on his hip and he's carryin' him over there and he's supervising ever' tree that goes in that ground." And Bruce carried Uncle Alton through that whole 40-acre or better grove. There was a love there between Bruce and Uncle Alton that you can't imagine. Uncle Alton had had his leg amputated so he had to be carried around when he'd come out there. I looked at that grove the other day and it's still a beautiful grove.

Merle, my husband, went into the post office and he was quite adamant about the American flag, how it should be displayed and so forth. He was a B-17 airplane pilot in World War II and flew 51 missions, part of them over the Pulaski oil fields. He went in the post office to get flag stamps and the lady said, "We don't have any flag stamps but I can give you chrysanthemums." He said, "Well, I'll tell you right now I think it's a plain disgrace that the United States Post Office and what I fought for and you can't buy a flag stamp in here today. I'm calling my senator today and I'm telling him that somebody needs to come down here and talk to this bunch at this post office." He went on and on, and there was a man waiting in line behind him and he went up to the lady and said, "Do you think that man will really call Washington about not having any flag stamps?" She said, "Knowing him I know he will!" After that he would drive out to Ona to get his flag stamps and they would keep them for him. So after he was gone I needed some flag stamps so I went out there and they said, "Yes, sir, we always keep flag stamps. We never will be without flag stamps because we know what somebody thinks about flag stamps."

So that's the story of him and the flag stamps. And I mean he meant that thing and when I see flag stamps I think of that… and I still go to Ona and buy my stamps.

There was a man who lived around the corner down there… his name was Roy Hodges. Roy was at that age that a lot of young people are… about 16, sometime in 1938 and Roy didn't know anyway to drive his daddy's old car but to push that pedal down to the metal! I mean that thing would come by here smoking and gasping and Roy just a-flyin'! One of the neighbors said, "Well, there's one thing for sure. Roy Hodges won't never be killed in an automobile, the way he drives all the time. He drives so fast he can slide out from under anything that happens to him and he'll never be killed in an automobile. And by George he wasn't. I can just see that car flyin' down that road and that car wasn't in very good shape but boy, he was gettin' all out of it he could.

Have you seen the new signs they've got down in the Castalia community and recently in Lily? They've just put 'em up for the community. I just saw them last week. Just ride along in Castalia community… this is all south of here in the Lily community. This was Indian country then, when they were settling there they were killing the Indians off the land because it's that old. That New Zion Church was founded in 1866 and there was a fort right there on Horse Creek. There were about six forts around here… it was big Indian country. This is where Lt. Alderman Carlton was killed by the Indians in 1856, north of here at the Tillis place. There's a lot of Indian history in this area.

When we went to school, of course, we rode the school bus and I remember that the school bus would pick up the children out there at the county line past New Zion and all back in there. They would get on that bus before seven o'clock in the morning and by the time we got to school in town it was eight o'clock. They were so tired out they didn't know whether they wanted to go to school that day or not.

They had to ride the bus for a good hour, stopping and starting on the whole route. This was the Wauchula grammar and high school in town. 'Specially in the wintertime you'd get on the bus and you ride that bus till eight o'clock and by that time you'd had a pretty good day's work. There were some good kids that came out of there. They stuck with it. That school bus was not a "bluebird" school bus by any means. It was a home-made, hand-made school bus and I'll never forget it as long as I live. It was put on a truck chassis and on either side it had benches that went down the sides… no seats in the middle. They were just little wooden benches and that was the school bus.

I remember the first time we ever got a real school bus… we thought we were up town!

Mr. Will Moore was a native of Zanesville, Ohio, and he had read in the paper that you could make a fortune in Florida in the wintertime growing strawberries.

He had been a coal miner and so that really struck his fancy. They had saved up what they called "Baby Bonds" back in World War I and he cashed in all of those bonds and came down and bought ten acres over 'cross the field from our homestead. Well, they didn't have any children and she had been a school teacher and she was a very cultured lady. She was the librarian in town later. Anyhow, he had read in a book how to grow strawberries and told my daddy, "I'm gonna make a fortune growing strawberries." Daddy said, "Oh… you are Will?" "Yeah," he said, "I've got this book and I've been studyin' it…" Well, I don't know what Daddy told him but he didn't tell him that you learned how to grow strawberries out of a book.

Anyway, then one day he came over and said, "Well, Mr. Carlton, I bought a mule. I know I have to have some help on my field over there. I want you to come over and see my mule." So Daddy went over, and pretty soon, he said, "Will, you've bought a good strong animal but your problem is the mule's blind."

Will didn't take anyone with him to buy the mule. It would be kinda like me going to buy an automobile… I wouldn't know anything about it.

I don't know what disposition they made of the mule but my daddy was so exasperated with Will because… he came down here like I've got the book and I know how to do it and you don't know anything about it, you might have been here all your life but you don't know anything and I go buy a mule and the mule's blind.

They lived over there and what money they brought with them was gone and they had a terrible time. He didn't know how to raise a crop and he didn't have the where-with to do it right and so finally the WPA came along and she got a job. They opened the library and hired ladies to bind all the books and bring the library up to par. And she got a job there and it really saved their lives because they really would not have had food to eat. She worked up there for years and years and they redid all the books in that library and it gave those women an income and helped the community too. I imagine some of the books that they rebound are still up there.

He stayed on the farm and they had a Model T Ford. One time he came over here, my daddy was gone then, and they said they had a little money ahead, I think it was $30, and we've got enough to drive back to Ohio. My mother was so worried and so upset with them she didn't know what to do. But she didn't dare tell them not to go. They went up there but it didn't take many days until they came back and they were so glad to get back home. You wouldn't have gone to Bartow, 30 miles distant, in that Model T but they struck out and went to Ohio in it.

Barbara Carlton: *I can remember when I first got married. Will got sick and I made a house call to that little old house which wasn't as big as this room. His wife had died by then and he was an old hermit back in there. Well, I treated him and he sorta recuperated and I could see him in town in that old Model T. The top was wrapped in bailing wire to keep it from falling completely to one side. And it was all rusted and looked like a big rusty tin can. Everybody called out… Ya'll watch out… Mr. Will is on the road. He'd go into town and he might make it back…*

Every day when I'd cook a meal at noon I'd always put a basket with fruit and food in it and I'd put it on his mail box which was right by ours. So every day I'd know when he'd get his mail. And so one day I put his food out and when I went to get the mail and it wasn't gone, it scared me… I thought: Something's wrong… something's wrong. So when Merle came home I said, "We've got to go over there and see about him because he didn't come for his mail today and to get his basket of food." So sure enough, he was down sick. That's when Coker had the ambulance service and we called him, and I remember they put him on the stretcher and they had to walk him out clear to that fence line in the pasture 'cause it was so boggy and bad they couldn't get in there to his house to get him. But he got better and so then I told Dr. Franks who was seeing him to let me know when they got ready to discharge him because I knew he couldn't go back where he'd been. There wasn't any point in asking him: do you want to go back home?

They called and said that he would be discharged and I said, "Okay, when he's ready to come out I'll send a lady in there from Rest Haven to get him. He's going to be living at Rest Haven, an assisted living facility." I happened to be over there and I told them to go in there and get him and bring him back. When he came in I said, "Now Will, you remember in your younger days you used to go to those lodges in the Wisconsin woods and what good times you had and this is going to be just like one of those lodges…" Boy, did I sell that thing to him! And I said, "I promise you that I'll come to see you. I'm not gonna leave you out here by yourself… I'll see about you."

I was as good as my word… I went to see him. And I remember one of the first trips I made out there, he said, "Alberta, this is the finest lodge I was ever in. You know it's warm in here all day and all night… I never get cold."

I could have just squalled. I'm telling you the truth… I can hear him now: this is the finest lodge I was ever in. And that's where he died.

There was no point in leaving him over there where he'd been living because I couldn't get to him anyhow. It's all right if you tell a little exaggeration if you get what needs to be done, isn't it?

Aunt Ella was in the hospital in her final hours. All of her life, her chore had been to wash the little boys' feet before they could come in the house… the nine brothers who were all younger than she was. That was her job every day, because the floors were scrubbed and if they tracked in there with their dirty feet it would mess up the clean floors. She was delirious and she kept saying, "The sun's going down… the sun's going down, I've got to get home…" She was so troubled and nothing the nurse could do would quieten her. She was just really, really troubled and the nurse was one of the most thoughtful people. She picked up a little hand towel that was on the end of the bed and draped it over Aunt Ella's head and said, "OK, Ella, you can go, you've got on your bonnet now, so you can go see about the boys' feet." This quietened her right off. I've always loved and appreciated Myra for that. She was Myra McCall. She trained at Gordon Keller Nursing School in Tampa. Everybody thought that she was just a miracle worker because she could get her to be quiet right off.

This is a hallmark of southern living – the rocking chair – symbolic of porch living which was well enjoyed by the Carltons and their friends.

PART TWO
THE LITTLE WHITE HOUSE

Kate Reichart 2005

"Carlton Country" had its Florida beginnings in Hardee County when Carl S. Carlton married Daisy Platt and began their lives together in what they called the Carlton Homeplace at Oak Grove circa 1904.

A substantial barn was built in 1905 to house the stock, mules, horses, and cattle as well as hay in the loft. The barn still stands today.

The original well which supplied water to the home and barn continues to this day... almost spring-like water.

Carl and Daisy Platt lived in the original homeplace, The Little White House, from 1904 to 1913, the time of Daisy's death.

In existence for over a century, The Little White House has endured births and deaths, searing heat and devastating cold, drenching storms and rain as well as droughts and hurricanes.

Yet through the love and respect of the Carltons, The Little White House has persevered, has sheltered and comforted those who have lived and loved there from one generation to another.

In 2005, the Carl S. Carlton homestead, The Little White House, was designated as a Pioneer Family Farm by the Florida Department of Agriculture, having been established for over 100 years.

73

CARL SIMEON CARLTON
1880-1932

A scion of the pioneer Carlton-McEwen families of Wauchula, was a citrus grower, cattle rancher and banker.

CARL SIMEON CARLTON

Carl S. Carlton was married twice. His first marriage was to Daisy Platt, she was born at Lily, Florida on July 16, 1881 and died at the Little White House on April 12, 1913

Daisy Platt   **Carl S. Carlton**

Carl and Daisy had two daughters Matred and Mattie Mae. They lived in The Little White House until their mother's death in 1913. Subsequently, Carl and his daughters, Matred, age eight, and Mattie Mae, age five, moved to the home of his parents, Albert and Martha Carlton at "Azalea Hill."

Later, Carl moved across from "Azalea Hill" into a home he had built on Bay Street where he lived until his marriage to Emma Edwards, a bank teller at the Carlton Bank. Carl and Emma produced one son.

Carl Simeon Carlton was born September 3, 1880, in the Oak Grove community, five miles west of present day Wauchula. Carl was raised in the Oak Grove community having lived in a log cabin near Troublesome Creek. Later the family moved to a two-story house that his father built on the Vandolah Road in 1885 for his growing family, where his parents, Albert and Martha (McEwen)

The Little White House circa 1908 Daisy, daughter Matred (about three years old) and Carl Carlton.

Carlton, had settled after their marriage in 1868. Albert, his father, had obtained some land from his parents, Daniel Wilson and Sallie Ann (Murphy) Carlton, to which he added onto until he had 340 acres. He planted 80 acres in oranges and the balance became pasture for his cattle.

In 1903, his father, Albert, bought about 30 acres in Wauchula, on which he built a two-story, Queen Anne 10-room house and planted 12 acres in oranges. He also had a mercantile business which he operated about two years before selling it. He then opened a bank of which he was president until his death in September 1925.

Carl S. Carlton attended public schools in Oak Grove and Wauchula. Attending Stetson University is a century-old tradition for the Carlton family. Early records are a bit unclear but indicate that Carl S. Carlton was the first in the family to enroll for a bookkeeping course in the 1900-1901 academic year.

After returning home from Stetson, Carl Carlton was employed in the or-

Oak Grove, four miles west of Wauchula, on Main St. (formerly 64-A).
The Little White House is in the background.

ange groves for about four years. Then for two years he was assistant bookkeeper at the Carlton Bank. Citrus growing and cattle ranching then received his attention but he returned to banking in 1906 and stayed with it until it failed in February 1929. However, he maintained his agricultural interests. In the 1920s he owned valuable rural property of which 35 acres were set in oranges.

Carlton & Carlton Bank, the first banking institution in what is now Hardee County, had opened for business in Wauchula in March 1904, with Albert Carlton as president and Charles J. Carlton (son of Albert) as cashier. The bank was incorporated in February 1915 as Carlton National Bank, with Albert Carlton as president, Charles J. Carlton as first vice president and cashier, J. W. Earnest as second vice president and Carl S. Carlton and W. D. McInnis as cashiers.

Ronald Lambert documents Carl Carlton's empathy... as Ronald Lambert's father stepped off the train in Wauchula, he was immediately given a job by Carl Carlton, the business man.

He was very active in the community where he lived. He was a member of the First Baptist Church of Wauchula where he served as its treasurer. A very generous and giving man, Carl Carlton set an excellent example to his family, friends, and citizens of the community.

Albert Carlton gave each of his children small tracts of land and in 1904 Carl built a home on one of these tracts and was then married to Daisy Platt that year. (This is the home now known as The Little White House located at the original homeplace in the Oak Grove Community, the Bar $\bar{\wedge}$ Ranch.)

In September 1920, Carl married Emma Edwards who was a teller at the Carlton Bank. She was born in August 1893 and died in June 1933.

Carl and Emma (Edwards) Carlton had one son, William Albert Carlton, born May 1, 1927. He married Dr. Barbara Castleberry in 1959.

Five years later when their little son was only five years old, Carl was accidentally killed in a hunting accident. Carl and his friends had been making regular hunting trips to the Everglades and this was planned as just another trip. On December 21, 1932, Carl and his brother, Alton, along with J. R. Rooney and Ander Marsh set out together on yet another hunt. During this hunt, Alton, Carl's own brother, fired at a deer, the bullet ricocheted off a tree causing a fatal blow to his brother. Alton tried valiantly to carry his brother out of the Everglades; however, being a small man, he could not physically carry his six-foot-two brother but a short distance. Those who were in the hunting party said later that it took all day to get Carl out of the place where they were hunting. Six months later, Albert lost his mother.

Little five-year-old Albert went to live with Matred and her husband A. Z. Olliff in Wauchula. A. Z. was said to be a very strict and a very ungiving person. He was named the executor-administrator of the Carl S. Carlton estate. To his credit through the years, A. Z. relentlessly protected Albert's financial interests until he (Albert) became of age.

An orphan, Albert was being raised by a family, a tremendous challenge to him as a child. He spent a lot of time alone, by himself, playing the piano at which he excelled. He was also very good in school, so good, in fact that he was allowed to skip the third grade entirely.

After finishing elementary school in 1941, he was admitted to Bolles Prep School in Jacksonville, Florida. Upon graduation from Bolles in 1943, he attended the University of Florida but shortly afterwards enlisted in the Navy. Returning from the Navy in 1945 he re-entered the University and graduated in 1948 earning his degree in Agricultural Business.

After graduation from the University, he became the recipient of his father's estate. There were vast land-holdings, the majority being ranchlands, however, there were some citrus groves, plus a partnership in a car business in Wauchula, an auto dealership, with his first cousin, Odell Carlton.

On the land at Vandolah, included in his inheritance, is one of the oldest citrus groves in Hardee County which has always been known as the Old Carlton Place.

Carl Carlton, the banker

Carl Carlton, the avid hunter with his dog.

Carl Carlton hunting in the Everglades, circa 1930.

EMMA EDWARDS CARLTON

After being a widower for seven years, Carl S. Carlton met and married Emma Edwards a teller at the Carlton & Carlton Bank. Emma was the daughter of W. H. and Emma Edwards Sr., of Lakeland.

They were a blissfully happy couple, deeply devoted to each other and very active in the surrounding community in which they lived and the First Baptist Church of Wauchula.

Seven years after their marriage in 1920, Carl and Emma were blessed with the birth of a son, William Albert Carlton. Immediately after the birth, it is said that Carl vigorously cranked their hand-crank telephone shouting to family and

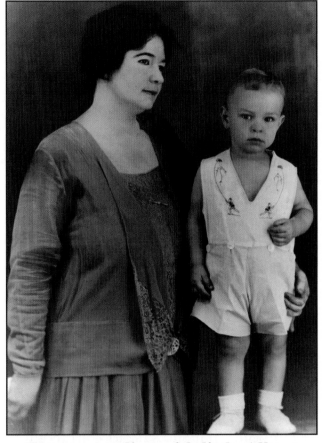

Emma standing with little Albert

friends... "It's a boy! It's a boy! It's a boy!" His happiness was shared by the entire community. William Albert Carlton, was born May 1, 1927.

It has been said that little Albert was totally idolized by both his family and the entire Carlton family.

After Carl's untimely death in 1932 Emma regularly took her little son to the Carlton Homeplace, The Little White House.

Mrs. Marsh, Ander Marsh's wife, cared for the family clothes. She washed and ironed little Albert's clothes. Emma was determined that he not only be clean but immaculate. He was the perfect little gentleman and she always dressed him in white.

Emma and little Albert often stayed for the noon-dinner at The Little White House. She was especially fond of Mrs. Marsh's "small, soft, round" biscuits made to perfection and baked fresh every day.

As time passed, family and friends thought Emma would recover from the loss of her husband. Instead, she sank into depths of depression from which she could not rise. Her general health was visibly failing and it appeared that nothing could be done.

As her depression deepened, she clung to her little son, a quiet child, the only person she appeared to have had any connection.

About six months after the accident that took Carl's life, in early June, Emma Carlton went to the home of John C. McEwen on Bay Street, went into a bedroom and took her own life with a bullet wound to the heart. At that time, little Albert and his cousin, Tom McEwen, were playing on the porch and heard the shot.

During this period of grief friends remembered that she was a very depressed woman. Her undying love for Carl was expressed openly prior to the hunting accident in that she intuitively did not want him to make the trip, even to the point that she said to Carl as he was leaving, "I hope I never see you alive again."

Emma left notes trying to explain her actions. In one of those notes, she wrote that she "preferred to join her husband rather than live without him." Other notes explained her actions to the point that Judge H. M. Hammell decided there would be no inquisition.

Emma Edwards Carlton died June 8, 1933, and was buried beside Carl at Wauchula Cementary. She was 39 years old.

On June 9, 1933, the local paper, *The Florida Advocate*, stated: The death of Mrs. Carlton has cast a gloom over the entire community where she was well known and so beloved.

TOM McEWEN

Linda and Tom McEwen with Dr. Barbara Carlton

Tom McEwen was about eight years old when Emma Carlton died. At the time he was sitting on the porch where he lived. He was with his cousin, six-year-old Albert Carlton. Tom recalls that sad day, more than eighty years later, with poignant clarity:

Carl Carlton was the father of five-year-old Albert and a leading citrus grower and cattle rancher in central Florida, one of the famous Carlton brothers. His first wife was Daisy Platt. They had two daughters Matred and Mattie Mae. Daisy Platt Carlton died of cancer in 1913. Some few years later, Carl met and married Emma Edwards. Their son, Albert, was born in 1927.

Some time after Carl's two daughters were born, he and his brother, Alton, went on a hunting trip in the Everglades. During this trip, brother Alton fired at a deer. The bullet hit a cypress tree, then ricocheted, hitting Carl in the eyeball, killing him instantly.

Tom McEwen's father, John, was among those who went in to recover and bring Carl's body out of the Everglades. Alton was a small man but very wiry and strong, while his brother was large and heavy. Alton desperately wanted to personally bring out his brother's body; however, even though he was extremely strong, it was too much. He could not carry his brother by himself.

Tom McEwen: "The closeness of the Carltons with our family, the McEwens, was due to the fact that several years after Daisy's death, Carl married Emma Edwards from Frostproof who was a niece of my mother, Mary Virginia Milton McEwen from Olustee near Lake City. Incidentally, Olustee is the one site in Florida where the only battle in the Civil War was fought. Emma's father was a bugler in that war. Our side won that battle.

"Later on, Mary Virginia came to Wauchula and married my father who was at that time a cowboy working with the Carltons. My mother was the aunt of Emma Edwards Carlton, second wife of Carl Carlton, the mother of Albert Carlton.

"One day Albert and I were on the screened porch at our home on North 6th Avenue in Wauchula. He and I were in the swing. The memory of that day is very vivid. Albert and I were just swinging and talking like boys do, laughing and having a good time together. All of a sudden we heard an unusual sound that came from the rear of the house. It was a very loud pop that to us sounded like a gunshot. We ran back to the room that Albert's mother had taken as her home after her husband had died. When Albert and I got to that back room my mother was already there, desperately trying to tend to the wounds. Albert's mother was in the bed badly bleeding from a self-inflicted gunshot wound. It seemed that there was blood everywhere. Little Albert was so shocked and stunned, not a sound came from him. His mother had shot herself and would die from the wound."

Emma Carlton was buried in the Wauchula Cemetery beside her husband Carl.

Thus Albert Carlton was orphaned at age six. Arrangements were made for him to live with his half-sister Matred, and her husband, Allen Olliff. They did what they had to do in caring for him until he reached maturity.

Albert would eventually inherit a large amount of property in Hardee County... orange groves and cattle as well, but he could not claim or take charge of his inheritance until he became of age. When that time arrived, this was in 1948, Albert was the most popular sought after bachelor in the entire region. Later on, in 1958, he met the beauteous Dr. Barbara Castleberry of Georgia who was practicing at the Wauchula Infirmary (Dr. Collier's hospital) in Wauchula. Albert and Barbara married in 1959.

"Throughout all those years, from the time he was five years old, Albert and I remained more than cousins.

"As a result of the gun accident that killed his father, as far as I know, Albert Carlton never hunted. However, he and his wife, Barbara, staged hunts for deer and birds on their ranches. They became famous for the barbecues that took place following these hunts. Barbara, an avid hunter, became a dynamic shot but without fail, safety was always first."

While Albert did not hunt, he attended all the hunts and was in charge of the refreshment trucks that were abundantly equipped to supply the hunters with anything and everything they needed to eat or drink.

Tom McEwen concludes, "But at no time in his life did Albert Carlton ever take up a gun."

MAE FRANK HIMROD
The Little White House in the Oak Grove Community

Mae Frank Marsh Himrod

It was in 1921 when Mae Frank Marsh (Himrod) first came in contact with the Carltons. She was eight years old, the daughter of Ander Marsh, the foreman for Carl Carlton's citrus and cattle business in Oak Grove for many years.

The Marshes had moved from Wauchula to the country so that Mr. Marsh could be the manager and take care of Mr. Carl's groves. There was a lot of new land and since Ander Marsh was a truck farmer there was all the farmland he needed on which to grow cucumbers and tomatoes and other vegetables that would be shipped north.

Mae Frank Himrod:

We had moved to the Little White House (Carl Carlton's homestead) where we are now. We children fell in love with this place. We moved in July 1921 and the county had just been changed from DeSoto County to Hardee. From DeSoto County, in that split, was Hardee and Glades, Highlands, Charlotte and DeSoto. Arcadia had been the county seat of DeSoto County… they had made five counties from the one big county of DeSoto. So Wauchula was made the county seat of Hardee, named for the governor of Florida at that time, Cary A. Hardee (1876-1957) who was the 23rd governor of the state. This was in 1921. We moved right after the county was divided and we were still living in Wauchula and we heard all the bells and whistles, the horns and people singing and everything ringing when it became Hardee County, which meant we had our own county.

Mr. Carl was married the second time; his first wife (Daisy Platt) had died. This home was his and Daisy's until her death. They had built the house originally... His wife's sister lived just south of them, she had married a Whidden. The Whiddens were some of the old pioneers in this area. Another brother had married an Altman… Tom Carlton lived around there, then Alton Carlton was another one of the boys... men, so it made a little village of the Carlton brothers. Mr.

Alton Carlton was the older, I think he was the second of 10 boys, Charlie was the oldest, well, Alton married Melt Whidden's sister, she was Mary Whidden, and Mr. Carl married Daisy Platt and Melt Whidden married Ona Platt and that's who the little town of Ona is named for.

Mr. Melt (Milton) started the Post Office at Ona that's on the railroad and he built the first little cabinet that held the mail. His real name was Milton but everybody just called him Melt. And I now have that little cabinet that held the mail on my back porch.

This was a nice little village and this was when we all learned to say Carlton Country because their dad lived down on the Vandolah Road

The original Post Office at Ona, Florida, established October 11, 1897. Mae Frank Himrod has the first cabinet used in the post office. It's on her porch now.

and that's where the Polish people came to and they named that little country village Vandolah. There are still a lot of houses there, it's grown quite a little bit and that's where a lot of the cattle ranches are. Probably the biggest one is the Susan-Duck Smith Ranch, I think it's several sections.

Most of the Carltons had moved to town… back to Wauchula and left the countryside. Mr. Carl, he and my dad got along real well.

They, the brothers Carl and Charles, owned the bank, the only bank in town before they all went broke in the '30s during the Depression when they all closed. That was the Carlton & Carlton Bank. My dad lost a little bit of money… several hundred but we had a good living here. My dad would clear land, he liked to have new land for growing cucumbers more than anything else. My brothers and I used to work in the grove and it was so different from what it is now. We didn't have tractors back then. We used mules to plow with and they used plain hoes to hoe the weeds from around the trees. All this was in the late '20s and '30s.

We hauled the vegetables into Wauchula and then they were shipped north by train to New York and other places. It seemed like my dad's favorite vegetable was cucumbers but of course we always had squash in the garden with greens and tomatoes but his main crop was always cucumbers... he really enjoyed them.

We lived here in the Little White House sixteen years. I married in 1929. I was 16 years old.

Mr. Carl was very fond of canning and beef. We'd butcher beef and can the meat in quart cans. We had a cannery in the house which had a sealer on it that just rolled the edges around the can and sealed it. Then we'd put all the cans in a big copper kettle outside and build a fire under it. We had different cuts of beef… steak, which we cooked and made the gravy before putting it in the cans. Then, there was stew beef and I don't remember canning hamburger but we had it. And we had a big furnace and a smoke house, too. The smoke house is gone now and there's farm land where it used to be.

That canned beef was delicious. In Georgia, I was told that beef was "put up" in glass jars, not cans.

And we'd do peas, black-eyed peas the same way. And one year Mr. Carl said, "Ander, you know when you hear of 'pork and beans'... why can't we have 'pork and peas'?" And he went to town and bought a whole side of white bacon, had it sliced at the grocery store, so we could have peas and white bacon. They were delicious! My dad would go out to Ed Davis' who grew black-eyed peas and they liked purple-hull peas, different kinds of peas, but we didn't have conchs back then. They were little-tiny peas... called white acre peas... small... tiny. And we canned tomatoes. The garden was right here close to the house.

Butchering and canning the beef went on until the late '20s.

We had one big out-house with two seats, some places had three. Everybody used it and of course we used chamber pots during the night.

Troublesome Creek wound around from its spring-fed source in Hardee County which has two branches. One branch flows north from Fort Green and then on up into Polk County. I don't know where it goes out from up there but down here it flows south winding around in so many places and finally flows into Peace River in Hardee County, which of course used to be DeSoto. We think the fork of the creek is between Vandolah Road and what is now Highway 64-A.

Dr. Barbara Carlton: *I am told that the initial log cabin that Albert and Martha had before they built the house on their knoll on Vandolah Road, was on Troublesome Creek, and that it was built with timber cut from their land. There's a lot of history on that creek! You just come down Troublesome and meet all kinds of folks and hear all kinds of stories.*

Way back when the first pioneers moved into this area in the mid - 1800s, the Seminole Indians were living here. One of them had gotten real old and they put him out because they thought he'd die. He'd gotten sick and they brought a little chickee down near a creek which was Troublesome Creek but back then it had no name. Well, he got better… he got over his sickness. Then he started stealing chickens from the pioneers so he could have meat. And the Indians started saying 'It's just that old troublesome Indian.' And so that's where the name came from. Troublesome Creek. But some people say that when the rains came back then, and occasionally, now that the creek overflows its banks and it becomes really troublesome. So you can take your choice as to where and how the name came to be. It winds down around the Oak Grove Cemetery and where the school house used to be near the cemetery. It has a lot of fish in it and people have fished it for years. And there are otters in it which are pretty bad ever' once in a while.

In the summertime the hardest work would be over. My dad could plant two crops a year, spring and fall. Mr. Carl was interested, he'd provide the fertilizer, they'd split the costs, then they'd split the profits each year. They got wages for taking care of the groves. Oranges brought a good price. My dad didn't pick them but we took care of the groves. Crews were formed with a foreman and men in the area who were called "pickers." These weren't foreigners, they were regular white men. Mr. Carl had different fruits… grapefruit, oranges and for his own enjoyment they had tangerines and mandarin oranges. It was a great big grove, twenty acres. Then we'd plant more groves. I remember my dad planting a five-acre grove with young trees but sometimes there'd come a freeze and they'd have pinewood fires in the groves and that helped to keep the trees from freezing… of course, depending on how bad the freeze was.

It was also in the summer when we always canned food. Many times we'd go to the lakes and pick berries. We enjoyed fishing and berry-picking… huckleberries and blackberries. There used to be many, many huckleberries in the early summertime. My dad loved huckleberry pie. Huckleberries are different from blueberries and we made pies from the blackberries too.

Mr. Tom Carlton (Carl Carlton's brother), who lived just a little ways from us, had sheep and I remember as a child when they'd bring the sheep in from the pastures and shear them for the wool. We children would hold the sheep while they were being sheared and that's something we enjoyed so much. My favorite sheep shearer was one of the Carlton boys. Maurice was his name, he was the oldest and Winston was the youngest. Mr. Tom had children but he and his wife had separated so he was a bachelor for a while. My older brother and his youngest son were real good friends. Both of them were Boy Scouts and they'd make their flags and do the other scouting things.

Another thing we were all so crazy about was the Carlton wash hole. There's a big place down there where the old Indian lived at Troublesome Creek and that's where we'd go swimming every day through the summertime. At noontime when our dad would be restin' after the field work and we ate dinner, we'd go straight to the creek and swim. Maurice Carlton taught us how to swim… we learned that first summer. He had gallon syrup cans that he'd tie a rope on two cans and we learned to swim. We taught Naomi to swim before she could walk. We'd take the baby with us so Mama could rest, too.

Mae Frank Himrod standing in Troublesome Creek

The swimming hole was the deepest place in Troublesome Creek to the left of the bridge going north. And there was a tree we could dive from. Paul, Jr. was always talking about how to dive like Tarzan. That hole was deep... like 30 feet deep and, of course, it shallowed around the edges. The swimming hole was about two miles from the headwaters of the creek.

In January all of the boys would get together and go swimming at the swimming hole. That was a big deal. It was cold in the summer but I went swimming in January on the 6th which was my birthday and I'd walked all the way from the Wauchula school. I was determined I was going to jump in that water. I stripped off all my clothes and dived in the water. I was fifteen. I told the garden club ladies from all over the state never thinking that it would be retold. Our president was Bern Davis from Fort Myers and she got up and told this story to a hundred women! I turned beet-red I was so embarrassed. But everybody had a good laugh.

One day Jack and I decided to go fishing down at the fishing hole. That particular day we hadn't had much luck... I think we caught a couple trout. Just as we started back before we got to the cemetery I turned my ankle bad, it hurt just terribly bad. Jack picked me up and carried me... he toted me a little ways, then I'd hobble hanging onto him until he'd rest then he carried me on 'til we got to the car. When we got home he put my ankle in hot water... just as hot as I could bear it. He said that was what his granddaddy did, he was William Altman. Everybody called him Uncle Bill, he was a cowhunter. The cattlemen, they used to all get together and go cow-huntin'. They didn't have trailers to haul the horses in in those days. Jack's granddaddy was a county commissioner for DeSoto County and he'd go to Arcadia in a horse and buggy once a month for meetings. Grandpa always did the horses this way... soak their feet in hot water. And it really wasn't very long until my ankle was all well.

You being a doctor, you may not agree with the treatment but it worked with me.

Dr. Barbara Carlton: *Usually, we recommend cold first, then hot, but who knows, that, too may have changed. Maybe it depends on who you talk to!*

Mae Frank Himrod's story continues...

After Daisy Platt died in 1913, Mr. Carl married a teller at the bank, Miss Emma Edwards, in 1920. They had their first and only child seven years later.

Mr. Carl was so thrilled even though they didn't know if they'd have a girl or a boy. He was just thrilled to have another child because Mattie and Matred were both grown. The night Albert was born, three o'clock in the morning, he turned the hand-crank telephone, rang up Mr. Alton, woke him up saying, "Alton, it's a boy, it's a boy, it's a boy!" Not many people then had telephones. So Alton, about daylight, came down to tell my daddy that Mr. Carl had a boy. And so they were real thrilled about that.

When Albert got a little older, Miss Emma, his mother, would come out once a week and eat dinner with us and bring us pretty clothes which I understand she'd bought from Uncle Charles Himrod's wife. One of her children had been stillborn.

That's Joe Himrod's mother. She had made beautiful little embroidered clothes from beautiful white cloth and Miss Emma didn't want them to turn brown and dark and the diapers too. So I'd do the wash and boil the clothes in the well water. That was wonderful water. And we'd eat dinner and have left-overs for supper. My mother would make yeast rolls and Miss Emma would eat three or four. My youngest sister and Albert were close to the same age and they played together... they were so cute. We loved Albert like he was our own baby.

Our refrigerator sat here in The Little White House, with a drip pan under it. My dad bored a hole in the floor under it for the water to drip through. We'd get ice about three times a week, a 50-pound block. It wasn't a real refrigerator... it was an ice-box.

We had to draw our water from the well, of course, and we boiled the

Original well at The Little White House, homeplace of Carl S. Carlton

clothes in the copper kettle. And another thing we used the well for, the water was so cool and we always had a milking cow and my dad loved buttermilk. So he took an enamel kettle and made a tight lid for it, then he'd lower the kettle or bucket into the well and by noon it was just real cool and he'd eat cornbread and buttermilk with his vegetables.

We used to get syrup, sugarcane syrup from Alabama. It came in barrels by train, and we'd keep it in the big old smokehouse. Mr. Carl liked the syrup, too, and he liked to come eat with us quite a bit. He'd come out and eat breakfast with us some days. We'd have hot biscuits twice a day, and that's one thing we had hot for supper, those hot biscuits. Cornbread we had at dinner time.

Daddy said he had to teach Mama how to cook because she didn't know how when they married. She'd make the little flat biscuits that were soft which he really liked. Then we'd have jelly. He learned to eat guavas after we moved out here. When we first came he never would eat guavas, he said they smelled like cat pee. And so many of them do, but there are so many different flavors, however Mr. Carl had found some white guavas and they were so different, he planted them and made a nice little patch. That was our snack after we'd come from school.

My dad loved guava cobbler that Mama would make with the pie crust and we had pure cream from our cow. And one year he decided he'd dry some. So we picked the guavas; we had lots of them. He'd split them twice, take the seeds out, leave the skin on and then he'd put them on a screen which he'd put on top of the smoke house. They were sun-dried and Mama made real good pies with them. They turned brown, of course, but they were delicious.

Besides the syrup my dad had something sweet twice a day so that's how I became a sweet-a-holic.

Dr. Barbara Carlton: *I treated Mae Frank's daddy, Ander Marsh, through all the years and made house calls in his last days. He died in the hospital at age 91, one month after his 91st birthday. He was a wonderful man, gentle and easy-going and never complained all those years.*

Papa would plant our garden every year. In the wintertime, fall, he'd plant lettuce and turnips and mustard greens. Then one year, in spring, he had fresh land that he'd just cleared right near Troublesome Creek and A. M. was maybe eight years old. His real name was Alex Mitchell. He said, "Papa, we've got tomatoes and they're gettin' ripe and so good why don't we plant some mayonnaise so we can have some good old tomato and mayonnaise sandwiches."

Anyway, oh my, history's so interesting to me!

The Carlton men would come out to Oak Grove where they used to have singing conventions at the church and some times all-day sings. They were all good singers and sometimes they'd sing in a quartet… Gettis, Carl, Charlie and Doyle, they'd sing in the quartet and sit in the choir loft. They were all dressed up in their suits and each one had a lapel pin. I think they were Masons. They were handsome men.

A lot of them would sing acappella because they just had the shaped notes and some of our men who were members of the church couldn't sing round notes. They only had six shaped notes. They had the old paper back hymnals and they'd sing acappella because they didn't have a pianist that could play the shaped notes. But they'd just sing on and on… all day.

Uncle Alton had bought a big touring car and he and his wife would come out to see us. Uncle Albert's brother, Lewis, married Aunt Martha's sister, Mary. So there was Martha and Mary and Albert and Lewis had married sisters. The women were McEwens.

When Uncle Albert's father moved to this county, this area, his name was Daniel, he started a school for the community. He built a little school house near

The Carlton Quartet, circa 1895. Left to right, Gettis, Carl, Charlie and Doyle

his home up in the Vandolah area. They called it the Oak Grove School. Later, the school was moved down to the cemetery. My mother-in-law was a teacher there and she taught the Carlton boys.

Then when they built the church in 1895 at Oak Grove, they moved the school to the church house.

Dr. Barbara Carlton: *In 1904, Carl Carlton married Daisy Platt and they moved into a house we presume they built, until 1913 when Daisy died. They lived here (Little White House) eight years and both their daughters, Mattie Mae and Matred, were born here. After Daisy died in 1913, Carl moved to town (Wauchula) with the two girls and lived with his mother and father, Albert and Martha, at "Azalea Hill."*

In 1920 after Carl and Miss Emma Edwards were married, they lived on East Bay Street across from "Azalea Hill" in the C. J. Carlton House. Emma was a bank teller in the Carlton & Carlton Bank.

A short time later Mr. Marsh and his family moved to The Little White House. He was called Ander Marsh, a local way of pronouncing the name Andrew. There's even a road named "Ander Marsh." Some time after Carl and the two girls moved to town to live with his parents, this house was used for the managers of the Carlton estates and later after he (Carl) was killed in 1932. So there were managers who lived here all that time.

This was for the groves and the cattle because this was the time of open range and that's what the cattleman would do, mark and brand the cattle. They all had different brands because the Altmans were pioneers, my husband's mother, and the Altmans and the Carltons had more cattle than any of the others. They worked the cattle and many times they'd camp overnight for several nights.

I know Jack loved to tell tales about going with his granddad who also had a big family, five boys and six girls. It was all about cattle and citrus.

I lived across Troublesome Creek when I married, as the crow flies about a mile from here, on the hill. We made sugarcane syrup and Albert loved that syrup.

He and Barbara would come over and watch it being made. Sometimes people would come and we sold a lot of syrup. Jack would make it because he wanted to do it like his granddad. Everybody used to make it and sometimes we'd make raw sugar and molasses, too. There's a big difference in the syrup and molasses.

In fact when we lived in Clewiston he worked with the sugarcane company.

$$\overline{A}\ \overline{A}\ \overline{A}$$

I had gone to town and had my hair done and was sitting in the parlor and I noticed that nobody was talking much, nobody was smiling and I finally asked why everybody was sad… not smiling. And the beautician said, "Haven't you heard the bad news?" And I said, "What bad news?" And she said, "Mr. Carl Carlton was killed in the Everglades…" I started crying and said, "My daddy was with him…" The beautician then said, "I'm, sorry, I didn't know that you knew him so well."

Later, I wrote the story about it. My daddy told me what had happened… they had gone to the Everglades hunting for deer shortly before Christmas. There was John Rooney, school superintendent for a long time, and Mr. Alton, the older brother of Mr. Carl's and my dad, Ander Marsh. There were four of them. They had walked five miles from the highway when Mr. Alton shot at a deer but his bullet didn't hit the deer, it hit a cypress tree and ricocheted hitting Mr. Carl in the middle of his forehead. It was instant death.

It was the biggest shock of their lives. Mr. Alton just went to pieces. The others were trying to console him and Mr. Rooney said he would walk out and phone Dr. Leland Carlton, his brother, in Tampa, and they'd get help. It was late

98

that afternoon before they got help.

I gave what I had written to daddy and when I asked him for it he said he gave it to one of the girls. I think he gave it to Mattie Mae or Matred and I think they burned it.

Mr. Carl begged daddy into going with him that day and he said, "I just can't Carl, I don't really need to go." Mama's health was not too good and Mr. Carl said, "If you're not going, we won't go." But he was so disappointed that daddy told him, "If you really want to go, I'll go," and Mr. Alton wanted to go too. So when they went by to pick up Mr. Carl that morning to go to the Everglades, Miss Emma said, in an effort to persuade him not to go, "Well, you won't do like I told you, I don't want you to go, and I just hope I don't ever see you alive again."

He was killed just before Christmas. Her remarks, as he was leaving that day, preyed on her mind, and in addition, the timing of the death at Christmas and the tragic loss of her husband whom she dearly loved, resulted in a deep depression that she was unable to overcome, resulting in her taking her own life six months later in June 1933. (This story is closely substantiated by Tom McEwen, the great-grandson of Rutha and Rev. William Penn McEwen. Tom was present with six-year-old Albert at the time of his mother's death. They were on the porch together.)

I was living somewhere else then and was told that Emma had taken her own life, leaving Albert an orphan, and that Matred, his half sister, was going to take care of him. He was certainly one wonderful boy. Matred was so good to him, she dearly loved him and he loved her just as much.

I remember hearing the story of how little Albert started calling Matred Sistoria. Back in those days it was the usual thing to give children Castoria for just about anything that they came down with whether they needed it or not. Well, I guess little Albert didn't know exactly how to pronounce the word, so he called it Sistoria, and that's what he always called Matred. Sistoria.

I learned to milk the cow when my brother got tired of milking. He insisted on teaching me and I enjoyed it. I was a person who was always curious and wanted to know how to do everything. This was before he ran away, about the time he was 15 and I was about 13. We'd churn about three times a week making butter. I'd sit and churn with one hand, about an eight-gallon crock. Daddy had made a lid to fit on it and a dasher. He was a jack-of-all-trades, and my husband was even better than that. The churn was in the corner of the kitchen when we lived in The Little White House.

Our youngest brother was born in 1922; my mother's health was so bad she wasn't able to nurse him very long. Well, the doctor had told my dad to get Eagle Brand milk which was real condensed and thick, so we'd boil the water and mix it and give him a bottle. It tasted so good my younger sister would take her finger and rub it around in the can and lick it and one day she said, "Papa would you buy an Eagle so we can have Eagle Brand milk?"

At times I'd be churning with one hand and holding the baby in my lap and giving him a bottle with the other and a book between the bottle and the churn so I could read. I was a voracious reader. One of the things I did in this house was there was a closet in the front bedroom which had a second story up there and I would climb that closet up to the ceiling and crack the door open. That was one of my hiding places to read. And then on cloudy, rainy days when we weren't working out I'd go out to the barn and climb up in the loft where there was a crack that let enough light in and I'd lie in the haystack and read a whole book if they'd let me alone!

It was just a wonderful life... went to school through the week and walked a mile to get there. My brother, Cecil, stayed awhile and helped Papa Marsh when everybody else had walked on to school and I'd stay and help my mother. He'd hold my hand and I'd have to take three steps to his one... he had such long legs so I'd just go trottin' along. Anything I couldn't do I just wanted to learn how to do it.

I was the number four child, my oldest sister was almost 10 years older than I was. I was different from the rest of them... one reason I think is because I thought I was kind of ugly. My aunts used to talk about how beautiful my sisters, Doris and Ruth were. Doris had shining black hair, straight but it was beautiful. And I had freckles. Ruth had curly hair; she was the baby for five years and was really spoiled. When my aunts were talking 'bout how beautiful they were, I thought to myself, "they're not saying a word 'bout me," so I remember thinking... "if I can't be pretty I can be smart," and so I learned to read when I was four years old. My health was kinda puny.

Dr. Barbara Carlton: *She survived being puny... she's now 97.*

I almost died with whooping cough and always had colds in the wintertime but I did love to study and they wouldn't let me go to school until we moved to Florida so I was six years old when I entered the first grade.

When my brother, Luther, who was three years older than I, ran away and joined the wild west show I was devastated. I cried myself to sleep many nights. My mother grieved over it but he began to write to us and Mr. Carl told my dad he would have the sheriff bring him back. The sheriff was Chester Dishong. Everybody loved Chester. My dad said, "No, don't bring him back, he'll just run away again." But it really grieved our mother. And it really grieved me. The first letter I had he wrote that he'd left a pair of shoes in the shoe shop and he wanted me to get them out and put them with his shirts. He said I could have his overalls but he wanted the shirts.

So I put on the overalls and began to learn how to hitch up the mules to the wagon and go with my dad to the field where he had planted a crop of cucumbers but he never would let me plough. He said that was for men, not women. In our cook stove we burned pinewood and I learned to pull the big saw. I just wanted to learn everything that my brothers had to do.

And we had a little rodeo. Mr. Tom Carlton let us have some of his cattle.

Bing Crosby's brother was with them. After a short time they went down around the big lake to Pahokee and had a big rodeo but they didn't come back here.

We've just had such an exciting life, all the time.

Later on when I married, I had to help my husband cut down big pine trees.

Mr. Carl really loved to come out and help. We had an old mowing machine that was pulled by a mule and my dad was mowing the grass... it was tall and nice, wonderful hay. Our old hen was setting in the grass and he mowed right over the nest which cut her legs off, so we had to kill her. But we took the little biddies and brought them in the house. That was the year I was in the 4-H Club and my mother gave me the choice of taking care of the chickens, the poultry, and I had hatched a lot of biddies and we'd eat the hens later on in the summer. I won a trip to Tallahassee for the 4-H Club for ten days and I was the only girl in the county and there were two boys who went to Gainesville. I went with girls

Carl S. Carlton, homeplace barn, circa 1905, which still stands.

from Polk County. That was a highlight of my teenage life! It was a wonderful, wonderful trip.

We'd cut the hay and let it lay in the sun for a couple days to dry; then we'd load it on the big wagon. Mr. Carl and I would load the hay; Daddy was driving and the two mules pulling the wagon. Then we'd pitch the hay through a big hole in the end of the barn and every summer we'd have that loft full of hay.

I first heard about my husband, Jack Himrod, from my brother, who was a friend of his in high school. Then later, after Luke had already run away (we called him Luke instead of Luther most of the time), I met Jack but I had known his uncle who was his mother's brother, and he was dating a young woman in Oak Grove who was our leader in Sunday School. His name was Mel Altman and he kept telling Jack there was a real pretty little girl over at Oak Grove playing basketball that he wanted him to meet. She'll make some man a fine wife one of these years and before Luke ran away he'd talk about Jack Himrod all the time. He had a good horse and they'd ride horses down by the Peace River but I never met him until Uncle Mel decided he'd have a party so I could meet Jack. He had the party and there were about 18 teenagers around Oak Grove who were there. He came down where we were and jumped the fence! I saw him because I was looking for him. Uncle Mel had told me he was coming. Pretty soon we started playing a game "March Around the Level." We formed a big circle and marched around it and we'd drop a handkerchief behind a person and if that person didn't pick it up real quick, somebody next to him would pick it up, then they'd have to drop the handkerchief. Anyway, I found the handkerchief and I dropped it right behind Jack and he started around. And when he looked at me and I looked at him we fell deeply in love. And we were in love as long as he lived. When we married two years later. One of my cousins said, "It won't last two years. He's only 18 and you're only 16." But it lasted 55 years and five months.

Jack had gone to work after he graduated. He was a senior when I met him and I was a freshman. He'd come and help me with my algebra which was a weak point with me. I loved everything else but math. The first time I got my report card, I got an "F," and it nearly broke my heart, so after that he'd come and help me and I got my grade up to a "B." He graduated in '28 and I went on to high school another year and he went to Clewiston to help build the smokestacks for U. S. Sugar Corporation and he was good at that. Then we decided to get married. He had to borrow a car to come to church over at Oak Grove because he didn't have a car. He'd walk across the woods to Troublesome Creek and that's where we courted. We'd just sit and talk. I knew not to pet, I knew it wouldn't work and I might get in trouble. Anyway, talk about suspicious, one day Papa got suspicious. I'd just take a walk down by the grove and nobody would mind, but he knew there was something drawing me to Troublesome Creek. Well, one day my mother was going to town to spend the day with my sister, she was married and had a little child, and he insisted on my going with my mother. I said, "No, Papa, I don't want to go. I want to stay here and I'll fix your dinner and so forth." And he said, "No, you're going." Anyway, Jack came that afternoon and he told me later, "I saw your dad and figured he was getting suspicious so I stayed hid. I knew you wouldn't come that day."

He brought me from church one Sunday night and he said, "Mrs. Marsh, Mae Frank and I want to get married." She said, "Jack, you're asking for my best youngun." He said, "I know it... that's why I want her." She said, "Well, let me go ask her daddy." He had already gone to bed but he was not asleep. Mama talked to him and he said, "I guess you might as well let her go, she'll just run away if we don't let her go." Mama came back and said, "Jack, I guess you can have her but I sure will miss her."

We were married 55 years and some months. We had lost our first baby. A lot of kids said... they need to get married, she's pregnant. We were both virgins, we didn't even have sex the first night or two which is another story. We didn't know how! We didn't know what we were supposed to do!

Jack's mother decided I should go back to school after our first baby died. We didn't have a baby for two years. I carried our first one ten months and he was born double-breach, I could not deliver him. I'd been in labor for 18 hours, Jack's grandmother and his aunt, Raymond Chambless' grandmother, Della Hendry, from Fort Green was a midwife, and she came and saw what shape I was in and I just said, "Dr. Spears, leave me alone. I'm tired and I'm not afraid to die..." He said, "Good God, woman, don't say that..." Aunt Della got up and said, "Dr. Spears, would you like for me to help you?" He said, "Yes, oh yes, Mrs. Hendry, if you would I'll be forever grateful." So she said, "Mae Frank, can you hear me now?" Tears were running down my face and I said, "Yes, ma'am." She said, "You know what shape it's in. The baby is breach and my hands are not strong... I'm going to get right up in bed with you between your legs so I can get my fingers around the baby's hips. When you have a pain give it all you've got! Push! When it subsides you take a deep breath and the next time you be ready to give it all you've got!" Well, with the third pain she had that baby out of there. But he was just as blue as he could be. He died in the birth canal, but he was active when I first started in labor.

She said, "You need to go back to school. You're a born teacher." She had taught nearly 50 years before she retired. So she made me clothes, pretty little dresses to wear to school and just about the time school started she found out that I was pregnant again... with Margaret. There went my schooling.

My Daddy told me not long after we'd been married... he said, "Mae Frank, Carl told me the other day that you didn't need to get married, he was going to pay your way to Tallahassee where Mattie Mae had finished getting her degree. I told him it was too late now. He didn't tell me about it but Mr. Carl thought I should have finished school and gone into teaching.

When Marge and Peggy Hanson were staying with us, we decided we'd have a party one night and I fixed food for all 12 of them. We had an old grass rug that we had in our living room. We put it out on the lawn and we had one of those old phonographs and we had some good records to dance to. I was dancing with the cowboys and we were having a lot of fun. Jack was playing the music... he never learned to dance. I learned to dance down in Felda and LaBelle... all sorts of dancing. I just loved to dance. And there was a man, I can't think of his name, and I was dancing with him and he said, "I never danced with a real lady before in all my life." 'Course that made me feel good.

When we lived in Alabama I didn't realize that my daddy could play the fiddle but he loved to and they'd have barn dances. Uncle Jim, his older brother and he had two pianos in his living room. One was a player piano and that's the one I played... just pedal it and play. Anyway, one time we were there for Christmas and several of the brothers had gone to a cane grinding and they got hold of some juice that they'd let sour... wine or something and they came back and Papa had had an overdose of wine and started vomiting. My mother said, "You deserve that! I'm glad to see you like this!" I thought she was so mean. I didn't know that he was drunk.

Barn dancing is old timey dancing and they did take place in barns at times. They would celebrate with parties after getting the hay in, and I remember although I was a small child, in Alabama we'd have peanut shelling and corn shucking and if one of the young men found an ear of red corn, then he'd get to kiss his sweetheart. That was with farming... country people.

After we were married there were square dances in Felda. And the Maddox boys were crazy about dancing, they really had rhythm. One of the Townsend boys, brother of the one who went to Australia, he couldn't dance but he wanted to try in his old cowboy boots stomping up and down, swing your partner and I had to watch so he wouldn't step on my feet. And my husband didn't mind my dancing... they were all his first cousins.

One time I asked my Mama "Where do babies come from?" And she said, "Out of a hollow stump." After that every where I'd go in the woods with my brothers I'd look in every hollow stump or log to see if I could find a baby.

Another thing I did when I was older, Luke was my favorite brother but I loved Tim and Cecil in a different way. Luke would have me tramping all over the woods, all over Carlton Country up and down Troublesome Creek hunting little animals with steel traps which was very cruel but he wanted to make money. We'd skin right through the woods, the palmettos and thorny places and I'd help him set his traps. When we'd get home I'd hold the little animals while he skinned them and cleaned them out. Then he'd tack them up on the smoke house wall to sun dry. Eventually, he'd mail them to Missouri, the Bungston-Burke Company. The low pole cats and the civet cats and opossum... there wasn't much money in them but every little bit counted back in those days. Once in a while he'd catch a raccoon and that would be a nice big catch. And the tail was really important, too. After all this was done he'd roll them up in a bundle, mail them out and he'd get some money back in the mail.

And then there was this: We were just teenagers when we did this and I can hardly believe that we didn't kill ourselves. (Mae Frank was pointing to the top dormer on the second floor of The Little White House) See that top dormer... that peak right at the top? Well, we'd take a 2 X 8 or a 2 X 10 plank, most any plank that was long enough, and we'd climb up there with it and put it over that top peak to make a see-saw. We loved being up so high – almost in the trees! Don't know why we didn't kill ourselves! We could have fallen off that see-saw plank and plunged down the roof to the ground.

I guess "Somebody" higher than we was looking after us.

WILLIAM ELMO REDDING

William Elmo Redding

Elmo Redding was one of the sons of Bob Redding who was the foreman for Albert Carlton and he (Elmo) resided in the Carlton Homeplace (The Little White House). He is a living historian regarding his experiences with the Carlton Family.

Elmo Redding: The Redding family moved to The Little White House in 1946; there were three of us kids. I had a brother and a sister. Three of my other family was born here… Ronnie Redding, Gayle Redding and R. W, the Third, who was Buck. He's an agriculture teacher at Hardee High.

Barbara Carlton: *The property, the estate, was settled in 1948. Albert had two half-sisters, but Albert was the main heir to the estate. His half-sister, Matred, raised him; her husband was the administrator of the estate. They divided the estate among those three in '48 when Albert became 21.*

Daddy was working at that time for Miss Matred, Mattie Mae and Albert, and they asked him if he would take care of Albert and that's when he left them and came to Oak Grove in 1946. And he stayed here until 1976 when he died. He moved about three years before he died out to New Zion and that's where he was living when he passed away. To me this is home, this little house, the Carlton Homeplace, The Little White House. When we moved here there wasn't indoor plumbing, nor bathroom, we had lights but that was it. This was a screened porch. Then they made a jalousied porch out of it, now it's back to what y'all had which is a lot better. That jalousied porch would freeze you to death in the wintertime.

It'll always be home.

I left here in '58 and went in the Army and when I came back I went to work for Mr. Doyle, Sr. because it was Dec. of '54 when Daddy broke his neck. All of 'em asked me if I could get out of school, I was in high school doctorin' on screw worms. I talked to Judge Evers who was the principal and he told me they'd let me out at noon in agriculture. So they had to have a horse saddled and I'd go to wherever they were. I did the doctoring for screw worms for Albert; I doctored screw worms for Doyle. Then you didn't have day workers and you didn't have but two or three employees and everybody came together to work the cattle. I've worked for all of Albert's uncles but two and they were both dead before I was born, that was Albert's daddy, Carl, and Uncle Ab. The rest of 'em I have worked for… weekend work, Uncle Alton, Uncle Tom, he's the one that brought my daddy here in '36.

My daddy was a quarter-breed Cherokee, my granddaddy was a half-breed. When you read the book *Peace River Pioneers of Florida* and they refer to the half-breed, that was my granddaddy.

When we first came here, the barn didn't have this side built on it, that was built later. The smoke house used to set right there and the outdoor toilet just over in the edge of the grove. They put an electric pump in… on the well out there and daddy and I built a shower right on the side of the wall out there, outside y'all's front porch. We could get us a shower… it was cold but it was a shower.

Back then where Dr. Barbara's house is now was a set of cow pens… that was before the house was set there. We'd feed-lot steers out there. We'd put four or five hundred head of steers in there then we'd ship 'em. We found out it was too expensive to do that, it just cost too much money to bring grain and you wouldn't make that much off of 'em so Doyle and a bunch of 'em went out west and got them boys out there to build a bunch of feed lots and we shipped the cattle to them because they had the grain. This was back in the late '50s and early '60s.

There's a lot of history on this place. I don't know other than the people who have lived here including Uncle Carl. The two girls were born here but Albert was born in town. Ander Marsh lived here with his family and he was the foreman for Uncle Carl. After he left the Howze family moved in here and then after they left, we moved in... And these are the only people who have ever lived here up until after daddy left here. I b'lieve Otto Whaley lived here for a while and then I can't remember anybody after Otto ever living here.

Dr. Barbara Carlton: *There was one other family... Vivian, she married one of the Whaleys. She was my housekeeper. They were the last people who lived here.*

Randy was still at home when Otto lived here. One of them married my wife's sister, Otto's brother, Roy.

There were horses here and five milk cows and what hogs we had we'd catch out of the woods and bring in and fatten 'em on out. Most all the hogs were wild. In fact, in the old smoke house, syrup kettle set right beside it. We scalded the hogs in the kettle and when we'd get through scalding the hogs we'd render the meat out in it. We'd cook the cracklins down to get the lard.

Then we cut up the white meat (called fat back) and put it in five-gallon crocks, five gallon lard cans we called 'em. Then we'd pour the lard back over it and seal it. Set it in the corner of the smoke house and when you wanted meat you'd just go in there and get it out and all you had to do was heat it and that kept the meat. It was too hot to smoke and cure meat, you could smoke some but not all. Hog killing always come on the first frost in November or December. We'd kill 20 to 25 head at the time. You could get almost a year out of that meat staying good. Long as you kept that lard over the meat when you pulled it out and put that lard back, it kept it rancid but once you cooked it and dripped that rancid fat out of it that left it good. We only salted the fat meat like bacon. We built salt bins down each side of the smoke house. You just put a layer of salt and you hand-rubbed that bacon and you laid in the salt and you covered it up with salt and ever' day you went out there and turned it over and redid the process… the salt would draw the liquid out and you'd replace the salt. And you just kept doing that until it got just as firm as that table. (He knocked his fist on the table to show how firm the meat and salt would get.) And it never would spoil. We would smoke some beef but it was hog-smoked hams. But sometimes they'd start rotting before we could get 'em cured. You cured them in a vat of water with salt. Salt the water till it would float an egg – just pour the salt to it 'til that egg floats, then submerge the meat in it and in five days you change it, and you continue to do that until there is no blood left in the water… it's clear. Then you could smoke it. That was the hams. But sometimes it would get so hot they'd start rotting. We still do it for Cracker Country at the Florida State Fair.

I can't talk plain with no teeth no more. A horse kicked me right there under that barn and messed up my jaw and they can't get no bottom plate to fit it. So I don't talk plain.

The first room here on the left of the living room of the Carlton Homeplace, that's where Mama and Daddy stayed. My sister Jeanette and Gail stayed in the room on the right of the boys room, us boys stayed in the second room on the left, and my baby brother, Buck, slept with Mama and Daddy in the big room. They had two beds. Me and Bobby Joe and Frog, we called him Frog... his name was Ronnie, we slept in this room here. I slept on a single bed and they had bunk beds.

There were six of us kids, and the

Bob and Fannie Redding, mother and father of Elmo Redding. Bob was Albert Carlton's foreman.

Marshes had four girls and two boys so this is a six-children house.

Of course, now that (he points to what looks like a corner closet in the dining room which turns out to be a closet for housing the air conditioning unit) wasn't here whenever we lived here and later on we built this and Mama made a pantry out of it. We'd go picking huckleberries and stuff and she made preserves and pie fillings and that's where they were put.

Normally of a morning Daddy would holler about four or four-thirty. I got up and went to the barn and feed Nick, but before I went out the house I had to build a fire if it was cold. Mama had a wood stove. Well, Daddy would come and get the stove going and I'd go feed the horses and milk. When I'd be on my way back to the house with the milk I could smell Mama's cookin' and I'd be so hungry I'd 'most run. Smellin' her soft, brown biscuits made my mouth water. And sometimes the milk started splashin' out the bucket so I had to slow down. Some mornings the dark was so black I had to feel my way, and some mornings in mostly early spring, fog was so heavy it was like I'd haf to push my way through it. Mama would have breakfast ready by five o'clock. We'd eat, then ever'body got ready to go to school.

During summer we were all working ever'day with the cows and we'd saddle up at the Carlton Homeplace in Oak Grove. In the beginning we didn't have trucks and trailers so we rode horses to New Zion. It was 10 miles. We'd leave the Carlton Homeplace in Oak Grove at five or five-thirty on horseback and be out there just a little bit after crack o' day. We'd start gatherin' cattle there on the east side o' Brushy near New Zion[1]. There was about a thousand acre crevice that was built during the dipping in the '30s when the dippin' vats were put in. We'd put the cattle in there and we'd gather cattle for two-three days and then we'd put 'em into pens and we'd work 'em. I can still smell all

(1): The original Bar-Ā Ranch that Albert inherited was at New Zion. The oldest Baptist Church in the Orange Blossom Association is there. It was founded as Maple Branch in 1866 on the Alafia River and moved to New Zion in 1873 and it's still standin' there, cemetery and all. Elmo says, "At noon we'd go to the church and Albert would play the piano. That's why I spent so much time there."

that heat and mess from them cattle and their bellerin' got to be deaf'nin'.

Sometimes Albert would drive out there, we'd leave his horses, or sometimes he'd meet us at the Bar Ⱥ Ranch at New Zion. If Carl was with him, Carl Saunders, they'd usually meet us here at the homeplace. And sometimes if Carl had to go they'd drive on… it just depended on where he needed to be.

Ever'thing was done by hand, you done ever'thing by hand. We worked four or five hundred head a day just depending on how big the crew was and who'd come in to help. We'd all be taking turns. When you git hot you sit down and somebody else would take over. The cows didn't stop but you did, you had to take a break once in a while.

I was leaning up against a chute out there, I b'lieve it was 'round '56, in the shade up against an oak tree and an old cow hooked me in the back through the fence.

I was not doin' a thing to her, she just wanted to hook me and she did! I've still got that scar today.

That's where we started out and 'course as we got trucks and trailers, specially the trucks, Albert got a '53 two and half-ton Ford truck and we built a bull rack on it out there under the barn, my daddy and I. It was called a straight job, it doesn't have a trailer, it's just the truck and the bed with a cow rack on it. We always called it a bull rack. Then we'd haul our horses out to New Zion. That was a lot better.

I grew up here in the Oak Grove Church, fact is, I went to grade school there, it was an old country school. I walked 'til I bought me a bicycle. Then I rode that bicycle 'til some old boy took the air out of the tires so I'd have to walk back home. So I just left my bicycle and kept walkin'. Ken McLeod… that's who it was.

Basically this was our day, nothing but work. Like I say, we'd be out there at daylight, specially doctoring screw worms you wanted to be there to see the cattle and you didn't leave 'em until you couldn't see 'em that night.

Then you rode home and you'd bed up, get a bath, eat supper and go to bed. That was the schedule. We didn't have television and telephones. This was our day and that was seven days a week.

Albert had a horse named Hitler before we came here, so I don't remember him but he rode a little old mare that we called Jackie, a little horse, a mare and that's who he rode most of the time. Daddy had an old horse called Pepper, and then a strawberry roan mare called Chula and then there was Syrup and Clabber, a pinto horse named Trigger. And Carl Saunders rode Trigger. Carl was Albert's nephew.

Like I said, when he came here, Albert to me was like a bigger brother, course I didn't have anybody else. Uncle Tom Carlton lived right down the road here. I think I was 10 or 11 years old when he died. But I've always been right here in this family. I was born in it and my granddaddy hauled oranges in oxcarts and my daddy after him and I'm still workin' for 'em. They won't let me retire right now. Which I'm glad.

Now here's something else. The old Carlton swimming hole. That was the community hole. We baptized in that hole right down here on the creek (Troublesome Creek). There used to be another house that set down there that I lived in when I came back out of service and went back to work for Mr. Doyle.

I lived in it for a year till we got the other house rebuilt over there below Alberta's where Red Wiggins lives now. Donna blew the roof off o' that one in 1960. I was already working for Doyle but I was living out on the Dallas Road… remember Doyle sold all that out there when he bought the Horse Creek pasture. Albert let me stay in that place till we got the other'n fixed where I could move back in the company house. Then Albert moved my daddy to New Zion and bought Bobby Joe and Irene a place when they first got married. Right there in that hole is where my sister and all of us learned to swim. Used to be a big old oak tree limb that went out over that hole and I let some of them older boys talk me into crawling up there one day and they just shoved me off. And said … "swim or drown" and that's how you learned. And that's how all of us learned.

But ever' Sunday afternoon that's where the whole community was in the summer. Ever'body went there to go swimmin'. That hole was prob'bly as big as this part of this house (20 X 40 feet) maybe a little bit wider. It was a nice hole and deep. That oak tree limb was 'bout 20-foot up in the air and we could dive off it without hittin' bottom. It had to be a good 18 to 20 foot deep I know. The last time I was there was when Donna came through. We were living there and we didn't have electricity and we went down to the creek with our baby diapers, we had the twins then. They were born in '59.

We've always been here since my granddaddy (after World War I) married my grandmother. At that time, Miss Louise (Alberta Albritton's mother) was married to her first husband before she married Uncle Ab. Granddaddy hauled oranges for Uncle Ab in an ox cart to Bradenton. And then Granddaddy left here because he said he couldn't make a living and he went back to Immokalee, that's where my granddaddy was raised. And he took my granddaddy back to Immokalee when he was two years old and he was raised there. Then during the dipping in the '30s my daddy was ridin' with a man out of Okeechobee named Zeb Williams. He was hired by the state to dip the cattle and Uncle Tom called and had the pasture at Micco Bluff (north of the Pearce Ranch) on the Kissimmee River and he brought Daddy back to Hardee County in 1936. In the meantime, Mr. Carl went into the bank. Daddy went to work for Mr. Doyle, Sr... Daddy lived over there where I live now off the Vandolah Road, and that's where I was born.

The only farming we did back then was for personal use… corn and peas… just what you needed to eat… about five or six acres because the whole family would eat out of it. Daddy planted the peas with the corn so the peas would grow up the cornstalk.

Uncle Tom Carlton owned a ranch at Micco Bluff on the Kissimmee River, in fact, Winston wound up with that. Winston was Uncle Tom Carlton's son, Albert's uncle also.

From 1946 my daddy stayed right here with Albert until he died in August 1976.

Elmo's recollections of the fatal shooting of Carl Carlton:

When Uncle Albert's father was killed the only thing I remember is what Uncle Ander Marsh used to tell me. He was there when Carl got killed. Uncle Alton wouldn't talk much because it still upset him till he died. Uncle Alton was there and he told me the story a lot of times and he never changed it... it was always the same. Onlyst part they never did understand was how that buckshot hit Uncle Carl at the angle it was. The onlyst thing it coulda been was it had to have ricocheted off one of those hard cypress trees.

Uncle Ander told me that Uncle Alton just lost his mind at the time of the accident. He just went crazy. He said sometimes they had to lay Uncle Carl down and try to get Alton to gather his senses before they could start totin' Uncle Carl out again. John Rooney and Uncle Ander actually toted Uncle Carl out.

We were told that Uncle Alton at first wanted to carry him out himself but he wasn't half as big at Uncle Carl, he was the smallest one of the bunch... he was a little man, a little fella.

When my wife, Annie, and I got married in 1958 Uncle Alton and Aunt Mary lived there in town at "Azalea Hill." We lived in that little house at the back, there was nothing to do but for me and my wife to live in that house till I went in the Army. In three months I was gone. I tried to get my wife to wait till I got back to marry but no she said I may not be here when you get back... you gonna marry me before you go. And I said, "Yes Ma'am!" and I'm still saying "Yes Ma'am!"

And this comin' June it'll be 50 years.

The biggest thing I remember about Albert was back when we were doctorin' screw worms. You know Albert always went at things 90 miles an hour and daddy had to get him slowed down. He said, "Albert, you're runnin' them cows to death! Slow down!" He told me one day, "If you two don't slow down I'm gonna put my belt on both o' you!"

Dr. Barbara Carlton: *When we got married we lived in a little house in town and then started building. And I remember Albert saying, "We're going to build just one house." Well, since then we've added to it a couple times but we never built another home.*

During the time that Albert was building the new home in Oak Grove, it was formerly the feed lot site, Daddy would drive by and say, "Albert I want you to put up about a 10-foot fence around this house… only way I'm gonna get anything out of you is to come by and throw groceries over the fence ever' once in a while." That's where Albert stayed. He stayed right there until it was finished. He'd come out here of a morning and Daddy would say, "You gonna help me today?" And Albert said, "Nope… I'll be right here."

Albert loved building… he sure loved it. And he loved the piano as good as anybody I've ever known. My wife went and got a death certificate the other day on one of her grandmothers and guess who played the piano at her funeral? Albert. He sure did. We didn't even know that. She died in 1949 and Albert played the piano at her funeral. She was my wife's great-grandmother, Georgia McCaskill. Now Annie, my wife, is back working on her genealogy… you know how that is for her. Albert's mama was Emma Edwards and my wife's grandmother was a Platt. Daisy Platt married Carl Carlton and had two daughters Matred and Mattie Mae.

There's a lot of history in this family. I was a lot younger than the Carlton family but I used to listen to the stories of the nine Carlton brothers especially Doyle, Sr., Uncle Tom, Uncle Charlie and Uncle Alton. All of us used to sit out on the porch and they'd chew their tobacco and smoke their pipes and I'd sit and listen and that's how I learned.

My wife, she and I were dating, she didn't want to go to town, she wanted to go to my granddaddy's and we'd set on the porch and he'd tell her stories about my daddy growing up in Immokalee and different ones in the family.

With daddy, Bob Redding, you didn't have a single job, you did it all. You ride the horse, work cattle, you worked on the road, you planted grass, you built fence. Nobody had a specialty. You did it all. Buddy (Colson) will tell you, he works for Dr. Carlton... started some 40 years ago.

Standing on the bridge that traverses Troublesome Creek where so much of the rich history of the Carltons embraces the true roots of this great family, Elmo Redding relates more of his vivid and colorful memories that span decades of his life:

Elmo Redding "The Professor," faithful ranch and grove hand still works for one of the Carltons.

This is a story about Uncle Alton Carlton who was one of the nine sons of Albert and Martha McEwen Carlton and lived in the Oak Grove community. This is about a grubbing hoe.

One day I was driving down the Alton Carlton Road and I saw Uncle Alton out there in the "stasher" side of the creek walking 'round like he was lost. So I stopped and said, "Unc... whatta you need?" And he said, "Well, somebody has stole my grubbin' hoe... and I can't find it."

I said, "Just a minute..." So I got out and walked down there with him, walked 'round a little bit and I found it hanging up in an oak tree. And that made him happy 'cause he had grubbed ever' palmetto and "burl" that ever grew up and down this creek... he grubbed 'em out. He was in his '80s then, and he lived until he was 89... and he was still grubbin' in spite of having one leg amputated.

Now this-here story is about Mabry Carlton, Sr. We called him Uncle Jack.

He used to tell me that there used to be an Indian village up there on the east branch of Troublesome. And I know at one time there probably was because there are banana trees that grows up there and there's Indian mounds. Well, he was born around 1901 and he said that when he was a boy there was still an Indian village there.

The mounds are still there but now they're protected by state law. One of 'em got a big old seedlin' orange tree growing right up through the middle of it. I haven't been in there to it since my kids were home. My children are all grown now, but when they're home I'd take them down there once in a while then I'd take 'em down behind my house on Troublesome Creek and they'd find a lot of arrowheads, spearheads and different Indian artifacts. In fact, a lot of those artifacts they give 'em to Uncle Jack and he put 'em in the museum down at Pioneer Park at Zolfo Springs. That's the Cracker Town park. When they started that, that's where they went.

When I was nothing but a little boy ever' where my daddy went he'd take me with him. And that's where I learned a lot about the history of the family...just settin' and listenin'. You didn't talk then, you listened. And so that's how I found out that little bit I know about this family... and spending a lot of time with Uncle Jack because he's the one that knew the history of this family. He would tell me stories.

When I'd come in from work, him and Mrs. Septa, his wife, she taught school here for years. She died here in Hardee County. They'd be tellin' my wife stories 'cause my wife is distant kin to 'em. That's how the stories were learnt was just by listenin' to the old people.

But whenever I was a boy and they'd go to Sidell in Sarasota County, my daddy would take me with him before I even started to school. And I'd hold onto the back of his saddle while we were going down there. And then I had to stay with the cook and wash pots and pans in the creek while he cooked and they worked cattle and that's how I found out a lot of the family history.

The family on weekends... my daddy usually went somewhere and I'd always go with him to help him work their own personal cattle, doctoring the screw worms back in the '50s, and that's how I knew just about ever' member of the Carlton family except for the two before I was born.

And that's the way it was... that's how I got what education I got and having a good memory and lovin' to tell the stories about it.

Dr. Barbara Carlton: *Elmo Redding was labeled "The Professor" because of his extensive knowledge and intended exaggerations.*

PART THREE
DORIS SPEARMAN LAMBERT
ALBERT'S CHILDHOOD
Vividly recalling her memories from early school days

Doris Spearman Lambert is a native of Wauchula where she grew up and went to school with little Albert Carlton. She has remained a devoted friend of the Carlton Family all her life.

Albert and I first met on the school yard at Wauchula Elementary School when we were both in the first grade. We were playing on the swings. My absolute first impression of him was seeing a very hurtful grimace on his face when a little girl, one of our classmates, walked up and said to me, "Did you know that his mother killed herself?" Of course, Albert heard the remark but he did not say a word. I didn't know anything about what she said but I changed the subject and even though little as I was I thought: *this is not right... we shouldn't be talking about this.*

Albert and I went all the

Albert Carlton at five years old

121

way through elementary and high school through the tenth grade and during that time I became aware of a lot of people who loved Al. He was always available. I do not know how he learned to play the piano, who taught him, I just knew that suddenly he was by far the best musician we had in school. I was a singer and he encouraged me greatly in my singing. We just seemed to have the very same feeling about music. I think if it had not been for his music I don't know how he would have gotten through his early years.

Both his mother and father suffered early tragic deaths and he was left to live with a half-sister and her husband, Matred and Allen Olliff, when he was only six years old. Although she took good care of him, I'm sure that living with that sister was not the most pleasant time in his life. I can remember that during high school years he wore faded plaid shirts and faded jeans, sometimes with holes in them because they didn't treat him any different than other children in those days. I don't know how much money there was in the family… I just didn't know. I do know that he was a little introverted, a little shy, never did he want to stand out in class or anywhere but Albert was probably one of the most brilliant people I have ever known as far as his lessons were concerned. He always made the best grades. I'm sure that if he had graduated from high school with us, which he didn't, he would have been the valedictorian. There's no doubt in my mind about that. But to go back to the high school years… he went to Bolles Military School in Jacksonville. From there I sorta lost track of him until he finished college and came back at which time he was 21, the age that he could take over his inheritance. His fortune had been preserved for him by the family who raised him… his half-sister and her husband. I never got the impression that they were a happy family but at least they did preserve his fortune for him and that I thought was a great thing to do.

During those years he was always available and he was an absolute wizard at the piano. He played by ear; he could read music but he preferred not to. So we'd say *let's sing so-and-so* and he'd say *start it off.* I'd begin and he'd immediately pick it up and play whatever it was perfectly… it was just wonderful.

And we did pep rallies at the school and he was always the one who'd play the piano. A unique thing was this: later in life, Albert had three sons and while we talk about Pat, the second son, being more like Albert, and he is in a lot of ways, as Albert was in later years, but Will was the one who was more like Albert as he was growing up. Will was a little bit shy, another very, very intelligent, smart boy but a little introverted. In other words he was not all that outgoing. These are my impressions as he grew up with one of my sons. As he grew older he came into his own and he's fine now and like Albert, he gained his confidence.

He had a special friend in one of his cousins, Dot Carlton Campbell. She was his special ally, his special friend and they spent a lot of time together. Albert was not athletically inclined at all but he was an all 'round friend. I never knew him to have an enemy of any description, no enemies. When I was asked to sing some place, he was always available. He'd practice with us as a trio, he'd save time on a certain day of the week… this was after he got out of school and came home before he was married.

I have several pictures of him but all that shows is his back because he'd be playing the piano and pictures were being made of the performers so naturally it was Albert's back that was in the pictures. But to me that depicted Al as he was growing up. He'd have his back to the group or the crowd. And those who heard his music loved every note but his face was never shown. To me, knowing him as I did, he should have been the one they celebrated because he was the most talented of all. I almost get overcome when I think about it because he was so sweet and he was such a wonderful, unusual person.

I remember we used to go to the drugstore and I was just a poor little mechanic's daughter and he'd go just with me, and sometimes we'd go as a crowd after school in the afternoon. And sometimes he didn't have a nickel to buy a

Coke… maybe I would have an extra nickel and I'd give it to him and never thought any more about it. Then of course, he came into his fortune because I don't think his family, the Olliffs, treated him any differently. They didn't furnish him with a lot of money, or a car… most young people in those days didn't have a car.

I want everybody who reads this book to know the heart of Albert and I feel that I know the heart of Albert Carlton. He and I would get together and he'd play the piano and I'd sing. We had the exact same feeling whatever the music was. It didn't make any difference; I knew we were in tune with one another. There was never any girlfriend-boyfriend, that never entered the picture. I think he played his feelings out on the piano. If it was joy, the music was joyful, if it was sad he'd play a sadder piece. He had a unique feeling for music and what it meant to him. I don't know of anyone who had the very same unique feeling that I had with him.

He was born with an absolute God-given talent that he could play by notes but he preferred to play by ear… and as he played, he played in silence. You could see his feelings on his face. I wish I could express what I remember about that.

My impression of his growing up in the home that he grew up in was that it was cold, it was *come in, get your dinner, go to bed, get up, get dressed, go to school.* There was never, as I remember, anyone who came with him to any school functions as a parent. There may have been, but if there was it was beyond my recollections. I got the impression that the man in the family, the husband of Albert's half-sister, was a hard, cold man. And some people will tell you that he had a soft side, but if he did I never saw it. As a matter of fact, I never saw the man smile. I got the feeling there was never any joy or happiness in that family. Albert got his joy and happiness with his friends at school, but for the most part he stood in the background... most of all with his music.

I gave Dr. Barbara a picture not too long ago of Albert leaning against a tree, which to me depicted Albert. Dr. Barbara said, *"He always liked to lean against a tree and put his foot up."* But I saw something else in that picture that she couldn't possibly see because when she met him –as far as I know—he was out of school and into his own and seemed to be happy as a lark. I don't know how anybody could come out of what he came out of and be as happy as he was in his later years. I got to know him again after school and he and Barbara got married and I know all men love their children but I think he was the proudest father I have known in a long, long time. And he said to me and my husband one night as we walked out of their home and he walked us to the car, "You know I could buy Will, my oldest son, a car if I wanted to but I don't want Will to have a car yet. I want him to know what it's like to do without a car."

I thought this was a wonderful thing because most parents the minute they can they buy their children automobiles. He didn't and I admired him so much for that. Their children have great values… they're genuine and friendly. It's unreal how they came out of these genetics.

I have to say that Albert, instead of standing out, he was outstanding. In his quiet way he was truly an outstanding man. All the teachers loved him. And some of the teachers were his cousins but they never treated him any different. You had to be nice to him because he wasn't anything but nice which was in a masculine way, not at all sissy. He was a genuine, genuine person. The heart of Albert was so good and how I wished for him that he'd had a mother and a father to follow and support him when he needed support. But that he didn't have.

His half-sister, Mattie Mae Saunders, did all she could do but she had more than she could do herself. She was a teacher and had two boys of her own to raise which was probably hard for her.

Sometimes Albert was like a shadow. He never stood out unless he played the piano, and he played for many, many functions… for the fairs, all kinds of meetings and programs, stage plays, whatever, and you didn't have to wonder would he do it, he did it. He really gave of himself to this county.

Albert was a special, special person. When he passed away I thought my entire family would absolutely collapse. My children had grown to love him… he was so special. There was something sad about him and to think that he had to die so young and he had such a struggle even before he had his first heart attack… so young. He and Barbara were so happy… they had the children… but then, it looked like the world turned upside down for them.

I remember that we felt we could not do anything good enough for the family when Albert died. My oldest son was very close to his children. My youngest son is Will's age. When he was younger, Will was a little bit introverted and he was another one who didn't stand out but he was outstanding… a fine outstanding young man. As Pat grew older he took on his dad's characteristics. Pat's smile is so friendly, he's so much like his dad during the last years of his dad's life.

But I thought in his growing up years, Will was more like Albert. I don't know if anyone else will agree with me but that's the way I saw it.

Albert was a great man. Sometimes we have to wonder why people like him have to go when he had so much to give. But he left a great legacy and his children… Barbara has done wonders with all of his legacy. The children will carry on, they're well-educated, they have good common sense and each one has something of their father. So as long as they live he will never die.

Julie is beautiful… a beautiful girl. The older she gets the more beautiful she becomes. She has her father's face and her mother's looks. Pat, characteristically, is like his dad. Charlie is a cross between a Castleberry and a Carlton. He looks a little like Barbara and a little like Al. But each one of the children has something that looks like their father. That happens to a lot of us but in some families you don't see such traits. In this family you can tell where these children came from!

There are no doubt many people who see and remember Albert in a different light than I do. There are very few people who knew him as I did… who knew his heart. I know that I knew his heart, as a child and growing up and as an adult.

Never was there anything… you might think I was in love with him but that's not true. I loved him but I was not in love with him. And he loved me … he was such a great encourager to me. I thought everybody in the world could sing but he'd say I had a special talent and he enhanced anything I did on the stage with his playing. It was just wonderful! And the backup was equally wonderful. Always, he was the backup, you could depend on him.

These are all impressions of mine. I did not go into the family but I know that when we had functions that students needed their parents, they were there for them, however, Albert didn't have anybody there. I guess that's one reason that I loved him so. I felt sorry for him at times. And I was so happy for him when he came into his own, and I was grateful to the people who raised him for having preserved his fortune for him and kept it intact so that when he became of age it would be there for him.

And the first thing he did when he received his inheritance was to go to the Buick agency and buy a brand new red convertible. He was the happiest person in the world! He'd never owned anything even near like that and I'll never forget it… the Buick agency was right down the street here. He wanted to take everybody for a ride, he was simply ecstatic over that car.

Then, of course, I don't know how he managed between the time that he came into his own and married Barbara. She, being the person that she is, was a great help-mate in managing everything and helping with investments, etc.

Albert deserved all the good things that he got, he just didn't deserve to die so young and leave them all because they all loved each other. Theirs was a wonderful family… they loved each other so much. That's why the children are so happy that this book is being written. They really have nothing to hide as far as their father is concerned. It was truly tragic the way his life began in his early years. The Carltons came from a great family, my father used to do all their mechanic work… all the Carlton's mechanic work. While I don't remember his father I remember the original family, some of them were my teachers, too. They were all wonderful people.

The heart of Al was what I knew. The older friends do not know what I know about him, they couldn't have. We were friends with all the school children… we ran and we played tag and played all kinds of games and he liked to do these things. And then I'd go to my home and he'd go to his and the others we played with would go to theirs, but then as he grew older and played the piano in school, I watched him. He wasn't happy-happy all the time because too frequently he just didn't have what other kids had. To me, he really was the poor little rich boy but he wasn't even rich back in those days because he had not come into control of his own inheritance.

I guess everybody knew that he would come into his own when he became of age but I don't think I knew that. You see, my folks did not talk about people who had money or fortunes like some people do. I never knew that until he actually did come into his own inheritance. That's what I'm so glad about. Even though it appeared to me that the family was very cold and they never smiled… I never saw any of them smile. And their son killed himself when he was probably in his mid-forties. He had alcoholism more than anything else. There just wasn't any happiness there in that home that I could see, and yet Albert grew up to be a happy person. He was smart, he knew how to be happy. He did not let his childhood days get the best of him. We don't know what he felt inside because he did not let it be known but you could read some of it, a lot of it, on his face. And I know I did read a lot of unhappiness on Albert's face.

I can not say enough good things about him. I've said all this from my

Albert Carlton on his tricycle, age four

heart. I loved him as a friend and his passing was one of the most tragic things I've ever been through. It was such a waste…

He was truly beloved by everyone who knew him. Regardless of the sadness, the tragedy of his early years even before he went to school, Albert Carlton emerged as a great, extraordinary human being.

DOYLE CARLTON SPEARS

Doyle Carlton Spears is the grandson of Alton Carlton, the fourth son of Albert and Martha McEwen Carlton..

Albert Carlton and I rode our bicycles every day together... he lived "right over there" and I lived "right over here." in the same neighborhood across the street from each other on Bay Street. On Saturdays Albert had to mow the grass. He had to use a big mower and it was hard work, but he could not play until he'd mowed. So I'd sit right there on my bicycle and wait for him.

We used to play neighborhood hide-and-go-seek on our bicycles with Jean Burton and Brunell Payton..

Albert was always very smart and liked to do his homework. He'd sit for hours doing his homework… writing… and practicing at the piano which would irritate me because I wanted to play but he wanted to play that piano.

We went to Bolles together, a prep school up in Jacksonville. He was in his junior year and I was in my freshman year. He was in the band. We did that because that was a "strawberry school."

(Doyle explained that a "strawberry school" is one that offers students summertime school in order that students can be out of school in the wintertime to

Petty Officer Doyle Spears in 1944 at Bolles School in Jacksonville, Florida. He is the first officer on the left in the third row.

work in the strawberry fields.)

Edgar Davis of Wauchula also went to Bolles. Albert joined the band, Edgar was in the military company and I was in a naval unit.

Edgar and Albert were there two years, their junior and senior years, I was there four years.

Albert and I used to ride the train back to Wauchula. We'd leave Jacksonville at eleven o'clock at night; and we'd get to Wauchula at sunup. Usually Booger man (Matred's husband Allen Olliff) met Albert. Mr. Davis would meet Edgar and Daddy (Dr. Spears) would meet me unless he was busy in which case I'd walk home.

Albert was in all the societies at Bolles, the honor societies, and he made all A's. I was in the naval unit, period! Albert graduated at the head of his class and Edgar did quite well, too.

Albert Carlton playing piano for the Bolles Glee Club.

But then we separated because Albert went to Gainesville. I think he joined the Navy as soon as he graduated. And we sorta lost touch there for a good while.

I came back to Wauchula and Albert and Odell Carlton had formed the Buick agency which was probably in 1948 or '49. It was a real good business but then I don't know what happened to it.

Their chief mechanic was C. H. Farabee, who was self-taught, and a patient of Dr. Carlton. He could spend all your money… Oh Lord, did he cost me! C. H., and his wife were good people. I can't say as much for his brother Bud!

I remember Uncle Tom quite well. Alton was my granddaddy and he had three girls, my mother and two others. He married Mary Whidden. He and Uncle Tom lived within fifty yards of each other. Papa was quite often trying to get Uncle Tom out of trouble.

Dr. Barbara Carlton: *It was said by more than a few that Uncle Tom was a roust-a-bout in all directions! When asked how many wives he had, Doyle Spears said, "He claimed two, but I don't think one of them claimed him!"*

Tom was a different character and he wasn't always straightforward in his dealings. If somebody bothered his hogs he'd go and whip 'em and Papa would get involved. Papa was a little man while Tom was a big ole tall raw-boned fellow. Uncle Tom would take off and was gonna kill him and Papa would try to get between 'em. So he got the worst part of that deal.

One of the best stories about Uncle Tom I ever heard was when he bought some Texas steers, longhorn steers, ugly looking things… mean. Robert Ray was working for him and they were out rounding up cows. He said, "Grab him! Go in that clump of palmettos and run that heifer out." Robert Ray rode in there but it wasn't no heifer, it was a longhorn steer. So Robert rode back and said, "Tom, that's no heifer… it's one of them longhorns!"

Tom says, "Well, Rabbit, I'll show you what to do with him." So he rode into that clump of palmettos and he had a .44 caliber pistol. He put it right between the horns and fired off a round. Robert said he'd never seen such a terrible thing in his life. He said, the steer came out one end and the horns came out the other and Uncle Tom came walking out, and Uncle Tom was cussin' with ever' breath.

J. D. Snell lived in what was just called a little frame house by the main house, and his wife was there and she ironed clothes and cooked. J. D. woke up one night with a terrible toothache. Well, he went and called granddaddy. Now granddaddy didn't like to get up for anything at night. But he got up and went out to the barn and they got these tools that were used to trim horse hoofs. They're like a big pair of pliers. He's gonna take care of J. D.'s toothache. But you know he got more than that one tooth. However before he got busy pulling J. D's. tooth –or as it turned out he'd pulled several – he went by the watering trough and sloshed those pliers around in the water to "sterilize" his tool.

That was a long time ago.

Grandpa Alton was addicted to a grubbing hoe. Oh he loved grubbing! He lost one of his legs due to bad circulation. Well, he had a black woman who would pick him up and carry him in his wheelchair out to the orange trees. Then they decided they'd cut him off of that so they hid his hoe. Bill Davis, Davis Feed & Fertilizer (Farm Supply) that sold everything from clothes to fertilizer was asked not to sell Papa any more hoes and that just about killed him.

Papa would like to take a little snort and Mama didn't like that at all. So she made him keep it out in the barn. And I went out one day and he was over in the orange trees and he said, "Come on, Son, let's go to the barn." He had an old dirty ice tea glass and he took it and down between the walls of the barn he had his bottle. He got it out and poured him some bourbon, the ice tea glass was about half-full. And he had a jar of sugar. He put about three tablespoon of sugar in the bourbon, stirred it in and then poured spigot water in it… hot spigot water and he drank it down. And then he said, "Alright, Son, it's your turn."

I said, "Papa, I think I'll pass on that."

Dr. Barbara Carlton: *I remember Uncle Alton telling the story about how he would come in every once in a while drinking his "stuff" and Aunt Mary asked him where he'd been. And he'd say, "I been drinkin' beer, Mary."*

He was physically a little man, very petite. I think he got up to 114 pounds one time… wet.

This is the story I've been told about the tragedy in the Everglades. Alton, Carl, Ander Marsh and Rooney, went hunting down in the Everglades. They were stalking a deer which had run into a bayhead that came up to a flag pond. These men had stationed themselves around cypress and oak trees and when the deer jumped out, Carl jumped out from behind an oak tree and at the same time Papa fired. The bullet ricocheted off a cypress and struck Carl a fatal blow to the region of his head. Papa saw there was nothing they could do for him so he insisted on bringing his mortally wounded brother, Carl, out of the Everglades swamp on his back. My Uncle Carl was a big man and Papa was a little man but he carried Carl all the way out of the Everglades on his back. My Daddy said that on up in the day, he'd stop and rest, then he'd go on a little ways and he'd have to stop and rest again. As they proceeded, Alton would have to stop and rest very frequently because the task was too overwhelming. Nevertheless, Alton was insistent that no one else could carry him out. Finally Papa got Carl all the way out of the Everglades but he wouldn't let anyone else touch him.

Regardless of the stories that vary a bit from the telling, it was a bullet from Alton's gun that killed Uncle Carl. Papa never touched a gun again.

Dr. Barbara Carlton: *And it's easy to see why Albert never hunted. I think over time Albert became less of a cattleman and more of a citrus person. He just had that paradigm shift because of the tragic past, probably as much as anything.*

Albert was a very, very sensitive person... extremely sensitive. He cared about other people. He couldn't stand it if somebody was hurt. It would break his heart. Albert would hurt himself before he'd let anybody else be hurt.

I did not know Miss Daisy but I did know his mother, Miss Emma. Daisy died of cancer in 1913.

Albert carried the burden of premature death not only with his father but with his mother also. So I think he compensated for his own loss by reaching out to other people.

Doyle Carlton Spears continues:

My granddaddy would get up in the morning at five o'clock, drink his coffee, at six o'clock get his overalls on and his file in his back pocket and put on an overcoat, a sweater, he had on his long johns, his pants and he'd go to the orange grove. At nine o'clock the overcoat would come off, at 9:30, the sweater would come off, at ten o'clock the shirt would come off, and at eleven o'clock he was down to his skivvies.

He loved chicken and dumplin's but they'd make him dizzy... I guess it was all that salt that went in 'em...

I've got a picture somewhere, if I can find it, of Papa driving his 1908-1910 car. He'd drive his neighbors and my mother 'round, probably to Ona. Papa bought a tractor because Tom didn't have one and he put that tractor up on blocks and never used it. He just wanted to have something that Tom didn't have. He had some mules and he did everything with those mules.

Me and Tommy went down to the Carlton swimming hole on Troublesome Creek every chance we had. And my grandmother had a sister named Aunt B. So one Sunday she said, "It's so hot I'm going with you... and we'll go in swimming." So we went through the palmettos down to the swimming hole. We took our clothes off down to our drawers and jumped in the swimming hole. And Aunt B got down to her skivvies and jumped in with us! About that time three strange boys walked up. We said, "Boys, we don't know who you are but you better get away from here because you're getting' ready for the shock of your life." Aunt B did get out and put her clothes on but it wasn't a very pretty sight."

That was good swimming…

Albert was beloved by everyone. Regardless of the sadness, the tragedy in his early years, Albert Carlton emerged as a great and wonderful person.

BILLY LAMBERT

"Muley" was well named. He would not move an inch if it didn't suit him. It took Dr. Barbara with a 2X4 to convince him that he was to pull the wagon loaded with children and dutifully performed during the annual Pioneer Day in Wauchula. L-R: Pat Carlton, Julie Carlton, Robert Collins, "Muley," Larry Davis and Dr. Barbara.

Billy Lambert and his family are close friends of Dr. Barbara Carlton and the late Albert Carlton.

I did not get to spend nearly as much time as I would like to have spent with Albert. I enjoyed his company very much, and I don't blame him for this, I blame myself. But I do wish I could have spent more time with him than I did because he was such an enjoyable person to be around.

I want to say a few things about some of the times Albert and I had together.

A few minutes ago I took my hearing aids out which made me think about Albert at the time when he got hearing aids. I saw him in church one day and I said, "Well, Albert, what do you think about those hearing aids?" And he said, "The best thing I've found about these hearing aids is that they've got an 'off' and 'on' switch!"

One of the times that Albert and I got together was on an occasion when Barbara was giving a Christmas party, as she did frequently, for underprivileged kids in this area. She would invite my wife and me over and we'd try to help her out as best we could. She had a donkey that they'd hitch up to a cart to ride the kids around. Barbara gave Albert and me the job of hitching that donkey up to the cart. So Albert asked me if he thought we could do it and I said, "Well, I've ploughed a mule so we probably can."

We proceeded in trying to hook up the donkey to the cart but that donkey just didn't want to get hooked up to the cart. We wrestled with that donkey and the cart for a long time and finally Dr. Barbara comes out where we are and she sees that the donkey is not hitched to the cart, so she picks up a piece of wood about the size of a 2x4 and she beat that donkey on the side of his head. At that time, Barbara was pregnant, bad pregnant, she was showing real bad, she was probably seven or eight months, anyway, Dudley Putnam was standing there and he was really concerned about Barbara using all that strength beatin' on that donkey.

Well, she did get his attention, the donkey that is. He settled down and backed right into those traces. So we finally got the cart going and rode the kids all around. That was some episode which I'll never forget.

Landscaping was one of the things that Albert helped do when they first built the new First Baptist Church, circa 1985 on the west side of town on Main

Street. A lot of landscaping had to be done including a bunch of big oak trees that had to be moved Albert had a big spade on a truck so he was moving some oak trees for me and generally helping with the project. At one point I went around where he was and was talking to him and I said, "Albert, these sure do look good..." and I was bragging on how good what he was doing looked. He looked up at me and said, "I want you to do one thing for me which is: I want you to quit bragging on me because I'm working just as hard as I can work!"

We spent considerable time together when we were landscaping the grounds at the church .

Another thing about Albert's character was I never heard Albert Carlton ever speak a bad word about anybody. Never, ever in my life did I ever hear Albert say anything that was detrimental to another human being. This is a trait you find in few people. I remember this very well about Albert.

And something else I enjoyed about Albert so much was when we'd have a party or a get-together, whether it was a Sunday school party or whatever it might be, Albert and I would sit down and he'd start playing the piano.

People would sing and we just had a good time. Albert had a special touch with the piano and everybody enjoyed hearing him play. It seemed like there just had to be a piano wherever Albert was.

Albert's piano-playing was an inspiration to me. About four or five years ago when I was about 73 or 74 years old, I took up piano-playing on my own. A lot of inspiration for me to do this came from Albert Carlton and his playing. I'm to the point now that I enjoy what I'm doing, even though I'm not very accomplished – I've never had any piano lessons -- just took it up on my own but I've enjoyed playing the piano.

These are just a few things I remember about Albert. But the thing I wish most, and I guess this is true with people you think a lot of, you just wish you could have spent more time with them than you did.

I knew Albert Carlton many, many years ago... I don't even know when our acquaintance first started. We lived on the east side of town about five miles out and he lived on the west side. We went to the same church, the First Baptist Church. We went to the old Baptist Church for many years before the new one was built and then after the new one was built we went there for many years. Dr. Barbara was our family doctor... as long as she practiced. We got to see them quite often, Barbara as well as Albert, whether it was for our needs for a physician or it might be a social affair we were having here or at the church or whatever. That's how our relationship started. Now I live in Lake Placid. I've been living there now for eleven years.

We've got kids the same age as Barbara and Albert. They kind of grew up together, went to church together, had a lot of functions at school together being the same age. My daughter and Barbara's daughter, Julie, are about the same age. My Wayne and Barbara's son, Will, are also about the same age. They were in the band together and had a lot of school activities together.

You know, you go to school activities with your kids and you run into their parents all the time. In a small community, everyone knows everybody else.

We have a foliage nursery about three miles east of Zolfo Springs. Albert would visit me every so often at the nursery and when I saw him come up I knew it was gonna take some time because he loved that nursery. He liked to go through there and he'd pick out plants and say, "Well, I better have one of those..." It took a long time; we'd be out there two or three hours. He really enjoyed those visits to the nursery, he always had a good time going out there and picking out plants. We'd be ridin' along between the rows of plants and he'd say, "Well, I think I better have one of those, too." Before we got through, whatever he was driving, he'd have it full! Most of the time, I don't think I charged him too many times.

And when you all built your beach house he came out to the nursery with a big trailer and that was two day's worth of looking. I remember when he showed

141

up you might as well plan on taking hours, but it was all right. He loved it... those plants out there at that nursery. It was as bad as trying to show an absentee owner part of ownership of something. You would have thought he was an absentee owner. But we always had a good time.

Another thing about Albert was that he loved watching big equipment at work, clearing land that preceded any other agriculture venture whether the land was going to be planted in grass or orange trees. And he dearly loved roses, all kinds of roses. He loved everything about them... the irrigation, spraying, pruning, grooming or whatever. He didn't care how time-consuming it was. If it had to do with roses he loved it. And one time he decided he was going into town and buy some roses... I don't know how many. He said he was going to have a new rose garden. So he told a fellow who worked for him, I think his name was Warren, to dig the holes while he was gone to pick up the roses. So he told Warren how wide, how long and how deep to dig those holes. Well, when Albert got back the holes were dug and he said they could have been graves! They were so wide and deep! And he did grow some extraordinarily beautiful roses... big blooms and extra long stems.

Knowing Albert was great... all the way.

Photo: Luther W. Oehlbeck

Tropicana - Hybrid Tea
One of Albert's top favorites

BUD ADAMS

Alto "Bud" Adams, the son of Judge Alto Adams, was born and lived all his life in St. Lucie County on the Adams Ranch. Upon finishing high school and serving in the Navy, he entered the University of Florida. It was there that he met and became close friends with Albert Carlton.

"I wish I could have known him better and for a longer length of time," said Bud Adams. "But I lived on one side of Florida at Fort Pierce and he lived almost on the other side at Wauchula, and if you didn't have any business in Wauchula you didn't usually go there..."

Al Carlton was one of my favorite people.

I got out of the Navy along about 1946 and went to the University of Florida. It was not long before I met Al Carlton. He was a pretty famous guy. He was very entertaining, and he could play the piano better than anybody I ever heard, so he was naturally quite popular.

I was an ATO, and Al was a SAE, but I had a lot of friends at the SAE house so I spent a good bit of time with Al during that period. We had a common interest in cattle, but I must say that Al was a little better socializer than I was and I was a little more interested in cattle than he was. But we were good friends.

After I graduated in 1948, Al came down and rode around the ranch... he wanted to see what I was doing with the ranch. However, I think what he really wanted was to see a guy in Stuart name Zack Mosley that wrote the Smilin' Jack cartoon, an aviator, and I think what Al really wanted was to go visit with Zack Mosley. So Al and I and somebody else, I forget who it was, we called up Zack Mosley and asked if we could see him. He said yes, so we went down to see him. He was a delightful guy to visit with and took up a lot of time with us.

Al and I had a lot of good times together. He was a fabulous person.

At one time I visited Al at his ranch in Hardee County, beautiful country, and we rode horses and saw some of his cattle which I enjoyed very much.

But I was over here and he was over there, consequently I didn't get to see that much of him after that.

In later years we'd see him at meetings and such gatherings and we always exchanged Christmas cards. And we always enjoyed seeing his fabulous family and of course, we enjoyed showing off our family.

However, we really didn't work together that much because of where we lived... quite far apart geographically, and what we did. Wauchula is actually not that far from here, yet if you don't have business there you don't just drive through there.

Al had such a good personality that at fraternity houses and all, everybody enjoyed going over there and visiting with him.

After I got married, I had a full time job here and I'm sure he had the same thing over there. Consequently we really weren't much involved with each other after that, but I wish we had been.

Adams Ranch had its beginnings when Alto Adams, Sr. bought a tract of unfenced grassland in Fort Pierce, St. Lucie County. In 1937 the land was fenced and stocked. Ten years later, Alto Adams, Jr. became a partner in the cattle operation as Alto Adams & Son. In 1963 the ranch was incorporated as Adams Ranch, Inc.

Adams Ranch Brafords are the foundation herd for all Braford cattle in the United States.

"Bud" Adams has lived all his life on the ranch. His love and dedication for photography began at the tender age of ten and so it has continued ever since. As a gifted photographer and writer, Bud Adams' books have made their mark throughout Florida, the Southeast and elsewhere. All his subjects live on

the ranch as he does... the wildlife, plants, the prairies and pastures, hammocks, streams, sloughs and ponds. His photographs reflect his love for all these as well as Florida's incomparable skyscapes.

Bud Adams Ranch, circa 1960. L-R: Albert Carlton, Joe Michael, Ann Michael and Dr. Barbara Carlton.

CARL SIMMONS

Native Wauchulan Carl Simmons is kin to and a life-long friend of the Carlton Family. The friendship endures and is reflected in that Fran Hobson Simmons, who died in 2005 is buried in the Carlton Glenoka Family Cemetery with Albert. Carl, who is still living, has requested a burial site alongside his wife, Fran.

My relationship with the Carltons started April 26, 1925, my date of birth, in Brewster, Florida.

The first recollection I have is… we were living with my grandfather who was a Carlton, Bascom was his name and he lived at Bowling Green. He had homesteaded out east of Bowling Green in what is called the Lake Banks section. They came down there from Madison, Florida, right after the Civil War while the Carpetbaggers were still around.

His father was born in North Carolina in Jones County in 1820. He is buried over at Mt. Pisgah in Polk County.

When I was around three years old, I recall the Carltons, Carl C. and his family, Carl, Emma and Little Albert, living in Wauchula on Bay Street. My grandfather and I went by there to see them one day when he was a young baby, maybe six months old. I remember he had a lot of black hair. My next recollection was when his father got killed in a hunting accident in the Everglades. Uncle Charlie and Uncle Alton came up to Bowling Green to tell my grandfather, Joseph Bascom, about the incident. And of course, one thing led to another after that.

When I was eight years old we moved to Wauchula. By that time Albert was living with his half-sister, Matred. The home where they lived is still there.

In the seventh or eighth grade we took up playing musical instruments.

Albert was highly talented in all kinds of music. And some of the bully fellows in the band wanted to walk with him home and I walked home with him and I didn't let them jump on him. My grandfather had told me to take care of Albert who had been orphaned at age six and I did. I'm two years older than Albert was and I was big enough to take care of him.

Our association continued right on through 'til the time he went off to a military school, Bolles, in Jacksonville. He was probably in the 10th grade and he was there three years. He finished high school there at Bolles.

After that, Albert went in the Navy and after that he enrolled in the University of Florida. During his career in the Navy he was stationed outside of Washington, D. C. in Dalgren, Virginia, Naval Air Station. World War II had ended at that time.

I was in the crew on a troop transport and we were on a run between New York and Le Havre, France, bringing the troops back home. In my off-time when we were in port, I'd go down to Washington and Albert and I would visit. That probably occurred three or four times.

After that period of time and we all got back home. By virtue of my age difference with Albert, I spent 31 months and some few days on active duty.

Then I came back to Wauchula. Along the way, Albert picked up a friend named Edgar Davis, in our preteens, and the three of us ran around all the time, and got involved in water skiing. Back then you didn't just go to the store and buy skis, if you wanted them you had to make 'em. We built water skis for quite a long time. We had a press manufactured at a machine shop, we got the wood and learned how to handle it, how to make the skis. We'd go to a lake where the Davis family had a cottage and we'd water ski and have cook-outs and all that kind of stuff.

Albert was pretty much right-handed, he couldn't learn to turn to the left on those skis. So when we got tired of pulling him around on the boat we'd just make one left-hand turn and that's be the end of him... we just left him in the water. Naturally it would then be somebody else's turn.

During the course of the time that we'd be going back and forth they had a quarantine on every county line against anything you might be hauling that might carry fever ticks. And they had people with lanterns out there at night on the highway at roadblocks to inspect you. Edgar Davis had a little old fliver... a 1938 that we used. They'd have you open the door of your car and they'd inspect the inside and then open the trunk lid and if you didn't have anything they needed to confiscate, they'd close you back up and away you'd go. We were going and coming every two or three days and they'd always stop us and inspect our car.

So one day there was an alligator about four feet long floating around on the lake so we decided we'd just see how much wildlife that inspector could handle. We shot the alligator, put the alligator in the trunk of the car, tied a rope around his neck and tied it onto the back of the lid so when he'd jerk that trunk lid open that alligator would jump right out on him. We couldn't wait to see that inspector's reaction! So we cruised in there one night about nine o'clock and we were sitting up there in the seats and he checked all the inside and he went back to the trunk and got hold of the lid and jerked on it and of course, the alligator being a little heavy the slack went out of the rope and he gave a BIG jerk and he had uh armful of alligator! Well, he let that lid on the trunk go and from then on that inspector never stopped us again. Every time we come by he'd wave us on through. We were just good practical teenage jokers.

Albert was under the guardianship of his half-sister, Matred, and brother-in-law until he was 21. On his 21st birthday he came into his inheritance. The first thing he did was go down to the Ford place and buy a brand new

1946 two-door canary Ford sedan with a Venetian blind in the back window. So the rest of that day and into the night we traveled through Hardee and Polk Counties looking for every girl we ever knew showing off that new automobile. That was one funny occurrence.

He was enrolled in the University of Florida and I was over at Stetson University in DeLand, Florida, which, was not co-educational. Albert would come down to DeLand and we'd date some girls and go to dances and parties and whatever they were having.

In the meantime Edgar Davis had come over to DeLand and wanted to know if a date could be arranged and I told him I'd get hold of some of the brothers at the fraternity house and see what I could do. So we did and we went down to the dorm to pick up the two girls. When they came downstairs there was a short brunette and a tall redhead and I said I'd take the tall redhead and you take the brunette. The tall redhead later on became my wife… we had met on a blind date. She was Frances Hobson.

From that night on we were closely associated with Albert and after a while when things began to get a little serious, we talked it over, Albert and myself and how she'd fit into this small town. She was from St. Petersburg. We all decided it'd be fine but we didn't get married until after I'd graduated. I always told people that she was much older than I. She was a senior when I was a freshman but that was due to the inconvenience of Adolph and Tojo, World War II.

Over a period of time, Fran became equally closely associated with Albert as a third sister.

Fran and I used to chaperon Albert and his numerous dates on various occasions for a number of years. After my graduation from college, we lived in Miami but we were still closely associated back and forth. Somewhere during all this sequence of events a lady who worked in one of the local doctor's offices downtown called Albert one day and said there was a young, good looking doctor there and he ought to have a date with her. So he did and things started to progress very quickly and he called Fran and me saying, "I met this nice looking Georgia country girl who is a doctor and she's filling in for a local doctor and I want us to take her out and see if she will fit in." Well, we checked her out and decided it would work out real well… backgrounds being similar. So Barbara became the fourth member of the clan.

Until the day Albert passed away, he and Barbara were like a brother and sister to us, a family relationship.

One afternoon when Albert had got rid of the yellow 1946 Ford he got a 1949 Buick convertible. That was really classy. So we decided we'd go somewhere for the weekend, the two of us, actually we were headed to Naples. But at the first intersection we came to we flipped a coin to see if heads we turn right, tails we'd turn left. So we turned right and went through Arcadia and Punta Gorda, and Fort Myers and wound up at Punta Rassa where the ferry landing was late in the afternoon. We drove right up on the ramp where the ferry was loading and dumped us off on Sanibel Island. We flipped again and turned right and that took us to the north end of the island. There were some cottages there and a dining room and that kind of stuff. We parked and walked inside the dining room and we were still in work clothes. The manager came up and kinda looked at us and we weren't gettin' anywhere. We wanted to know what you did for entertainment 'round there. We asked her about a vacancy but we didn't get much of an answer on any of our questions. Then she turned around and saw that car and she began to warm up and started answering our questions. Then she went back and got her daughter who was about our age so we got all that out of the way pretty quick. Turned out, the entertainment in that area at that time consisted of a place called Daggley's Dock. We had toured the island before we went to the Gulf View and found that the next ferry going back to the mainland was tomorrow morning at ten o'clock. Well, our balloon deflated but we decided we'd make the best of it. And so were told that the party would start down at the dock about nine o'clock. We asked the lady's daughter if she would like to accompany us and she said she sure would. We drove down there and walked out on the dock and it's got a little place about a 16 by 30 with a little bar in one end and a place where people could dance, and some tables. Then just as I stuck my head around the door to step aside, the biggest, ugliest looking guy I ever saw in my life hit me full in the face with ice and ice water. What had happened was the waitress had bent over to get something out of the cooler and she took off toward me and he was throwing that stuff to her. Well, he came around and apologized and I told him not to worry about that.

To make a long story short, after while things began to happen but we

Albert at the piano dubbing in with the performers at hand.

151

didn't have any music. Albert, being an accomplished musician, particularly on the piano, somebody brought up the idea that there was a piano in reasonable tune at the church and if we could get it down there we could use it. So we went and got the piano and hauled it down there. And before this show was over we had a guy playing saxophone, one playing a clarinet and of course, Albert playing piano. We had a great time. He and I did that a long time. He and I had a bunch of crazy songs we sang like college people do. We did that from Daytona to Miami and Naples. That was over a period of years.

We were such good friends and our wives were such good friends and we were very fond of their children. My wife and I did not have children. We used to baby sit the kids and I'd spank them when they needed it, when they didn't, I didn't! They liked both of us... it was like we were family.

Albert grew from a child with an unusual up-bringing into a man of strong ideals, loyalty to family and friends and excellent moral character along with a strong desire to achieve excellence in his chosen pursuits during his lifetime... and he did. His greatest achievement in life was marrying Barbara.

During my association with him which began early in life and was still going on after almost 70 years, through those years we enjoyed many pleasant outings and spent much time together.

The impact he had on my life shall last until I pass from this earth.

~~~~~~~~~~~~~~~~

Carl and Fran were so close to the Carlton family, that when Fran died unexpectedly, Carl requested that she be buried in the Glenokra Cemetery (the Carlton Family Cemetery) at the Homeplace Ranch in Oak Grove.

(The name Glenokra was derived from the Kennedy Compound at Hyannis Port.)

Top row, left to right: George Heine, Albert Carlton
Seated left to right: Elmer Boree, Carl Simmons,
Bill Lanigan, Bobby Lambert and Bed Prescott, circa 1943

CARL SAUNDERS
SON OF MATTIE MAE AND JAMES ROSWELL SAUNDERS

Carl Saunders

Carl Saunders is the great-great-grandson of Albert Carlton and the grandson of Carl Carlton.

I was born in Augusta, Georgia, where my mother was a school teacher, having graduated from Florida State Teachers College for Women, now known as Florida State University. We lived there for six months then moved to Wauchula in 1932 at the height of the depression. At that time mother had some land out in the Vandolah area along with Matred and my uncle, Albert Carlton. My dad died in 1941. First, he was trying to make a living down here… he had a sawmill across from our house on West Main Street where the junior high is now. He had a sawmill and tried to make a go there, and he sold automobiles for Ford Motor Company over in Sebring. Later he developed tuberculosis and was in the sanitarium about six months before he died in '41. I was eight years old and my brother, Jimmy, was six and a half.

After that, during the war, my uncle Allan Olliff was married to Matred, mother's sister, and Albert's half-sister. We couldn't maintain the acreage out there so it sorta traded around, mother obtained a 10-acre orange grove out of it and paid off the house she owed for… house, lot, and everything for $2500. That was paid off which was a God-send because she had two children to raise on a teacher's salary. For many years she was declared a farmer because she made more on the orange grove than she did teaching school with a master's degree!

Yet we all survived. My brother and I grew up here in Wauchula… played ball, went to the University of Florida and played baseball there. I was All-State High School in baseball but when I got to Florida it turned into a curved ball. They just looked at it and hit it. Well, I started to develop a fast ball and a little movement on the fast ball and when I did my elbow started bothering me. I had two years up there in the University and then I enlisted in the Air Force… went through navigation training first, then pilot training.

I remember working for Albert during summers. It was 75 cents an hour, $25.00 a week, five days a week and a half-day on Saturday. These were very enjoyable times. $25.00 was $25.00… it was decent money for work at that time.

I thoroughly enjoyed riding horses with Albert and Bob Redding, Albert's foreman and the other cowboys at the Strickland place - the Bar $\overline{\mathsf{A}}$ Ranch. They would hire cowboys from several ranches around when they decided they'd round up the cattle. They usta have old "yellars," an old Spanish breed, but later they brought in Brahmas, Herefords, and Angus to improve the stock but they still had some of the "yellars" in the herd. They tried to breed the "yellars" out with Brahma bulls that were supposed to be more heat resistant, and as a result better calves would be produced. Selling calves at that time usually brought around 14, 15, 16 cents a pound. I remember when the calf market went up to 21 cents a pound, this was in '48-'49. Albert thought we ought to sell everything we had out there! Now it's $1.15 to $1.25 a pound for calves when you take them to market!

Every morning we usta go cow huntin'. Bob Redding had an old Morgan, a breed that was a big, big horse but he was feisty, he was still a stud. Every morning it was a rodeo when Bob first got on that horse till he got it quieted down and we were able to load him up on the truck. One time I remember they put me on a mare and I hadn't ridden that much but I loved it and we were gonna go cow-hunting. G. B. Gause, Albert, and Herbie Kay and some of the other cowboys... six, eight, ten of 'em were on the backside of these bayheads and Bob Redding and I were going through the bayhead to chase the cows out of the bayhead up the hill where other cowboys would get 'em and push 'em toward the fence and on into the pens. Bob being a quarter Cherokee Indian headed for that bayhead and he let out an Indian whoop and that big old Morgan took off making noises through the bayhead trying to chase the cows out. Well, this mare I was on got her teeth in the bit and she started running. She was following big Morgan and I had that horse's head just about in my lap and I didn't know enough to let the bit go and jerk it… let it go and jerk it, and eventually the horse would let go of the bit and get the bit in the back of the mouth where you could control it. That blankety-blank horse headed right through some pine saplings that had grown to about the size of my leg and I'm holding onto the horn and she aimed at a stump and aimed me for it. And she got to that stump and put on brakes, slid and I went off to the side and I just barely missed that stump… it went right by me. I had hold of the reins and I dropped the reins, got back on that horse and went over to where Bob and 'em had got the cows up on the hill by then and by this time the horse was suckin' her breath in and out, in and out, and Bob says, "Oh, my gosh, you wind-broke that horse."

About that time, Albert said, "No, that horse has been wind-broke a long time before that."

Bob Redding was a character. I remember following him… we were cow-huntin' and we were going into a store I guess it was Ona. Bob needed to get tobacco of some sort. I used to buy what was called a rum-crook, a cigar that was dipped in rum. You'd smoke that until it was down pretty short and you wouldn't get thirsty the rest of the afternoon. We went to the store and had a pop or some-thin' and on the way back if you didn't get one of those things you'd get thirsty. Bob stopped and there was some water there that was contaminated with cow manure… a little pond. Bob went down like he was gonna drink some water and he looked over at me. Well, at that time I was 16 or 17 years old. I started to drink that water but I thought… I don't think I'm gonna do that… I'm not that thirsty. I think he just wanted to see if I'd take a drink. Bob was a character.

Another story: He and G. B. Gause. He worked with Dr. Leland Carlton. Herbie was our resident Yankee for years. He was still that when he died 60 years later. Herbie Kay was one of the best guys who ever came around here. He was our cousin.

Herbie and G. B. and Bob were out, and they had this bull that had gotten loose and Bob was going to lasso him and bring him back in. G. B. and Bob had this arrangement that they were going to miss with the lasso and let Herbie lasso it. Bob threw the lasso at the bull and he missed, G. B. threw his lasso and he missed and he said, "Get him Herbie."

Herbie was sittin' on that little old mare of his, but Herbie had sense enough to pass on trying to lasso that bull. Those Brahma bulls at that time were big and they were mean.

G. B. and Bob Redding were the epitome of the Florida cowboy. We were lucky to have Bob those years. Barbara had to train Bob Redding not to shoot quail in bunches on the ground. Bob had a sawed-off automatic shotgun and when he found a covey of quail he would just go bam… bam… bam and wipe out the whole covey. Barbara was prompt about setting him straight.

In his early years, Albert was interested in airplanes. I was pitching baseball for the University of Florida, and I got a job pitching for Ocala for $25.00 a game and I'd cut an economics class on Monday morning to fly airplanes at $5.00 an hour at a field in Gainesville and I got my license. I was back here one summer and found out there was an airplane up in Lake Wales that the fellow was trying to sell for storage charges. So I went up there, I was working for the Buick place at the time. Well, I found the airplane, the right tire was flat, the left panel of the wing was floppy where the paint need rejuvenating… you put rejuvenating fluid on this fabric and it tightens it back up. There were dirt dobbers in the feed-out tube, and the engine hadn't been run for about eighteen years. But the fellow at the Buick place had worked on B-17s during the war so I took him up there with me and we put air in the tires, and the windshield was green and glazed over... Plexiglas, the green was cracked and you couldn't see out of it. This was in 1949. Anyway, we drug it out of the hanger, got the engine started and ran it for about 45 minutes to make sure it'd run, and changed the oil. It was a Continental 65 which is a small engine, called a Veronica L 3 used as an Army Observation Plane for training pilots in the Army Air Force.

I negotiated for $200... for an airplane that was flying... air-worthy. It was Albert's $200 that he loaned me. I was just making $25.00 a week.

After we got the engine running and everything I flew it back down here to Wauchula. I had to stick my head out the window because you couldn't see out of the windshield. I took off from Lake Wales and I followed the road to 17. When I was on the road there, the Bartow Air Base was still active at that time and they had T-6s and this fellow saw that the windshield was green and he circled over me in a T-6 so I'd know where I was going in that airplane that you couldn't see out of. I flew it on down here to Wauchula. We had a Taylor craft at that time and I flew it from here to Avon Park.

The fellow there told me what I needed so I got the materials at Tampa, the airport over there... new Plexiglas, rejuvenating the section of the wing, checking the cylinders, getting the spark plugs off, cleaning those off... the annual inspection. It cost me $50.00 for that and $35 for the materials. So I had an airplane licensed for one year for $285.00. Cheapest airplane I've ever owned in my life. Now I have one that cost a hundred thousand dollars!

The mechanic over there, when he signed it off, said, "Don't you get into any rough weather because... I'll show you." He went over to the fuselage and took his finger and hit the fuselage and the paint was so dried it would ring... like a ring around it where you'd punch it. It would crack. "So don't get in any real rough weather."

There's no way that thing should ever have been declared airworthy… but I didn't know it. I flew it around a lot of times. I went up to a football game at the university… and I went up to the airport and flew a girlfriend of mine at that time up to Gainesville. Mother drove from here and she got there before I did!

My cowboying was just part time. Thank God Albert gave me the job because it was thoroughly enjoyable. I enjoyed working with those people. They were good solid Americans. Course they'd play tricks on you. Mother had a plastic tin, a triangular shaped plastic container and we'd go out and take our lunch. She put a piece of pie in that plastic tin so I'd have something to eat. And I never did hear the end of that… those cowboys riding me about that fancy container with a piece of pie.

Albert and my cousin, Odell Carlton, had the Buick place right across from the drive-in teller's window at the bank. About 1951 some fellow drove a '35 Packard limousine down here from up north… Canada. That was the loveliest automobile I have ever seen. It was as long as from here to the other side of this house! I think it had 12 cylinders. I had a chauffeur's cap and I'd go round to the fraternity house to pick up some of the guys and take 'em 'round to the dorms, open the door for them and I'd drive that down to Ocala to play ball. At 25 to 30-cents a gallon, I'd get paid $15.00 a game and I'd spend about $8.00 on gas going down there and back. That '35 Packard limousine had the original paint job on it. This fellow from Canada traded it in on a new Buick. He had a resort up in Canada and he'd meet the people at the train station and drive 'em up to the resort in the limousine. It was well cared for. When I had to leave and go in the Air Force I think they put it on the lot up there and some cotton-pickin' orange picker bought it. You could sleep in the back seat. The back seat of that limousine had about six or eight different lights and switches all around. One of the most interesting things about it was an oil container underneath the hood and when the engine was running it would pump oil to about eleven different universals to keep it greased all the time. It had a ride control… you could go from a smooth floating ride to a harsher ride. On a paved road, you'd take that smooth drive for a rough road. An interesting automobile.

I drove it from Gainesville up to Macon to visit Uncle Claude and Aunt Doris and on the way back around Fort Meade a cylinder or a spark plug blew out. It kept running' till I got it back down here and put a helix-coil in it.

Dr. Barbara Carlton: *We were always needing an airplane ride. Albert always wanted to own his own airplane. Carl was out of town and he had an airplane so one time we all piled in his Twin Beech. He had taken everything out of it to take crawfish down to the Bahamas, it was just bare back in the back. We were flying up to the mountains (Carl did put seats in for us but we had to strap them in) and we got a parachute as a joke when we climbed in the airplane. Skeet (Mattie Mae) climbed in and thought she was going to have to use the parachute all the time just looking out that crack in the door that wouldn't close completely.*

It had a heater in it but I didn't know whether it would work or not so I didn't want to turn it on.

Dr. Barbara Carlton: *It was really cool! You can imagine our family just loading up in that thing…*

There was you (Dr. Barbara) and Albert and mother, Will and Julie, too, and myself. There were eight or nine of us. We had a lot of good times.

I'd been down in the islands ferrying some lobsters back in to try to make payments on this thing, part time with my American Air Line job and the custom people didn't like people coming in from the islands with twin engine airplanes because as paranoid as the custom people are, they were sure I was ferrying dope in. There's no way I'd give up an American Air Line's captain's job to ferry dope around. This is how paranoid custom people are. We'd left Treasure Key having carried a bunch of lobster in, Craig and I were flying it and I had my Cessna 182 down there also at Fort Lauderdale. We filled out all the paper work and customs inspected the airplane. There were two of 'em and one of them had disappeared. He was out on the ramp where my airplane was, and he stayed out there and stayed out there. And I said, "Look, we're ready to go... we need to get going."

One of the inspectors said, "Just hold on a minute." And I asked, "The paper work alright?" He replied, "Yeah, it's alright". We were there about thirty minutes. He looks out the window and says, "OK, you can go now."

I said, "Craig, I haven't flown Beulah for a while, you take the Cessna 182 back and I'll fly Beulah back."

I cranked up the engines, I knew it was taxiing a little bit sluggish but the tail wheel was sort of sluggish anyway, not sluggish just tricky but I went ahead and took off and I noticed it wanted to pull a little to the left but I went ahead and took off and came back here to land at Wauchula. It was grass... not paved at that time. It was light... about 9:30 at night. I touched down and it wanted to go to the left. I kept adding the right rudder, it kept going left... kept going left... I had full right rudder in, it still wanted to go left. (It had a ground loop in Tennessee... that V-18. They took the worst aspects of the large twin engine and the worst aspects of a small twin engine, put 'em together and made a V-18 out of it.) It was heading for the ditch. I said... you turkey you're not going in that ditch and I started putting the brake in. Well, the combination of the left tire, which I found out later was flat, and the right brake, it went up on its nose and slid about ten yards and turned upside down. I unstrapped my seat and landed on my head and reached up, turned the battery switch off at the ceiling and got out. Luckily the door was not jammed. So that was the end of our V-18 and Beulah.

Craig landed just about right behind me.

I will believe to my dying day that the people at customs did something ... you can take a match stem and put it inside the schraver valve, a valve that's on all tires that allows air to go in but not to come out. You can take a match stem and put it inside that schraver valve and it'll just leak out real slow. They did not want twin engine airplanes flying in there, especially when all the paper work was all filled out, everything was done. Usually it takes about ten or fifteen minutes to go through customs, but it took us 30 to 45 minutes to get outta there.

And they kept looking out there to see our airplane and see if the other guy was gone. I'll never believe that they didn't do something to that airplane, but there was no way to prove it.

I flew for the Air Force as a navigator then went into pilot training. In '67 the airlines were starting to hire, I made out an application and American accepted me and I flew for American for 27 years. The first base I was assigned to was Los Angeles. I was there for five or six years, then San Deigo opened up and I moved down there in '72 and was there for ten years, and then I started trying to do some avocado farming. A friend of mine was a vocational ag instructor in high school and also did free lance work on avocados. We got together, got some new trees and we were in that business for a while in California.

We raised our kids in California. They were either married or in college. Craig was going to school in California. We decided to think about moving back to Florida. So we rented our house in California, then rented a house in Lutz, up in North Tampa, on a lake and enjoyed that. Then this home in Wauchula came available with a 40-acre orange grove, 120 acres of pasture, and this house.

I knew I could commute from here just as well as from Tampa; I was flying out of Dallas at the time, a DC-9.

A preacher, Herschel Creasman, was using this house. Matred Olliff was letting him use it as a parsonage. He left earlier than we thought he was going to so the house became available in July '84, and we moved in here then. I commuted from here to Tampa, and from Tampa to Dallas and flew 747s from Dallas to Tokyo for a couple years. This worked out pretty good, it was three days and six days off because we were getting $25 on the three days that we were gone.

Anyway, we bought this place and thoroughly, thoroughly enjoyed it. *The adage that you can't go back is wrong, you can.* I've thoroughly enjoyed living here.

I'm trying to give back a little bit to a small hick town in the southeast when I was growing up, I've done a little bit but probably not as much as I could have done if I'd spent a little more time on other projects. Working 200 acres of orange groves, 150 head of cows, with just one other man has kept me busy.

That, and trying to beat my aunt (Dr. Barbara) at golf which I've just recently been able to do. She's starting to get older than I am. She's got her thumbs broken now so she's using this as an excuse... She used to beat me up all the time at golf.

We were out hunting, Barbara, Stan and I. And Barbara and Stan were up on the first covey and I waited back by the truck. Barbara was going to *share*, so it was my time to go shoot. She took the dogs back to the truck and I thought she'd stay back there, that's what she was supposed to do... stay back by the truck. She was not supposed to stick her nose up there where Stan and I were hunting. Stan is on the other side of these big bushes and I'm on this side and the dog's on point. A bird gets up and goes this way and I swung around and go BANG! and knocked the bird down and Barbara says, "Carl you shot me!" I didn't know she was there, she's back behind there and she should have been back at the truck. I get blamed for it, but she *shares*! Is this true or not? Here it is …

Dr. Barbara Carlton: *Well, I'm the one that got shot.*

You're the one that shoulda been back by the truck.

Dr. Barbara Carlton: *What is so ironic is when I have an X-ray, the technician says, "Hey! You mean you have bullets in you?" And I say, "Yes, and my nephew is the one that put 'em in there!"*

That shook me up.

EDGAR DAVIS

A native of Wauchula, where he has lived all his life, Edgar Davis, has been a life-long friend and a business associate. Not only were Edgar and Albert life-long friends but they enjoyed being SAE fraternity brothers at the University of Florida.

Front center, Albert Carlton at the piano,
back row, Edgar Davis
SAE House, Gainesville, Florida

I've lived in Wauchula, Florida, about all my life. My mother says I should be here 82 years in May '08.

Albert Carlton and I became acquainted in the third grade of school, possibly the fourth grade in Wauchula Elementary School here in Hardee County. At that time it was called Wauchula and now it's called Hardee Schools.

Albert and I went to Hardee County schools up until our junior year in high school at which point we transferred to Bolles School in Jacksonville, a military school that also had a naval unit and the band. I was in Company A, in the military school, Albert was in the band that was attached to the naval unit.

I went to summer school and that was really the first time Albert and I had been separated and as best I remember Albert did not go to summer school. I finished Bolles in February and went directly on to the University of Florida. Albert graduated from Bolles and immediately went into the Navy. He served until after the war and then he came to the University of Florida. At the University both Albert and I joined the Sigma Alpha Epsilon Fraternity which was also the fraternity of a couple of Bolles boys who were there, Tom Henderson and Dick Minton. Tom is still living but Dick passed away several years ago. Tom lives in Titusville; Dick lived in Fort Pierce.

Edgar Davis	SAE Fraternity House	Albert Carlton
U of F 1945	University of Florida	U of F 1945
Freshman	Gainesville, Florida	Freshman

At the University of Florida, Albert and I worked on publications. He was with the *Seminoles* which was the year book and I worked in the business side of the *Florida Alligator*. Later on Albert became the editor of the *Seminoles*. From there we were both inducted into the Florida Blue Key, the honorary society of the fraternity. After we graduated Albert and I moved back to Wauchula. He was busy with his ranching operations and I first went to teaching veterans up at Fort Meade for a year and a half. At the same time Albert was busy in both the cattle and citrus industry. We were friends... business and social until he passed away.

I was an avid hunter but Albert didn't like to hunt. I didn't like to play golf but he did so we had a running discussion and arguments about the virtues of hunting and the virtues of golf. Once in a while he might twist my arm, and I might carry his bags or hit a ball or two with him but seldom did that happen. And once in a while he'd go hunting with me. Basically it was with Robert Ray Smith, Rabbit, and I because Robert Ray and I hunted a lot together. Albert didn't care for hunting although he liked the outdoors and things like that. We had many pleasant times together.

We used to do a lot of water skiing. Albert was one of the hardest guys to get up or teach water skiing to that I've ever been associated with. I remember it took us a couple of summers to finally get him up to where he would be proficient enough to ski. After he learned how to ski you couldn't hardly get him off of 'em! He wanted to ski all the time. We did a lot of skiing out on Lake Viola... summers out there in Avon Park. My folks had built a log cabin there in 1939. My mother or my grandmother would stay with us and we had good times during the summer out there.

After we got a little older I did a lot of fishing; Albert, we called him Snow, he'd rather drive the boat than fish. One time we were going down to the Keys down to Marathon, from Boca Grande to Marathon. Albert practically piloted the boat all the way down there and all the way back because he really liked to pilot a boat... why I don't know 'cause once you get it set and going there's nothing to piloting. He just loved it and really he liked to fish but he'd rather pilot the boat than fish.

Dr. Barbara Carlton: *Albert was in the Navy, so his love of boats dated way back.*

One time when we were skiing at Avon Park, we had killed a three and a half to four-foot gator and Carl Simmons and Albert and I were coming back. This was during the time that Florida had the fever tick. One county might have the tick and the next one would not. Highlands County had the tick and Hardee County did not. You'd be stopped at the county line coming back from Highlands County where Avon Park is, and checked to see if you had any kind of animal that you were bringing back, not necessarily a water animal or a fish or something like that, say rabbits or something that might have a tick on it. They'd look in your car or truck, check out the trunk and see what you might be carrying that might possibly carry a fever tick on it. We had been by this check point several times between Hardee and Highlands County and the fellow was always kinda grumpy. So we decided to play a trick on him. At that time I had an old Ford coupe, it was called a business coupe. Well, it had a long lid on the trunk and you could get from the front seat back into the trunk. Well, we'd killed this alligator and we'd pulled the gator back up and tied him to that trunk so when you opened it up, he would just come out right on top of you if you weren't expecting it. As the fellow opened the trunk to see if we had anything that might carry a tick that alligator just covered him up. He wasn't very pleased at this happening. He might have beat us up but we had Carl Simmons along and he was pretty good size for his age. And all the guy did was give us a talkin' to. But I tell you what, he never did open up my trunk again!

Albert brought an alligator – and it might have been the same gator – which ended up on a roof in the sub-division for a while. I don't know if Albert put it up there or who it was but after two or three days it got to smellin' and then I don't know what happened to it. Albert may have buried it.

When we were in Gainesville in 1944, and I don't remember exactly when Albert got there because he'd been in the Navy, I was 4-F and never did get in the service. I believe he came a year or so after I got to Gainesville. We had very good times at the SAE house. I recall one happening there. We had a fraternity brother from South America by the name of Fernando Ortez de Savalos and ever'body called him Fergy for short. I remember that "Song of the Desert" was a movie and it was very popular back then and of course we went to see the movie once in a while, and we all slept in the dorm on the third floor of the SAE house. We had a cannon ball around the house and somebody would get at one end of the dorm that had a staircase there and another staircase on the other end of it and roll that cannon ball down through the dorm about twelve or one o'clock once in a while. It was a favorite joke. I remember when somebody had rolled that ball down there one time and Fergy hadn't been in the house very long and he got up and woke up and being very startled said, "What is theess? What is theess?"

Another thing that happened at the fraternity house was… after the war ended there were several brothers who played the piano, Brother Knauer and Charlie Bloom both from Jacksonville. Most of the songs we sang came from Jacksonville and Charlie Bloom, if he didn't know the words he'd make up words to a popular tune. We used to sing kinda risqué songs and there was a brother from Bradenton by the name of Brother Leach and he said, "If y'all don't quit singing those songs lightning's gonna hit the fraternity house." During the summertime lightning was rather prevalent up at Gainesville and sure enough lightning hit and knocked the chimney off one end of the house! After that Brother Leach got the proper sign for the second coming of the Lord.

We had many good times singing with Albert playing the piano, "Butter-beans… "all I want is a bowl of butterbeans, don't want no collard greens" and so many songs we can't remember 'em. There were ten or twelve of those songs we sang.

The house mother's name was Joe-ree. One of the songs was "Joe-ree don't let no risque songs in here." We had many good hours of Albert playing the piano and all of us singing and having a good time… something to recall.

Albert went to Tallahassee and I went mainly to Stetson because that's where Dot was and I'd go to see her… Dot Campbell, a cousin of Albert's. Of course, on big weekends I'd invite dates down and they'd come from Tallahassee and from Stetson. I graduated the year before Florida was made co-educational and Albert was still there and I don't know what happened after it became co-educational as far as his social life was concerned. (University of Florida was the boys school, Florida State University was girls, the year was 1948 when they became co-educational.) I graduated in '47 and Albert graduated sometime in '48.

When we started water skiing, the skis were so expensive we couldn't afford to buy 'em, so in order to water ski, you had to have water skis. So it was necessary that we build our own water skis. Albert had a syrup kettle some place, I don't remember where that was. Well, we took a cut-out of a couple of skis and we couldn't make a press but one at a time. We'd take that piece of plyboard and we made a pretty wide ski, it may have been eight inches wide at that time and cut that center ply out of it for about eight or ten inches and put that press in there and we'd pull that lip up where it'd have a curve at the end of the board. So in order to keep that curve after we took the press off in the board we took it and in this syrup kettle some place that Albert had and boil that sucker in that kettle for two or three hours to get the wood pliable and soft. After it dried out it did set to the extent that it had a little curve in it. That's the way we built our skis back then. This was a pretty good task. We probably spent as much time building skis as we did skiing.

DR· ALFRED SMITH

Alfred Smith was a childhood friend of Albert Carlton in Wauchula. He was later to become a distinguished pediatric ophthalmologist practicing in Miami.

Alfred Smith: I was named for my grandfather who would have been a contemporary of Albert's grandfather Albert. They all lived in Wauchula.

The crate mill was south of town, maybe closer to Zolfo Springs. I don't know whether they just made orange crates or if they made crates for everything. It was a big employer and was a landmark. When it burned down things moved away from Zolfo and that area. That was in the early days of the railroad. There was a round house there in Zolfo.

The Carltons were in Florida long before my grandfather, A. G. Smith, came. My grandfather was with the railroad, the Atlantic Coast Line railroad. He was a telegrapher and later the station depot agent.

Our family lived two blocks east of the tracks on East Orange Street. It ran east and west, parallel with Main Street and perpendicular to 4th Avenue. There was the City Hall, Mediterranean architectural style.

I'm not sure where Albert lived but they told me Albert's mother and my mother worked in a bank before the banks went to pieces in the depression. Actually, the Florida real estate boom peaked around '25-'26, Albert was born in '27 and I was born in '28. So their early motherhoods parallel but I'm not sure where they were living.

Albert had an uncle who lived up the hill from us on 4th Avenue. To the south on a hill they had guineas. They made lots of noise. There was an orange grove between that house and Albert's grandfather's house. Dale, Odell, and Golda lived there. I don't remember all of them but there were several more Carlton children.

Right across the street from them, not far, there was a family called Silverman. Todd Silverman was about Albert's age, maybe a year older, so he went in the Navy before Albert did. Todd now lives in Miami.

Sometime before this Albert may have lived on the north side of town and lived with his half-sister, Matred, who was married to Allen Olliff. The kids called him Booger Man. I guess because he was a stern supervisor.

We (Albert and I) somehow got into Wauchula grammar school a year apart. That doesn't seem to be a big age difference but when you're five and somebody else is six or seven you don't mix very much. We mixed more as we got closer to seventh and eighth grades.

Albert became such a good pianist they had him play for all the school functions; I particularly remember two songs that we sang at Wauchula Elementary School... one was "Marching Along Together." Albert came in and played the songs. He was playing the piano very well by the time he hit the sixth grade. Doris Lambert probably remembers the words and music because she was quite a vocalist. Possibly she was in Albert's class.

I thought some place along the line you'd like to listen to Todd Silverman because they were absolutely across the street from Albert's grandparents. Albert should have been a strong student. Half of his relatives were teaching school. I guess a lot of people were teaching then because there weren't a lot of jobs to be had. Hardee County and Wauchula were agricultural communities. Nobody ever really starved. I remember that people would come through and would want to chop wood or anything for a meal. That's all I remember of the depression.

This about sums up my early recollections.

We lived closer to the railroad. We were only one to two blocks to the east of the railroad on Orange Street. Orange St. and Main St. ran parallel. On the west side of the tracks were the Carlton Bank and the Simmons Hotel. The bank was closer to Main Street than the Simmons Hotel. Those were the landmarks.

There was a restaurant on Main Street on the south side closest to the railroad.

On the north side, J. W. Earnest Store was the landmark building. At the west corner of that same block was the Wauchula State Bank. The other banks had all closed. I was too young to remember their closures and I'm not sure at that time exactly where Albert lived.

Across from the bank was Beeson's Drug Store. It was popular because of the soda fountain. Later on the management discouraged our age group. We were probably noisy. Anyway, Albert's cousin, Dorothy, started a movement... "Buy bonds and boycott Beeson's for Victory." We took our business to Dasher's Drug Store. Albert and the Clavel children were close. Tiny Clavel I'm sure was in the same class with Albert. We began to hang out together as we moved into high school.

I was told that my father, A.B., used to hunt sometimes with the Carltons. He was not with them when Albert's father was killed. He hunted very little after that accident.

As we got older we became interested in water sports and particularly water skiing. Somehow we all got together... Carl Simmons, Edgar Davis and Albert and I. They were making the skis in Albert's garage. I think they took ply board and soaked

L-R: Simmons Hotel, Carlton and Carlton Bank, Wauchula, Florida, circa 1927

it and pulled it around a barrel to give it a bit of a tip upward. I wasn't much of a wood worker but I probably participated some; I know I participated in falling off the skis. That interest in water skiing was probably because they'd seen some of the activities up around Cypress Gardens in Winter Haven and when as we got closer to college age, the girls who worked there were more of an attraction than the aquatics.

Edgar Davis, who was older than all of us, went up to Bolles in Jacksonville. Edgar started in Gainesville well before the rest of us got ready to go to college. His family had a small place near Avon Park and I think the Olliffs had a place at Walking Water. There was water around to ski on. There was nothing to ski on in Hardee County.

The Peace River in our time looked like split pea soup. There was so much phosphate refuse in the water it had turned green. You could see gar fish in that water but not much else. It wasn't fit to swim in or fish in.

Another swimming hole was Kissingen Springs between Bartow and Ft. Meade. It dried up suddenly, probably because of the diversion of water by the phosphate wells.

Somewhere along in high school Albert cleared property out west of town. I think Bob Redding was the manager. They were clearing land (this would have been high school days) and they kept Albert working pretty much. He didn't have goofing off time. They had one of the first diesel powered tractors.

I do remember that he was part of the little Wauchula Band, but I'm almost sure he didn't play the piano in the band. He played the clarinet. He had some uncles who were musicians. This could have been about the time that we were in the eighth grade. This band was particularly interesting. Years later, I was in New York. Albert visited New York several times. We both remembered the man who led our band. His name was Harold Carr. Professor Carr went around and solicited parents to put their children in that band. Albert had a similar family set up. I lived with my grandparents and aunts and uncles. My grandmother was musical and she pushed me into music... never very successfully. I think Albert and I at one time had the same piano teacher, a lady named Kate Hadsell. When the band came together this Professor Harold Carr held forth in the city hall. We all met over there to take lessons. I don't think we were all there at the same time but occasionally we had to get together because we had to rehearse as a band. I was supposed to be playing trumpet (which I did poorly.) I don't think my brother was involved in that but Albert was and I think he was playing clarinet. The fire chief's son, Billy Barker, was quite a good horn player. Albert had an uncle (who could have been Uncle Will) played tuba. Part of this story is that Professor Carr decided that we should have uniforms.

They were able, I think to find enough people to play in a little band shell (near the goat shed) which was downtown. I remember being down there a few times. I think Albert and his uncle were there frequently playing in a gazebo.

Years later, they had a big hit, a musical, "The Music Man," and it was about a man who came to a small town, Professor Harold Hill. He was a lot more handsome than Professor Harold Carr. He fell in love with the librarian. Harold

L. Hill was a con man selling instruments and promoting himself in the musical. Professor Harold Hill was called "The Music Man." Years later we got together in New York and laughed about that particular play or show. It sounded like our Wauchula story. Professor Harold Carr in Wauchula had left with some deposits for instruments and uniforms and was never to be heard of again. When we looked in his locker we found one little baton and about a two-thirds empty gin bottle. I don't know where he went but that was the end of the Wauchula Municipal Band.

At that time we swam at a place called Zolfo Springs, but no one was really doing much on the river because it was so polluted it was not much fun.

Albert went to Bolles and Edgar and Doyle Spears but I can't say exactly when. It was probably 1942. By the time he finished Bolles, I got to Gainesville, he had enlisted in the Navy. I don't know how long he stayed. I think he probably went right after his first year in college.

At Gainesville, I was right across the street from Albert's SAE House. I was in the TKA Fraternity and he was in the SAE Fraternity. We were good friends by that time.

It was not unusual for most of us to go home on the weekends. Most of us did. There were no girls in the UF at Gainesville. We hitch-hiked. Some whose parents were more generous gave their children cars. Gene Lisely Leedy, another of Albert's friends eventually became an architect and designed the houses that Albert and I had side by side at Boca Grande.

Edgar Davis and a couple guys from around Winter Haven named Snively... the Snively that we rode with had a nice car and he lived in Dundee which is close to Winter Haven. We called him the Duke of Dundee. In one of these travels back and forth to Gainesville I remember coming back and they always stopped right outside of Paynes Prairie and had their last drink. By this time I think Mr. Olliff and maybe Horace McDonald were involved in a citrus juice plant and we drank

175

this grapefruit juice that they had processed. They weren't making concentrate at that time, they just did juice but they had quite a large operation there.

So we organized it and I don't know who gave it this name "The South Florida Grapefruit Juice Drinkers with Whiskey, Inc." That was just the place that we stopped. It's around Paynes Prairie. Then the race was to see if you could hold your breath when they drove all the way across Paynes Prairie. It would take you three to four minutes and I don't know that anyone ever could but we had 'em there gasping.

I told Barbara that I didn't have much interplay with Albert in that time but quite a bit later on. When we both finished school, and he finished first, he came back down to Wauchula and he had the Buick Agency. And he took one from

Albert Carlton at the Carlton family beach home in Boca Grande, circa 1982

Odell and I remember this trip when we went out to Orlando where we both had lady friends and I was real sleepy when we left. He was driving. I remember I had to stop him on the road because I saw this phenomenon, the moon was absolutely blue. There was a song "Blue Moon" and I had never seen anything that looked like this. He stopped and he said, "You don't see a thing." What happened was this was one of the first cars with a tinted windshield, the tint was heavy and the way I was laying I was looking up through that tint. So I thought I had had too much. We were drinking but we did not have much.

Booze was not a major part of my life or his but like most kids in college we went off and learned how to drink. Supervision in Wauchula was too tight, and, of course, the Baptist hated that activity. I guess Presbyterians tolerated it but no one endorsed alcohol, that is.

Somewhere along the line Albert went to Europe. No doubt he had finished college. I remember only one thing about the stories he told about eating abroad. There were no cornflakes to be found. That's what I wanted most on return.

When Albert graduated and came back to Wauchula I continued on. It was years before we spent much time together. We saw each other at Christmas vacation and for some reason we felt compelled to take New Year's Eve swims in a creek west of town. He became "The Greatest," a nick name bestowed on him by Carl Simmons. It was not a nickname. He was "The Greatest."

He set the music standard by which we judged all music at our parties. Now, when anyone plays "Lover" we think of that as his song.

Every year at the Scramble – we especially miss him then. He was the spice of that party.

Albert was the spice of our lives.

Albert Carlton at the piano at Boca Grande. This piano was a birthday gift to Albert, for the Boca Grande Beach House.

Albert Carlton and Dr. Alfred Smith on the beach at Boca Grande

L-R: Albert Carlton, Robert Ray Smith, Dale Carlton and H. A. Strickland at the Pinecrest Golf Course, Avon Park, Florida.

ROBERT RAY SMITH
"Rabbit"

Robert Ray Smith's friendship to Albert Carlton goes back to early childhood, and that friendship continues to the present day with the Carlton Family.

I suppose I was probably nine years old before I met Albert. We lived at Torrey, Florida. Mr. A. Z. Olliff owned a place which we called "The People's Place" across the road from where our homeplace was. And he would come out on Saturday, Mr. A. Z. , and he would drop Albert and Bob Redding off at the house and we would play. And we'd play there for several hours and then Mr. A. Z. would come back by and pick up the two boys and come back to town.

There was a period I guess about six years when Albert and I didn't see a whole lot of one another because we moved from Torrey to Lemon Grove, Florida. Times were tough and we didn't get into town but maybe once a week or once every two weeks. And the period from like the sixth grade and Albert hadn't gone off to Bolles to school and there was that period when we didn't see much of each other.

But after that, then the Navy came along. He served in the Navy. I was not caught up in World War II... I was 4-F. And then later, I got caught up in the Korean War where I spent two years. Albert's time with me being in Lemon Grove and him being at Bolles and then his time in the Navy there was a time when we didn't see each other.

But after that in going to the University of Florida there was another spell, I spent one year there, I was home here working. Albert came home from the University and I was working for Doyle Carlton, Jr, and the time came they would split the estate. I wanta say this was in '48.

In splitting the cattle, Albert came to Doyle and asked him for some help.

So Doyle sent me to work with Olliff and Albert in splitting up the cattle. We worked for several, several weeks there to split the cattle.

You see, after Albert's father died, A. Z. was administrator of the estate, Booger Man --- he was a Booger!

So in splitting up the estate, Mr. A. Z. was administrator, and, of course, he was tough and I remember it very, very well. In dividing the cattle, I told Albert that we'll take 'em, shoot and run. He gets one and we get two, so that didn't set very well with Mr. A. Z., he wanted to pick his own and we didn't go for that. Then, of course, we divided the cattle. All the outlaw cattle we had to rope and we hauled 'em to at that time it was Kingham Company, and the money was split that way but I stayed there with 'em for several weeks and we divided the estate cattle and I think Albert came out real, real good.

Albert and I would go to football games in Gainesville, and I can remember one of those – I'd never been anywhere – and he and I went to Atlanta to see Georgia Tech play Florida. Bobby Bowden was the coach and they beat us to death! But we had some great times, spending time at Walking Water Lake near Avon Lake, Florida, water skiing with Edgar and Carl Simmons. We just had the most fun even at Lake Viola.

And I'd like to tell one story when the state was quarantined for fever ticks, involving being stopped by a state inspector. We killed a gator and put him in the trunk of Albert's Ford, tied his lips to the bottom latch and then the top and seeing that inspector, of course we had to push the gator way back with a broom handle. We said, "Yeah, it's unlocked, just go ahead." Well, that gator come up, Lord have mercy, that inspector talked foul language! 'Course from that day on when we drove up he'd just wave us through. He never looked in that trunk again to my knowledge.

We had some excellent times... some wonderful times together.

Albert was in my wedding and I know that when Barbara and Al got married that Bob Gibson and I got up and stood with them at their elopement at Jensen Beach, Florida. It's been just a wonderful, wonderful relationship that I cherish forever.

That's about the sum of my experience with Albert. I just hate that period when we didn't get to see each other a great deal.

He was one of my favorite, favorite people. And I enjoyed him so much and I can remember another time when we were at the beach.

Al was playing the piano and we couldn't buy anything there because people were just enjoying our college songs. We weren't allowed to pay for anything, they treated us. We had some wonderful times... great times. We were over at Bradenton Beach... Anna Maria, Florida.

I rode with Al a number of times but I don't remember which horse he rode. Oh, we were out there lots and of course, when we were gathering those cattle to divide that estate, that was something.

We'd been through that screw worm program and all the cattle were just crazy. You couldn't have a dog because a dog would catch one and that was automatically a case of screw worm. And you talk about tough, whoeeee... daylight to dark and after dark we'd rope those cattle and Mr. A. Z. didn't want to pay too much money and we'd have to go back at night with a truck or trailer and haul 'em out. It was tough. Man, it was tough. No improved pasture, all rough land and it was some kind of tough.

Dr. Barbara Carlton: *The story that Albert told me was about the horse named "Hitler." And whenever he got on "Hitler" that was the end of any controlling the horse. He would take off and they always put Albert on Hitler for some reason. And Albert liked to do tricks; he rode sideways and it looked like he was falling off all the time. And every once in a while he'd be slipping off and he'd put one foot down and push himself back up. This is the story that I guess Bob Redding told.*

While I'm not familiar with that, I can remember that Mr. A. Z. had this horse – and I'm not sure that it wasn't "Hitler" – we were moving some cattle from Frostproof to Babcock Ranch. And King Kong Smith, Mr. A. Z. asked Uncle Tom Carlton if he would ride this horse that he'd got in Texas that had bucked ever'body off. Tom told him yeah I think we got $200 for him. Well, from west Frostproof to Bright Hour Ranch on Route 70 out of Arcadia, my print is on about every section of land from there on because he bucked me off at least once a day... my whole side, back and all. The first time he bucked me off was in a church yard and from there on, it was constantly. I could ride him and he'd buck and I'd ride him and he'd buck, no problem. But every time that I went to relax that's when he'd buck me off. He just knew exactly. I could take a feed bucket and catch him in forty acres and he'd be just as gentle as a dove but he was absolutely going to buck me off one time during the day. A beautiful horse... he really was a beautiful horse.

But we took him back to Mr. A. Z. and we rode him and he paid us.

But I think they just more or less let him go to pot because everybody was scared of him.

We had learned to shoot doves at New Zion and apparently the word got out and the game warden came. Of course they got there a little bit early that time and we didn't get caught. But then we got there about the second phase of the dove season and we were gonna shoot the same field again and the game warden came and all I can remember is they picked me up just before I went into Stewart's Ranch. There was a prearranged trade off. Where by the game warden checked Doyle, Jr.'s field one time but checked Albert's field seven times. You can imagine that Albert's group got caught a lot more that Doyle, Jr.'s. I happened to be with Doyle, Jr., whenever they were sent to the Strickland place which was out at Ona. And we got read the riot act there. I was totally safe when I was at Doyle, Jr.'s.

Lots of doves. You've got to feed 'em to have 'em. You got to put out a little corn and something to attract 'em. Then, of course, you couldn't have but 10 doves, but they did increase it to 12 and if you can shoot at all you can kill 12 or 15 out of the first box of shells and then after that it gets pretty rough on you. I got caught later in years. I got caught one Saturday. They charged me with 26 birds, I had 40-some hidden in the grove. The very next week they caught me in Glades County near Ortona on a Saturday and I had 44 that time. The game warden came and caught me with 44! It's pretty tough when you get caught twice in one week! Each Saturday $119.00. They withheld adjudication.

Corvil Justesen caught me when he was sittin' in an orange grove watching me shoot. But every time one would fall over in that young orange grove he'd pick it up before my little old retriever could get there and he'd pull its head off and give it to the dog. He was trying to tell me that he was out there.

Later he come up and he said, "You've got to be the dumbest so-and-so I have ever seen in my life. Look in there and see them with their heads pulled off." I said oh hell, I thought I was shootin' good! $119.

We'd go to put into Walkin' Waters over the weekends to go water skiing. We had so much fun, Edgar, Albert, and Adrian Chapman. We just had a great time... perfect going over that ski jump. Albert had a Chris Craft and if you ever got on the outside, it was tough, 'cause the ski jump wouldn't give.

The other outboards you could kinda stall them out a little bit back then. You couldn't stall one out now. But that Chris Craft didn't have any give in it. You got on the outside, you'd be doing a hundred in just a few minutes.

Great times! Great times! Those were the good old days.

Calves were going for 30 cents a pound. In fact, we sold a lot of 'em for 20 cents a pound. This was in the early '50s and get 'em up to six or seven hundred pounds and before you sold 'em for about $75 a head. It was hard to get $75 for 'em.

I can remember the first time I ever sold a calf. I got 50 cents per pound. They were what we'd call lightweight calves that weighed 200 pounds. In 2007 they brought $2.30 a pound. Our heavy weight cattle in 2007 averaged $435.48 per head.

Times have changed!

JOE L. DAVIS, SR.
Life-long friend of Albert Carlton

Joe L. Davis, Sr. played a vital role in the Carlton Family real estate business. His real estate company was responsible for several major transactions beginning in the 1960s and continuing through the 1980s.

Joe L. Davis, Sr., Governor Lawton Chiles and Dr. Barbara Carlton

Contrary to a few of these people you have talked to, I am just enough older than Albert that I really didn't grow up as a child with him. I was out and gone before he was a grown man. And so most of our relationship was after we came back home in '48.

Albert and I were friends, knew each other real well and enjoyed each

186

other. Then, there was a doctor from Georgia who came here and upset the whole damn thing! We were privileged to witness that romance and the production of their four fine children and we've been grateful for it.

My wife thought Albert was the greatest person in the world. Pat Davis. She and Albert had a unique little friendship. I don't know how it really developed but they really liked each other. We never did hunt together, but we did a little golfing here, and did a lot in North Carolina. They were the first ones, Barbara and Albert of our little group or our bunch, to own a place in North Carolina. They were very generous with it and shared it with all of us at High Hampton in Cashiers, North Carolina. They bought the first place up there. We all enjoyed it and for about 15 years, every Labor Day, we'd have a party, a stag party up there. We had a lot of fun and eight or nine of those years, it just so happened, I was shootin' white wing doves down in Mexico. On the way back, it just worked out for me to go by and catch the party at High Hampton. I'd bring the doves over and we'd cook the doves and that's where I learned to play Hearts… around that table. It's a great place.

Albert and Barbara, and Pat and I owned property together one time and made a little money out of it… a little bit. We had a great relationship. Two or three times we sold property for them and they were always very pleasant transactions.

When Barbara and Albert bought at High Hampton Country Club in 1965, most of us enjoyed their place so much we wound up buying a place there ourselves.

And we're at Highlands, North Carolina… Highlands Country Club which is about twelve miles from Barbara's place.

Two of the greatest things I remember about Albert: I never heard him say a negative thing about anybody in the world. He had a little trait there and a gift that most of us miss completely. And I've heard my wife say the same thing. She says, "Joe, you're so bad to criticize people, why don't you be like Albert. I've never heard him say a negative thing about anybody."

And what was so funny, Albert's first cousin, and my best friend, Doyle Carlton, Jr., who ran for governor in 1960, is the worst damn gossiper in the world! He was chairman of the deacons but he was also chairman of the gossip club. Then the other thing that was so great about Albert was his great gift of playing the piano. We never had any kind of a social event, no matter whether it was in North Carolina, Wauchula, or Boca Grande, before the night was over we wound up around the piano, Albert playing, and all of us singing and having a good time.

Dr. Barbara Carlton: *Albert did have music, piano lessons, I think starting at age nine. All I remember is being told that his teacher, Kate Hadsell, would crack his knuckles. He could read music but I don't think the lessons continued for very long.*

I think some tales got out that he couldn't read a note of music, that his playing was all by ear. He could and did read music but his playing was a pure gift… as Barbara has said many times, ninety percent of his playing was the result of his gift of music. He would much rather hear someone hum a tune and then he'd just play it. If you could hum the melody he could play it.

I think some of the greatest stories are about golfing in North Carolina… We buried him last year, one of Albert's dear friends and one of my dear friends, Dudley Putnam. His grandson, Adam Putnam, is now a member of the United States Congress. He is the fifth man in power up there. He's 31 years old and his hair is just as red as it can be. Dudley and I would go to North Carolina with Albert. Part of the time we'd ride with him and part of the time we wouldn't. Some of that time, Albert was President of Florida Citrus Mutual. At that time we couldn't sell our oranges. All in the world you could do was put them in participation, which means that they take your oranges and a year-and-a-half later they give you what they want you to have. So Dudley and I used to give Albert hell because he couldn't do better in getting the price up on oranges.

He was president of Mutual two terms and was on the Commission two terms. Later on I followed him on the Commission. I'd been on the Commission two years and I'd gotten myself elected Chairman. I never will forget, Albert called me and said, "My God, Joe, I didn't know you'd get the big thing!" And I said, "Well, when I went up there I decided I might as well run it."

"That's what some of those pictures are of the commission when I was on it, and I would guess that all four of them are of the four years I was Chairman," Joe said, pointing at the wall behind him.

But the Citrus Commission, actually at that time there were no Brazilians in here and there was very little fruit in Brazil. Most of it was in Florida. Actually, the Florida Citrus Commission ran the citrus business in the whole world. Twelve Commissioners are appointed by the governor and confirmed by the Senate and they have taxing power. In other words, the Commissioners put a box tax on every box of oranges that's picked and they collect that money which is used for advertising and promotion. It's a unique thing. Like I said, Albert served, then I was fortunate to serve and Albert's second son, Pat, also served.

Dr. Barbara Carlton: *One thing about this Florida citrus industry is we have, through our research at Lake Alfred called IFAS, been able to teach the world how to grow citrus and it's put us out of business. We taught Brazil how to grow citrus. We even sent people down there for that purpose.*

Yes, but we only did that after… Brazil had a pretty good citrus crop and it was all destroyed from tristezia, and they lay dormant in the citrus business except for a little fresh fruit until the freezes kept our production away from us. And that's when people like Lykes, Pasco, Minute Maid and a lot of others went down there and started planting citrus. And now they dominate the citrus market for the whole world.

But when Albert was on the Citrus Commission and the first part of when I was on it, Florida dominated the citrus business in the whole world. It's an amazing thing.

Albert was on the Commission in the '60s and early '70s, and I was appointed by Bob Graham in '79. I served nine and a half years. Then Bob Martinez got elected and he didn't need my services. Then our good friend, Lawton Chiles, kicked Martinez out and I served another nine years on the Citrus Commission. So I served 18 and a half years.

A big part of Albert's life was tagged to the citrus business, and the cattle business. I think he always had a little more interest in citrus than he did cattle and we did also. His cousin Doyle (Carlton) only had citrus because he had to. Ninety percent of his interest was in cattle. It was just according to which way you leaned. I think it was a decision all of us made that we would be more involved in cattle or on the other hand we'd be more involved in citrus. But Albert was deeply involved in both.

Joe L. Davis, Sr., Ted Williams and Dr. Barbara Carlton

I don't think of Albert as being a slow person. I think of him being active and moving along. I think in the later years he would have a little conversation with "the doctor" about big decisions. But she was even quicker than he was so you didn't have to wait too long on them... whether we were buying or selling. This is a pretty accurate statement.

The four of us had a mutual friend over here, Ted Williams, the baseball player.

190

We all enjoyed him very, very much. I think one of the greatest times that Barbara and Pat and Albert and I ever had was breakfast at our house when Ted would come up and eat with us. He had a private pilot and I said to Ted, "You know, that's a little funny that you have a lady pilot." He said "Well, I gave her a little test. I asked her if you took off with the wind or against it."

We had a little champagne… we had quite a breakfast… a great time.

Barbara had a time with golf. Albert was like some of the rest of us, he wasn't like his wife, he wasn't a gifted golfer… but she is, very talented.

Dr. Barbara Carlton: *Albert would hit the best shot and the worst shot, back to back, of any person I've ever seen, even Capt'n Jack Nicklaus.*

But he had a time getting ready. Maybe I shouldn't tell this, but I told somebody… when Albert is gettin' ready to hit, he looks like an elephant tryin' to screw a house cat!

With our friends, the Putnams, we had a lot of fun playing golf in North Carolina. We were up there one time when the ground was frozen and we found all the balls in the ground. The freeze had pushed 'em up to the top and we had a sackful of balls that we'd found out of the frozen ground.

Dr. Barbara Carlton: *Speaking of Dudley Putnam, Albert and Dudley would head up to N. C. and Dudley would go up there and stay two-three weeks with him. On the way up there Dudley would talk your ears off…. never stopped, just kept on talking. Well, after Dudley figured out that nobody was listening he'd just read the road signs. All the ads on the side of the road he'd read them. Albert said the only thing that kept him from going to sleep was because he had to listen to Dudley. That was eleven hours of driving with Dudley talking the whole time.*

The other thing is… Dudley told me, this was after Albert died, I went out for his 90th birthday and we were sitting on the porch and he said, "You know, Barbara, I loved that guy, I loved Albert. You know we never had a cross word."

They fussed and argued all the time! I guess when you get to be ninety, ev-

ery thing gets to be mellowed in your memory... it kinda flattens out.

Barbara made a good catch. I never could decide if she made the best catch or Albert made the best catch. I think maybe it was a toss-up.

Dr. Barbara Carlton: *Guess what... it was a jump ball. The Gators are getting ready to play UCLA tonight and it's a jump ball.*

We talked a little about Doyle but you know one of the greatest things that Albert enjoyed for years was when he went to Tallahassee with the senator as his administrative assistant. Somebody could probably explore that better than I could but he really liked and enjoyed his time there.

Dr. Barbara Carlton: *And when Doyle ran for Governor, Albert was his black-bag carrier. He collected all the money from the campaigns. That was the year we'd just gotten married... in 1959, and this was 1960 and he jumps right in this campaign and here I am this new bride and he's flitting around in this airplane all the time... I think that Albert never ran from anything and I believe that particular seven or eight years would be one of the highlights of his life as far as he was concerned. He thoroughly enjoyed it.*

We got in an argument one time sitting around the table at High Hampton about what the national debt was. We'd had a few martinis. And he asked how are we going to prove it? And I said let's call that man that writes the Washington Merry-go-round. It was a famous column at that time. I said he'll know what the national debt is. Sure 'nough we got some money put up, had one more martini and Albert called him and got him on the damn phone! And I won the bet!

Dr. Barbara Carlton: *You don't remember what the national debt was then do you?*

Well, I know it's nine trillion now. It wasn't even a trillion then, it was just a few billion. This would be in the late '60s or early '70s.

The best thing that ever happened to me was my coming back to Wauchula in 1948. I was here in time to catch the Carlton courtship. I left here in '41, went all over the south, was managing a Woolworth store, and then I came back in '48. You thought I was off in service but I wasn't.

I had come back home to Wauchula, Florida, where Pat and I would live the rest of our lives.

Doyle E. Carlton, Jr.
State Senator

BOB BARBEN
Citrus Grower

Bob Barben and Albert Carlton did not know each other in their growing up years. They met and became close friends as a result of both being in the citrus business at the same time, especially when they were both elected to the board of the Florida Citrus Mutual, a relationship that spanned nearly two decades.

The 1961-62 Mutual Board of Directors contained many industry notables. Seated, L-R: B. F. Wheeler, Ford Moody, John Parker, A. B. Michael, W. Max Acree, James C. Morton, J. J. Parrish Jr., <u>Bob Barben</u> and Vernon Conner. Standing, L-R: Charles Partin, L. W. Tilden, Henry Prine, Clayton Logan, W. Elton Clemmons, Tom Brown, Bill McMullen, Chester Karst, <u>Albert Carlton</u>, Herbert Massey, Fred Adkinson and Alexander Ryburn, Partin and McMullen still serve on the board!

Albert and I had been on the Florida Citrus Mutual board for 18 years, and I just happened to find the Florida Citrus Reporter that was put out May 24,1974, stating that Albert and I and another gentleman, Charlie Harrison, were kicked off the Mutual Board the same day. It says, "The revolution in Hardee County which ousted three directors of Mutual appears to be the result of grower anger and frustration, not necessarily at the organization or the men involved but at the situation."

At that time I was also president of Florida Ag Tax Council and they said I was going to have to get off that, too. But I never did. They kept reappointing me so I served on that council for about 20 years.

Anyway, I made a copy of this report. What really happened was some of the boys over there in Wauchula, they thought they could get the price of fruit up if they'd just get the three of us off the board. Of course they got on there and they found out that really wasn't the situation. And it's mentioned in the newsletter... saying, "The turnover can't possibly produce the results they hoped for. And the three new members from that district won't be able to perform any miracles."

Prior to the big "ousting" Albert had for years been giving parties before he and Barbara were married in 1959. I remember the first little house he and Barbara lived in as newlyweds. Bob Gibson would bring ice and chip it up so we had a lot of snow out in front of their little house on Turner Avenue. We'd been going over there for a long time for their annual Christmas party with snow and snowmen in their front yard. And so one day I ran into some of my friends over in Wauchula, and I said, "You know, you boys over here really didn't have to vote for me, but you know Albert has been wining and dining you bastards for years."

Albert and Barbara, Mary and John Rocker at 308 Turner Ave., Wauchula, Albert and Barbara's first home.

And I'd heard it even got so bad that when they'd see Albert coming they'd cross the street to the other side.

The situation was that we had a five or six county gentleman's agreement... one grower would come from Highlands County, one from Hardee and one from DeSoto because we were three of the biggest citrus producers in the area.

The other day Jane, my wife, was remembering one night when we were over where you lived at Glenokra. Barbara would always go to bed early. Even while we were visiting, she would disappear about nine o'clock, get undressed and go to bed. She'd go back and all the party would go back to their big bedroom. Jane said, "I remember one night Barbara went back and got in bed and we all went in there, and I can still see Albert sittin' by the fireplace taking his shoes and socks off." He was ready to go to bed, too.

Barbara was working, practicing medicine, so she had to get up the next morning and go to work.

I went on the Board of Florida Citrus Mutual in 1955, and of course, got kicked off in 1974. Bob Rutledge was Executive Director – and I know a lot about Bob that you can't put in this book – but one of the funniest things was that Bob was fooling around with some girl there in town and one of his main men was also going with the same girl. So the story that I heard was that Bob went over there one night to see his girl and was very shocked when he was in the bedroom and saw one of his employee's picture there.

Bob was an unusual sort of fellow, but he was good for the times. He came up with a lot of good things... I was thinking the other day that one time we had an awful lot of extra fruit and he came out with the idea that we'd put another orange in a can of concentrate. So instead of putting in nine oranges we'd put in 10 and that would take care of 10 percent of the crop.

And I remember Tom Brown telling me that when Claude Kirk was governor they had to pay Claude to go to Washington with them to do something but that wouldn't bother Bob... he'd get the money to make that happen.

Of course, Homer Hooks, Executive Director of the Florida Citrus Commission was at the Commission and Bob was just running Homer crazy because Homer had to comply with the statutes and Bob Rutledge could just do anything that he wanted to in his position.

Dr. Barbara Carlton: *Another thing that happened during this time was they were trying to get a spokesperson for the citrus industry. And they'd gone through all kinds all through the years but I guess it was Bob who came up with the name of Anita Bryant who was in her heyday (photo page 200). She was very, very popular. She was in the homecoming parade of the citrus festival at Winter Haven and rode in the parade in that '33 Rolls Royce convertible which was built by the Carlton Carriage Company. Then, right during her real heyday, it came out in Miami about the gays, and the citrus people didn't know what to do then. This was one of the first anti-gay movements and the citrus industry did not want to be identified with the anti-gay movement. Of course, Anita was ousted from her position as spokesperson. That was a critical thing.*

**Albert Carlton's '33 Rolls Royce roadster built
by the Carlton Carriage Company of England**

During those years when we had a citrus gathering, it was big news. A lot of people came. The occasion of the annual meeting of Florida Citrus Mutual that we had over at Nora Mayo Hall in Winter Haven which was named after the wife of Nathan Mayo.[1] Meanwhile Bob is up in the rafters in the auditorium. That was a real tall building and how he got up there I'll be damned if I know. Anyway, he was always coming up with something. He was a real showman and no one could imagine how he got up there or what he was doing.

Another time... we always had good speakers. We'd get the governor to come or I remember when Claude Kirk was governor and I was Master of Ceremonies. We met Governor Kirk at the plane and evidently he didn't have anything prepared to say. However he remarked to somebody, "What do you want me to talk about?"

Nevertheless, he gave a wonderful speech... it was really wonderful.

Then I guess the last year that Albert was president of Mutual, you, Barbara, and Albert had gone to Europe and I gave Albert's speech that somebody else wrote. I just read it. And that was in the Nora Mayo Hall also in 1965.

We continued to have some really big meetings and of course during that time, the citrus industry was kinda in bad shape. It was amazing, the worse shape we got in the more we got done! The reason was because everybody pulled together and came up with ideas as to how we could actually make things better – sell more orange juice!

As you look back, it might not have been doing as well financially but we did well lots of years. In the years when it was toughest seems like that's when we got more things done.

What year did Bob give Albert the car?

Dr. Barbara Carlton: *Bob Rutledge presented Albert, the outgoing*

---

(1) Nathan Mayo was the Florida Commissioner of Agriculture for 37 years. His father was Colonel James Micajak Mayo of the Confederate Army. In 1874, the city of Mayo was established.

president of Florida Citrus Mutual, a '47 Ford and that was one of the years when he was President. He got two gifts in appreciation of his years as president of Florida Citrus Mutual. One was the '47 Ford and the other was a clock which was eventually handed down to our fourth son, Charlie Carlton. We kept the '47 Ford. It was Will's first car and he drove it to high school and all the kids quit riding the school bus so they could ride in that '47 Ford and Will could take them to school.

It's amazing how all this sorta folds into the family life.

Bob Barben continues: I came down here from Pennsylvania to flying school in 1942. I was in Sebring learning to fly B17s. I was a Yankee but I got over it. And I flew the B29, too. I married a girl from here in 1945, then I went back up north and went to law school. Then we came back down here in 1950 and I went in business with my father-in-law. We were both lawyers but we loved to farm better than we did law.

**Florida Citrus Mutual Banquet, Albert Carlton, President FCM,
Bob Rutledge, Executive Director FCM and Doyle Conner,
Secretary of Agriculture, circa 1960**

199

I probably met Albert when we got on the board in 1955. In 1960 I was the campaign chairman in Highlands County for Doyle Carlton, Jr. when he was running for governor. Albert carried the black bag with the money in it. I always said if they'd had some other advertising outfit that would have done a good job for Doyle, he would have been governor.

Dr. Barbara Carlton: *Doyle was not politically motivated. He was not going to jeopardize his name for the sake of politics. He was a real statesman.*

Doyle and Albert landed out here at the airport one day in a DC3 and we were having a dinner for them at a restaurant out on the highway.

I got in and I had a clipboard with all the names of the people I'd invited to the party. I climbed up in that DC3 and handed Doyle the list. He went over the list and said, "Bob, I know everybody on this list except one." I said, "Who's that?" And he said, "Elton Crews." I said, "Certainly you know Elton... he was born in Hardee County." "I've never met Elton," he declared.

Later Elton told me it was true that he'd never met Doyle.

It was amazing how many people came up afterwards and said, "Alright, damnit, did you have to tell him who I was?"

I told Doyle one time, "Doyle, there's only one thing you have that I want..."

"What's that?" he asked.

I replied, "Your ability to remember people's names."

The funny thing was, the day of the election, my

Anita Bryant, Florida Citrus spokeswoman

wife, Jane, was pregnant and I was taking her to the hospital and she'll never let me forget it. I stopped down here at the headquarters just to check on things, and our son, John, was born that day. So I went to a party and everybody wanted me to name him Farris, for Farris Bryant who had won the election.

One of the things I remember is Albert and his straw hat, and his playing the piano. When we'd go over to their home he always played the piano. And he'd play at the Mutual meetings. He was assured that the entertainment would have a piano that he could go to and play.

We'd have several hundred people at those meetings. Anybody that was anybody in the citrus industry didn't miss those meetings. It was a big event, Bob Rutledge was a showman and everybody went to see what in the world he would do next. Bob was an idea man... he had lots of great ideas and few morals. That's common knowledge. He was something. I always felt sorry for his wife.

He had no compunction. Anything that wasn't his he'd give away. One day I went in and he had an unusual chair in his office. I sat down in the chair and remarked something about it and he said, "If you want it, take it."

Dr. Barbara Carlton: *Which makes me remember another incident that's similar. The leather couch that's out in the 'new room' at the ranch used to be in Albert's office. Bob Rutledge gave that to him and we still have it. Albert loved it! And Bob said, 'You can have it.' This is exactly what you're saying. The couch actually belonged to Florida Citrus Mutual, paid for by the members. Bob just wanted to distribute that wealth.*

JOHN V. D'ALBORA, JR.
Fellow Citrus Commissioner

From the time they were in military school, John V. D'Albora, Jr. and Albert Carlton were friends. After their time in school, John and Albert developed a mutual interest in the citrus industry which they pursued for many years.

Albert and I met when we were both at Bolles Military School in Jacksonville. Since we were a year apart we didn't really see a lot of each other yet we were good friends and I always felt I knew him as a person. I graduated in 1943 and he graduated in 1944.

Albert was a very studious person and he had a lot of personality. I knew he was unusually intelligent and that he carried himself well all through his life. He distinguished himself unconditionally... academically and materialistically as well as in the field of music.

A piano was like a magnet to Albert Carlton. His musical ability was such that he could not turn away when we'd be somewhere that there was a piano. Those who were within hearing distance of his playing were drawn to him. Albert had a unique gift of being able to play anything that he would hear. Everyone who ever heard him wanted to hear more and more.

Anyone could recognize Albert Carlton by his carriage.

PART FOUR
LOOKING BACK

Looking back, Barbara Castleberry Carlton recalls: The plane circled the airport before making a perfect landing, bringing me to the door of another world, a world that I began to embrace from the minute I stepped off that plane.

Dr. Miles Collier had called asking for a substitute physician to fill in for him at the hospital he ran in Wauchula, Florida during an unexpected illness.

Dr. Collier's practice covered everything from pediatrics, OB and general surgery to and including a full time family practice.

Having been in school in Georgia all my life up until that time, I had no idea what the back country of Florida was like. I remember seeing endless miles and miles of greenery... pastures and prairies and woodlands to the edge of the

203

world, dotted with sprawling ponds and lakes and rivers, all spreading below the bluest sky I had ever seen.

Now thinking back to 1958, I believe it was then I first began to realize that this world was different - unlike any I had known or seen up unto that time.

As the years passed, subconsciously the events that had shaped the lives and living in this part of the world began to emerge.

Thus this book that has come from the heart and soul of the characters on these pages. I could not let all this history drift downstream and be lost.

In the restoration of Carl Carlton's homeplace (The Little White House), I became enthralled with the rich history it represented. During the process of restoration it became evident that the photographs of the Carlton ancestors, as they hung on the walls from room to room, represented a calling to preserve and endear these vibrant figures for the Carlton descendants and generations to come. It was this calling which has inspired this book documenting an historical and personal perspective that must be preserved.

The year was 1849 when the first Carlton set foot on this land...

JEANNE ARCHAMBAULT

The story surrounding this book would never have happened had it not been for Dr. Miles Collier's "Girl Friday," Jean Archambault. Barbara Carlton

Wauchula Infirmary circa 1959. 1. Jeanne Archambault, 2. Ninfa Collier, 3. Dr. Miles Collier and 4. Dr. Barbara Carlton

I knew Albert way back but I did not socialize with him until after I was married... that was in the early forties.

My husband was a music nut. I mean he really liked music. He had all sorts of records and stuff and played the saxaphone, and naturally when we met Albert and he was playing the piano and they'd get together and sing and they'd just really have a good time.

Albert had more charisma, I think, than anybody I've ever met. He liked people and he loved to entertain people. We had lots of barbecues together. I think maybe he or some of his relatives had a place over at a lake and we'd go over there to barbecue... maybe four, five or six couples. And invariably they'd always end up at a piano, no matter where it was. Of course everybody knew he played by ear so he could play anything you wanted him to, even if you had to hum a few lines he could pick it up and play it beautifully. He was just a very outgoing individual.

Don, my husband, and Albert both liked the same type music. That was the connection for the friendship.

As I've said I had known Albert before, but he was so much younger than I that naturally I didn't socialize with him until after I married.

I think he and my husband first got together at the local Elk's club or some place like that where Albert was playing and my husband got up and went to the piano and they started talking about music. Louis Armstrong, Ella Fitzgerald and all the musicians they loved so much and then they started singing and that's how their relationship began. They just had a mutual love of that certain type music. And that's how the friendship started.

I can't remember some of the girls that Albert dated but when he'd have a date they'd go to a barbecue and he always depended on me to bring the salad or the pie or whatever he needed in the woman's line. Of course, he'd get the steaks and that's what we'd do to have a barbecue with whomever he was dating at the time... that is, until Barbara came along.

I worked for Dr. Collier at the hospital. I had been with him for quite a while. And when he'd leave, of course we had to have a locum tenum and it was my responsibility to find somebody at the hospital in Augusta, Georgia.

I would call up there to try to get someone to fill in. Dr. Collier always preferred a man if we could get one.

While I think he paid them adequately for being here, of course, they had room and board free, so whatever salary he paid them was free and clear. But in

Hardee County patients were not acclimated to a woman doctor. We'd never had one, so he always preferred that I get a man if possible. But then, if we couldn't we had to do something. So the very first time I could not get a man I said we'd just have to let a doctor named "Sarah" come, who just happened to be very rotund. When I told him about it, I said, "Dr. Collier, there's no one who wants to come, so we're just going to have to take this lady doctor." He said, "Well, I'm gonna go, so tell her to just come on."

Of course, she came and she was well received. But not long afterwards, Dr. Collier became ill. That was in the latter part of '58. So that's when I called up to Augusta again to have someone come and help out. Again, we couldn't get a man so that's when we got Dr. Barbara.

That was really comical when you think about it. Of course we were expecting a woman doctor and having had Sarah... she was a certain type lady, bustling bosom, I guess you'd say... but when my husband and I stood at the airport to meet the lady doctor we kept looking and waiting as the passengers disembarked and I said, "Oh... oh, there's no woman on this plane who looks like a doctor."

And my husband agreed. "I don't think so either..."

I don't know what I really expected but remembering Sarah I certainly didn't expect a very young, beautiful lady getting off that plane... I didn't expect her to be a doctor. Everybody else who got off that plane was either with a man or had a child by the hand or something so by the process of elimination I told my husband that's got to be her. We were looking at a young, very beautiful, slim, trim lady. Well, my husband agreed with me saying she didn't look like a doctor. And I said again, "No, she does not look like a doctor." So we just waited until she approached us and I said, "Dr. Castleberry... I presume?"

She was the only one left, so she had to be the doctor we were looking for.

She was certainly a surprise to us – and believe me, she was certainly a surprise to Al when he met her!

When I had talked to him on the phone, I told him, "You are really going to be surprised... she is just as cute as she can be and I went on to tell him about her but he was still reluctant to date a stranger. He thought I was pulling his leg! Anyway, I kept talking to him and he finally agreed to come and meet her. Naturally she was staying at the hospital but she was at my home at the time. So he came out there to meet her.

They visited a little while there in my home then she went to sleep on his shoulder. We didn't wake her up, we just let her sleep. She'd been up all night with emergencies at the hospital.

We, Albert, Don and I, went on visiting until after a while Albert said, "I guess I'd better be taking her home." And I agreed because as I told him, I knew tomorrow would be a hard day for her. Dr. Collier had a big practice so I knew that next day would be more than a little busy.

She was well received at the hospital and in the community and I was happy about that. I think her southern charm won over most of the patients even though they were not accustomed to a woman doctor.

We had had none in Hardee County. Barbara stayed there until Dr. Collier died... that was in March of 1960.

She and I together, it was our responsibility to find a doctor, hopefully to buy the practice. So she and I together interviewed a man and a woman doctor who at that time were in Bartow. They agreed to buy the practice. But I'm sorry to say we used poor judgement because that didn't work out. They were not at all suited to handle the practice and it did not work out at all.

I'm sure there's a lot I don't remember but I sure remember that we had a lot of good times together. Al and my husband were always at the piano. There could be 25 people at a party and the first thing you know Albert was off playing the piano and Don would be sitting there on the bench with him and finally everybody would file in and they'd sing for a long, long time... all evening.

I can't say that Don and I spent a lot of time together with Barbara and Albert but we did go to barbeques and things like that with them. We were so much older than they were and he had a ranch with cattle and groves to 'tend to but he still had time to socialize. And Barbara was more than a little busy with the practice. So there wasn't a lot of time that we could spend with each other. And after they married, she practiced for a while. Although there wasn't a lot of time for us to be together, what we did was sure fun!

I knew fairly soon that this was a good match. When she first came down as a locum tenum, I can't remember exactly how long she stayed that time and when she went back I can't remember if Albert went up there to see her or not. But when she came back, I knew he was very serious about her.

Later on, when Dr. Collier became very ill, we had to get Barbara back again, I knew it was serious between the two of them. In a way it was kinda funny because he had dated some very nice girls during the time I had socialized with him, two or three girls at that time, and he'd have a barbecue and he'd have a date but nothing serious. He was never very serious about any of them but he always had a date. He was certainly never serious until he met Barbara... that's for sure.

I don't think Albert was still living with Matred at that time but I'm not sure where he did live. Barbara lived at the hospital as long as she practiced there. She attended Dr. Collier all during his illness. He was home in bed about a month before he died and she, of course, took care of him during that time.

Dr. Collier came to Wauchula in either '39 or the early '40s. I went to work for him in 1945 and at that time he was using the Bartow General Hospital even though he had his practice in Wauchula but he had to use the Bartow hospital for surgery. Later on, however, he bought the infirmary which Dr. Poucher owned at that time in Wauchula. It was a little 25-bed hospital and Dr. Collier bought that in about 1948.

Original gurney used at Dr. Collier's hospital - Wauchula Infirmary - now restored and used as a rolling dessert cart for Carlton guests. Circa 1950

I was pregnant at the time he bought the infirmary and I was gonna retire but he didn't agree with that so I couldn't retire. He'd bought the hospital and he was going to build an office in front of it and he said, "No... you can't leave me now." So I didn't leave but it worked out OK.

After Barbara and Albert were married we didn't see too much of them because as I've said they were so much younger and Albert was friends with Carl and Fran, Doyle and Sarah, Edgar and Ruth and they were all the same age. They all lived here in Wauchula and had been to school together and my husband and I were considerably older than they were so we didn't socialize with them a lot... some, of course, but not a lot.

When they were first married they lived in a little subdivision, Relyea, on Turner Avenue. They lived there quite a little while.

We went there several times to that little house to eat with them and socialize before they built their house on the ranch.

The people in Wauchula who were "in the know" so to speak, who knew the Carltons real well, always complimented Mr. Olliff for taking such good care of Al's assets, his inheritance. Even though he was known to be a difficult man, the townspeople really thought he had taken good care of Albert's inheritance and they complimented him several times about that.

I think Barbara started practicing here –in this house, their Oak Grove home—maybe in the mid-'60s. I remember she called me wanting to know if I'd come and work for her. I think I had just started at the bank at that time and I didn't want to change. I was Vice President for 32 years! I just retired in 1999. I worked for Dr. Collier for 15 years, then I worked for a grove maintenance man for seven years, then at the bank for 32 years and before that I worked for Uncle Sam for three years. So I worked for 56 years and didn't retire until I was 75 years old.

When asked what she does in retirement, Jeanne said, "Oh man, I gad around the most you ever saw, I play a lot of bridge and do a lot of eatin' out!"

I think the most outstanding thing about Albert was his personality... his charisma... his love of people and his ability to fit in with any class of individual that he might meet. That's a rare talent... God-given, to be able to converse in any walk of life. That's the thing that always impressed me about him, definitely his personality and charisma. I don't think Albert Carlton ever met anyone he did not like, or that he didn't get along with.

He just had that personality that liked people.

After I met Barbara there was no question that the two of them, Barbara and Albert, should meet. She had that extroverted personality and he was extremely extroverted so it was almost natural that it would work out. They were so well suited for each other. Albert was an extremely likeable individual. I don't know of anyone who ever met him who didn't like him.

I've always felt that everybody felt the same way... everyone liked Albert Carlton.

PART FIVE

MERCER UNIVERSITY
MACON, GEORGIA

Mercer University became my home from 1949 to 1953. It was quite a transition from the Steward County days in Lumpkin, Georgia where there were peanuts, cotton, cane grinding, my horse and great country life. My daddy had instilled a strong work ethic and academia became my passion - - - graduating magna cum laude four years later.

While at Mercer, there were so many opportunities to make new friends and I pledged Alpha Delta Pi (ADPi) in 1951. In 1953 the Dorothy Shaw Lead-ership Award was presented to me by Alpha Delta Pi – it was the greatest honor in my college career. Two sorority sisters – Neva Jane Langley Fickling and Deen Smith Day Sanders attended our national convention in Banff Springs, Canada. Neva Jane was Miss America in 1953 and we have nurtured our friendship thru the years. Deen has been ac-tive in philanthropy and has a summer home nearby at High Hampton in Cashiers, North Carolnia.

In 1983, the board of trustees at Mer-cer University gave me the opportunity to serve on the board until 1988. While serving along with Deen Day and Jane Woodruff, new friendships emerged. Later on in 1988,

**Barbara Castleberry Carlton
and Deen Day**

Alpha Delta Pi Convention with Neva Jane Langley, 1953 Miss America

I was privileged to be President of the Presidents Club of Mercer University and held that position for two terms.

Jane Woodruff was awarded an honorary doctor of law by Mercer University and she has excelled in charitable causes since the death of her father and mother, George and June Woodruff. Her contributions in the field of education and medicine are extraordinary.

Jane Woodruff and Dr. Barbara Carlton

MEDICAL SCHOOL

After graduating from Mercer University in 1953, I was admitted to the Medical College of Georgia in Augusta, Georgia to start my long and arduous career toward being a medical doctor.

The freshman year in medical school was just eye-opening, scary at times; it was like being on a different planet. For example, one of the first exposures we had was to our cadaver, which is a dead body that each medical student would be carving on and dissecting for some four months. We would have a group of four medical students standing around the table with a body on it and we would start with the head and neck, dissecting every blood vessel, every vein, every nerve, every tendon, every muscle and to learn the names of these entities. Our cadaver happened to be a male, black male and he had been electrocuted, had gold teeth and I never will forget those gold teeth looking at us every day and we would start early in the morning and dissect until about noon and then after dissection all the extremities... the arms, the legs, but before dissecting anything else we had to coat it with Vaseline and wrap it with something like Ace bandage to preserve the body. Even though it was embalmed with embalming fluid, it would decay over time.

The first day that we were presented with the cadaver, it was on the second story of our medical school building. There was a big shaft with an elevator and they would transport the bodies up to the dissecting lab by this huge open elevator shaft. We were on the top floor looking down as they brought those bodies up stacked on top of each other.

They had attendants who would actually lift the bodies and place them randomly on the dissecting tables and then each group was assigned a table. I think we drew numbers to get the body that we were to work on. Ours was this black male.

There were three men at my dissecting table... partners, one woman, three men surrounding this black cadaver. They would always be playing tricks. There were four women in my medical school class, 78 total, men and women. The men would really play tricks on the women a lot. One of the tricks they played as we got into the lower part of the anatomy of a male... I went in one morning to be greeted by this projectile portion of the male anatomy that they had rigged up as a joke to tease me. I looked at that and I was mortified, turned away and they thought they'd gone far enough so they immediately corrected the position of this projected part of the anatomy and things sorta calmed down. That was just one of the tricks they'd play on the women.

The other trick they used was when we were quote "volunteering" for being selected to have blood drawn or to have the tube passed down your nose and experiment on each other to learn how to draw blood, put tubes down the nose and catheterize. We didn't actually practice catheterizing each other but we did draw blood and put tubes down the nose. What my three guys would do was we'd flip a coin and the odd person that got the odd coin had to do it. And they all agreed that they would always flip heads or tails... all three of them. So I was always the odd person. So I got all the tubes down my nose and the blood drawn. That was just another one of their pranks.

But I can say out of all this teasing and pranks if anybody went too far I would have a cadre of boys that would come to my aid. I never did get down to crying but I would have used that as a last resort if I had to.

That was sort of a little touch of what I was exposed to in medical school.

In my sophomore year I had to take physiology which was a tough, tough course. I had a tough time; I usually did very well in most of the courses but this one was awful. I had a professor, his name was Phillip Dow, he would give us pop quizzes. I would flunk 'em! I'd have an "F" and so would about ten, twelve, fifteen other students.

So we formed what we called "The Goon Squad." All those that were flunking would get together and we'd meet at night and we'd have special sessions trying to figure out what was going on with this physiology. The women were always singled out to be called upon for an answer to a question. So Dr. Dow, since I was a woman, he really picked on me a lot. I was really flunking but I finally passed. It was an effort but it took being a member of that "Goon Squad," a lot of studying and preparing for me to be able to pass physiology.

After dissecting on our cadaver we would go downstairs underneath the medical building, which was like a dungeon. That's where we would eat and I never will forget that formaldehyde smell – you've been working with your hands even though you had gloves on, but you never could get that smell off your hands. The first meal I ever ate, I remember trying to figure how to eat without using my hands. Even using a fork that smell was just awful, and you certainly couldn't pick it up any other way. Getting used to that was... well, it took weeks for me to be able to eat at all after dissecting on those bodies.

In my sophomore year I also remember very vividly an autopsy. We had to go see autopsies as part of our anatomy course. There was this young woman, an alcoholic, who had died of cirrhosis of the liver and that was the first autopsy I witnessed.

We were there looking at the autopsy and I did fine until all of a sudden they threw her black hair back over her head and started sawing into her skull and I just completely lost it. I passed out. I couldn't take that and I never will forget thinking about the life of that woman, her drinking all those years, and here a group of medical students trying to learn about what drinking does to the body, watching her being decapitated, taking her skullcap off, looking at her brain and my passing out... I guess that was part of the learning process. It created an indelible imprint on my memory and I guess you remember the traumatic things – that was very powerful for me to watch that, or not watch it!

Also in our sophomore year we took dog anatomy. It seems that the first two years you spent time on books and doing experiments in the lab on frogs and everything but humans and then all of a sudden you've got this live dog that you had to take its spleen out or its gall bladder and you're graded by how well you do. You have two surgical residents who supervise your quote "surgery." You'd have a team of three, one would put the dog to sleep, one would be the surgeon and one would be the assistant surgeon. There was the anesthetist who put the dog to sleep. Well, if the dog died from that procedure they'd get an "F" or if you lost the dog from bleeding or some accident like going through the gut then you'd get an "F." It was very, very anxiety-provoking to have two professors stand over you while you were doing this surgery. I somehow managed to come out on top on that course. I got an "A." And I didn't go into surgery. Doing dog surgery was enough for me!

Also during your sophomore year you started warming up to being with real patients. The first thing you'd do was to buy a little black bag and you'd get a stethoscope to hang around your neck and you'd feel like a real doctor. I would get my little black bag and I'd have an otoscope in there and ophthalmoscope and of course I kept my stethoscope in that little black bag and we'd run around the wards not knowing a patient from a frog. We'd go in a room and look at 'em and wonder what to do with the stethoscope, but it was fun just thinking about having two years behind you and you can be a real doctor. You can carry a black bag and look like one... of course, we didn't act like one but we felt like one.

The first patient, oh, how they did get through to us. We were scared of them but I'm sure they were more scared of us. And we would have all kinds of specialty clinics where you knew what you would be tackling like leg ulcers. That's all you did was tend to a leg ulcer. They would come into that clinic because they had a chronic leg ulcer, and you'd be on rotation and just tend to nothing but those for maybe two or three weeks at a time. And you'd have diabetic clinics where you'd just see diabetics, do urine sugars and the like and that was a learning process as well as learning how to be comfortable around a patient.

In your junior year you were on the wards more, got to see more and more patients and in your senior year it was the same thing. There was a lot of physical diagnosis and you were trying to decide what you wanted to do. During your junior and senior year you needed to know what you wanted to do after medical school, what kind of field you wanted to go into. I chose Internal Medicine. I just liked to figure out what was wrong with a patient so I pursued that course of direction and enjoyed family practice for seventeen years after that, which was very fulfilling and satisfying.

When I was a sophomore medical student I had a room mate, Nelle Strozier, and we'd go to the barbecue place every afternoon when we were taking anatomy. Part of the anatomy course was learning the bones so we had a box of bones, human bones... skull, legs, thighs, femur... we had all the bones of the body in a big box and we'd roll up to the barbecue place and order our barbecue. This black guy would wait on us and he'd come back with our order and by then we had our bones out of the box and we were reciting to each other what the grooves were on the bones, the articulations and the guy would come out to give us our sandwich and we'd be rattling those bones. He'd look at us and say, "What they be?" And we'd tell him they were skeletons, and he'd just turn around and run off. He was scared to death and he wouldn't wait on us any more. But when we took the skullcap it was really scary for him or anybody who'd come up to get our order. We'd have the skull with the teeth and the nose and you can imagine the reaction at a drive-in restaurant, how they'd feel when they would see that.

After four years of medical school, I was finally getting ready to be awarded my medical degree. And I can remember my daddy coming to my graduation, all my family coming, but especially my dad, who really was very, very hesitant about my venturing into a man's world to study medicine and then to become a doctor. But the pride on his face when he came to see this little country bumpkin from Lumpkin receive her medical degree... It was just about more than I could take.

To think about the sacrifice that he had made... He was a rural mail carrier and there were five children and not a lot of financial resources. But somehow he saved the money to enable me to go to medical school and that was such a wonderful, wonderful feeling and I guess it was a tribute to him, a thank-you to him to let him know that I was sincere in wanting to pursue this career and I was so thankful that he had the courage to invest in me and to trust me in my decision. That made me very, very proud.

Evelyn Dowd Castleberry and Troy Holder Castleberry,
Dr. Barbara Castleberry Carlton's parents

MEDICAL STORIES

As I opened my door in 1962 to practice medicine in our country home in the Oak Grove community near the Carl Carlton homeplace, one of my first experiences was to put my name plate on my desk.

I had gotten my medical degree under Barbara Cordeva Castleberry. So my name plate read Dr. Castleberry. I placed that on my desk to look official, to look professional.

Albert saw that Dr. Castleberry and he had a F-I-T, that spells "fit!" So I immediately had to discard that Dr. Castleberry and I don't even remember whether I got a Dr. Carlton plate to replace it, but the Dr. Castleberry plate went in the closet!

I did have a name plate put on my door, Barbara Carlton, MD which was required by state law that I had to identify my site of practice. So that was on the door of my office and also on the door to our front porch.

Thus I became a country doctor, seeing patients in my home from 8 o'clock to twelve every day referring any patient who required hospital care to nearby Lakeland, Florida, Watson Clinic.

In 1960, Will was born. We moved in to our house in 1962 when Pat was born, then I had Julie in '64, and Charlie in '67. So during my practice I had these four young children, knocking at my door trying to get in to see Mom. My waiting room was on the front porch... had six rocking chairs and, of course, my children sat in them most of the time and my patients had to stand up, but it was by appointment only so I didn't have a line of people on the front porch. They would just come at their appointment time, park out in front of the house and Betty Abbott, my nurse, would bring them in, check their blood pressure, get their weight and I'd find out what their chief complaint was.

I had a wonderful time seeing patients and really enjoyed the practice of medicine – that's truly what it was... a practice. Here is a quote to verify this statement:

Doctors are men or women who prescribe medicine
Of which they know little –
To cure diseases of which they know less
To human beings of which they know nothing.
                                        --Author unknown

Some of my most interesting patients were just pure redneck Florida crackers who came to my house for me to quote "fix 'em up" and I can remember one patient in particular, Joe Kersey. He was a great big guy -- you could strike a match on the bottom of his feet! He even came barefoot a lot of times into the office. He was a diabetic. And I recall one time he was gored by a hog on his shin and he came in, I looked at it and I said, "Gosh, we'll have to amputate that guy's leg!" But we started him on antibiotics and topical treatment to the big ulcerated lesion and showed him how to dress it every day and gave him ointment and Vaseline to clean it with and bandages to bandage it with.

I'd see him twice a week because it was so severe I felt it was gangrenous and he was going to lose his leg. Well, the first re-visit when he came back in, he presented himself with the same bandage that I'd put on three or four days before, so having found that out I made him come in every day for Betty to clean it and dress it because I knew we could not rely on him. Finally the ulcer did clear up and he got well and he would bring me chickens or sausage, ham or cane syrup. I almost had a love affair with old Joe Kersey and his wife Kate. They were both diabetic and I treated Kate until she died. I had retired from medicine before Joe died. They were some of my favorite patients. They were strictly Florida pioneers. They lived at the headquarters of the Myakka River in a little cabin. He'd grind cane every year and I'd take my kids out to the cane grinding. It was more than a doctor-patient relationship. It was a kindred feeling that I had with this wonderful husband and wife.

I can remember another patient, her name was Mrs. Hat Keene and this occurred before I started my office practice. I was still practicing with Dr. Collier. Mrs. Hat looked like Abe Lincoln... real tall and she had a little beard. She had a full length black trench coat which she always wore and a hat. She was called Mrs. Hat Keene. One day they told me that I needed to check on Mrs. Keene that she was in the emergency room. I went into the emergency room and there was this long body lying on the operating room table with a coat and hat on and she had these two huge "Q" sticks that were 8-inch long cotton applicator sticks stuck up her nose and the sticks were sticking out and I thought she was dead, that they wanted me to come in and pronounce her dead.

What had happened was anytime she'd come in with her sinuses bothering her, they'd put all this stuff on those big sticks and ram them up her nose and she'd lay there about 30 minutes and she'd be better. At times I would see her in town with her black coat and black hat and her beard... she was a character.

Another character was named Eddie who was the janitor at Dr. Collier's hospital. Eddie had a real high voice and he was always making me cookies, giving me something and I never will forget, when we moved into our new house out in Oak Grove we had a problem with the carpet curling in our family room and the bedroom. So Eddie comes out and says he could fix it. So he's out there trying to pull that carpet and trying to fix it and all he wanted to do was to come out and see my new house. He didn't know anything about fixing a carpet. He was another character.

When I started practicing out in the country besides getting the sign on my door, there were several other things in the little office. There was one room with a half bath with scales in it, lavatory, commode, and I had a small area in a closet which had a small lab where I could do urines, hemoglobins, white counts, I had a microscope to do differentials. Looking and talking to the patient, (physical diagnosis) enabled me to diagnose most patients. And I also had an EKG machine, an X-ray view box so I could have X-rays made elsewhere and look at them there in my office in the view box. So I had a country practice, mainly using my eyes and ears, my hands in trying to decide what was wrong with the patient... listening to them. No MRIs, no CAT Scans, no Sonograms! Patients know what's wrong with them if you'll listen to them. So I practiced in that environment. I had a way to do pelvic exams in my office, did a lot of annual physical exams on mainly women who didn't want to go to a male doctor.

The whole time I'd be seeing these patients, sitting out on the front porch in the rocking chairs would be four children taking up the places in the rocking chairs. My children had fun talking to the patients and vice versa. And when it would get cold my family room was the waiting room. So the patients were targets for the children inside because they didn't go to kindergarten, the only time they left home was when they started to school. They caught the school bus but they were under foot during my practice when not in school. Betty, my nurse, would masterfully maneuver them away from my door inside the office that led to the family room because they would want to see Mommy about something that would pop up. I did have a housekeeper so between the housekeeper and Betty and sometimes Albert, they would keep the children away from banging on the door so I could take care of my patients.

I practiced there for 10 years seeing patients from eight o'clock to noon, five days a week. I made house calls, that was in the days that doctors even made house calls. I felt like that was good medicine to see a patient in his home environment and because it was a family practice. When I saw a patient I assumed the whole practice of seeing the whole family so it took on a truly holistic approach to family practice.

The relationship that my patients had to my children was amazing. They would oftentimes, while sitting on the front in the rocking chairs, have them sitting in their laps playing games with them. I can recall one time when Albert was out in the grove and they had burned a bunch of orange trees and there was a big heap of ashes in a pile. The children were out there watching them burn and for some reason Julie ventured up on the pile of ashes. She sank into the ashes and had severe second and third degree burns on both feet. I was in the office seeing patients and they brought her up screaming and, of course I saw that we had to take her to the hospital in Lakeland immediately. My patients were there on the porch and they were helping to calm her down until I could get her feet wrapped and get her sedated so we could take her to Lakeland. It ended up that the burns were so severe that she was going to have to have skin grafts. Dr. Charles Lawson was her surgeon and he had wrapped both feet and she was scheduled to have the debriding in the operating room. So they took her into surgery and took the bandages off, debrided the burns, wrapped her back up and we brought her back home.

My mother (Lynmama) was there and she was trying to entertain Julie and was riding her around in a wagon. The wagon turned over and Julie ended up cutting her head, so she had the burned feet and the cut head that we had to get sewed up. Typical day with children and patients, but we survived. I can't say enough for the compassion that my patients had for my family and my children. It even made the practice a lot more satisfying to know that they recognized that I was a mother as well as a physician and that they were willing to participate and join in with the family in our emergency times.

In 1970 when the new hospital opened, Albert and I decided to build a new office for me across from the hospital in Wauchula. We had fun getting the new building designed by Harry McEwen, a prominent architect from Tampa, Florida and embarked on recruiting other doctors to fill the office building. There was room for four doctors with a central waiting room that was shared by the four physicians. I moved my practice there in 1971 and practiced there for seven years until I retired in '77.

The practice of medicine in the hospital was very, very strenuous. It was time-consuming, stressful because not only did I have patients to see in the morning, I had patients in the hospital to make rounds twice a day before eight o'clock and again before I went home. At one time I had 26 patients in that 50-bed hospital that were under my care so it was a huge load for two or three physicians, but we were trying to make the hospital a success. Since the early '70s we recruited a surgeon, Fausto Garcia M.D., and an ObGyn, Bill Black M.D., and later on a family physician, James Whitehurst M.D.. We had two family physicians, a surgeon and an ObGyn, and the hospital was doing very, very well. It was 50 beds and had a full operating and emergency rooms. We monitored coronary patients in their rooms with coronary monitors. It was a state of the art hospital in 1970, very upgraded. That hospital still stands today. It went through some upheavals including the baby-swapping scandal that occurred in '76 and '77 which eventually caused the downfall of the hospital and it was closed.

After two to three years of tumultuous times the hospital was finally reopened when Florida Hospital out of Orlando leased the hospital at which time it started an uphill climb again.

Hardee Memorial Hospital was very, very dear to my heart and I can remember when I was told it was closed. I was in North Carolina. It was one of the most traumatic, sad events of my life to know that all the years that we'd spent trying to have a community hospital, to know that now it was to be closed and there'd be no hospital care facilities available. (Every successful community needs a community hospital.)

So the campaign to reopen it became a challenge and later on we achieved the reopening of the hospital. In fact, in the year 2007, the hospital is open and running. We have two new family physicians who have moved into my old office just across the street and hopefully its future is bright which would make me very, very happy and fulfilled.

Dr. Barbara Carlton getting Albert Carlton to take his medicine, 1964

The sign on Dr. Barbara Carlton's door.

NINFA COLLIER
Mrs. (Dr.) Miles Collier

Dr. Barbara Carlton: *I would not be in Wauchula had it not been for Ninfa's husband, Dr. Miles Collier.*

Ninfa was very important to me in helping me adjust to life in a little small town about which I knew nothing. She is very loving and has meant the world to me in so many ways.

Ninfa Collier has been a supreme, lasting introduction to this communit, with her dedication to her husband and his practice and her friendliness to a stranger like me. I owe her a great debt of gratitude... she has helped me tremendously.

Dr. Barbara came to work for my husband, Dr. Miles Collier, when he became ill and had to go to the hospital. She stayed with me part of the time. Some days and nights she stayed at the hospital. She used his car and came back and forth here from our home. She worked for him two or three different times.

Then, every time he'd leave, he'd call Barbara. She had met a young man in Wauchula named Albert Carlton, so she didn't mind coming at all. She worked there at the hospital with my husband and all his patients loved her and talked about her, and men, of course, wanted to come to see Dr. Barbara.

After Albert and Barbara married, she continued to work at the hospital until after he, my husband, passed away in 1960.

Dr. Barbara did a lot of practice during this time because Dr. Collier was not well but he had a long, hard practice. He practiced for the whole county. He made house calls... all out in the county on country roads. In fact I went with him a lot just riding. Several times I was caught and had to help him deliver a baby. He worked all over Highlands County, Avon Park, Sebring... a lot of places. So he had a general practice plus the hospital and he did all the work. He, of course, had Barbara and a staff to help run the little private hospital as well as his full time office practice.

My husband set up his first practice in 1937 in Bartow, the Bartow Hospital. His practice was general... house calls, office calls, surgery, delivered babies, read his own X-rays and did all his own work.

In Bartow, we knew Dr. Hughes who was a general practitioner. He was a wonderful man and I think my husband picked up a lot of compassion, a lot of his traits, a lot of the ways he practiced which were all good. I've never known another doctor as wonderful as Dr. Hughes was with his patients. My husband practiced there at the hospital, the county hospital, as did Dr. Hughes.

Our daughter Ninfa, was born in 1936 so when we came here she was three years old.

After two years, my husband moved his practice to Wauchula.

Dr. Barbara Carlton: *He had a full service general hospital with a lab, X-ray, operating room, little emergency room plus an office, so he was a one-man show doing all that work himself with some very, very good nurses but there were no physician's assistants, and no practitioners. He just had good LPNs mainly, probably a couple RNs, but it was daylight to dawn, seven days a week, 365 days a year. Naturally he never knew when patients would get sick... when he had to do surgery, or when he'd have to deliver a baby.*

I can remember the first time I came to practice at his hospital... one of the first patients was a man with acute urinary retention. I had spent time doing internal medicine residency, had little surgical training and no urology training. Dr. Collier had a very good orderly and he, the orderly, took care of this patient who could not pass his urine. In a gnat's whisper he expertly inserted the catheter giving the patient prompt relief from his over - extended bladder. That was one of my first brushes with Dr. Collier's many, many challenges.

He loved medicine better than anything. It was his whole life and we understood it so we didn't bother him. Every time we'd pack to go off a few days, of course we never got off. He would come home and say, "I'm sorry..." We had very little time away but occasionally we tried to take some time. He became sick early, he was young. He got sick when he was 45 and he had practiced really hard up until that time.

I'm sure, as Barbara said, she saw things she'd never seen before. They didn't have assistants at that time, doctors mostly did everything themselves. He had a doctor come in and help when he'd leave... to take care of the business. But he did all the work. Then Barbara came along and she was broken into everything.

Hardee Memorial Hospital opened its doors June 1970, and is now one of the many divisions of Florida Hospital, a Seventh-day Adventist Hospital Corporation.

Dr. Barbara Carlton: *After his death, the practice was sold to a couple, Peggy and Gene Moore. He was a surgeon and she was internal medicine. They continued general practice plus the surgical practice and then they sold the hospital to Dr. Alfred Massam. He continued to practice till the new hospital became operational. Hardee Memorial it was called. This was in the summer of 1970.*

I always called it Dr. Collier's hospital but it was really Wauchula Infirmary. Before the Hardee Memorial new hospital opened there were two hospitals... Dr. Collier's, the Wauchula Infirmary, and the Palmetto Medical Clinic. These two hospitals operated as independent general hospitals until they were eventually closed because of the opening of the new community hospital called Hardee Memorial.

Back in 1977 when Hardee Memorial Hospital was still in its prime there was a baby-swapping scandal event that happened at Hardee Memorial and it

The Doctor's Center was the offices for Dr. Barbara Carlton, Dr. James Whitehurst, Dr. William Black, and Dr. Fausto Garcia. Built in 1971.

became a big media event on the news. It was finally resolved but eventually as the result of the bad publicity and because of poor administration the hospital was closed. And then after a couple years of its being closed, it was purchased by a group out of Atlanta. They ran it for about two years and then it was closed again after which Florida Hospitals out of Orlando, the Seventh-day Adventist Hospital, eventually took over and they have managed the hospital since that time.

The thing I remember most is when that new hospital was opened, it was imperative that we recruit doctors here. So my husband, Albert, and I decided to build an office across from the hospital. After it was constructed we were able to attract a general surgeon, Dr. Fausto Garcia, Dr. William Black, OBGYN, and Dr. James Whitehurst, a family physician. The hospital really flourished during this time from the early '70s 'til the late '70s. All of a sudden four to five doctors were doing what Dr. Collier did single handedly. That's the evolution of medicine, medical practice today that you have specialists doing general medical and surgical work and we've lost the hands-on powers of a family physician. Unfortunately it's made the practice of medicine a business not a passion, not a profession. It's sad but this is the way it is.

After Dr. Collier died our family sorta began to really want to know Ninfa, now a widow, a lot better. Will was our first child, born in 1960, and I would corner Ninfa in helping me to baby-sit and we'd go fishing while she'd baby-sit Will on the creek banks. And my mother, LynMama, would go and we'd drag Ninfa along. A lot of the time we'd end up going to the strawberry patch and she'd sit there with a big hat on watching Will in the stroller while we picked strawberries. I even took her golfing with me, even took her hunting with me and I'm sure she can recount some of those tales the two of us, plus my mother. We'd all load however many children I had at the time and we'd go turkey hunting. We'd build a campfire and LynMama would stay there with the little ones and Ninfa and I *would slip down to the turkey blind and shoot at the turkeys and LynMama and the children could hear bang! bang! from afar and we'd come back and they'd be fixing breakfast 'round the campfire and we'd be dragging in two or three turkeys.*

Barbara would shoot all of them. Remember when a turkey came right up and we were right on him? Barbara said, "Shoot... shoot!" But he passed right on by me. However, when he came back by, Barbara let him have it!

Dr. Barbara Carlton: *And then when the children got a little older I had a Jeep and we'd go out there in that Jeep quail hunting.*

Barbara and I would be out in the field and we'd hear the Jeep and I said, "Barbara, I can't see anybody in it... it's an empty Jeep... I guess it's Charlie..." He was so little we couldn't see him, but he was just going everywhere. And he did the same thing with the golf cart in North Carolina. He'd drive the golf cart and Barbara and I would walk and play golf and he'd carry the clubs. He turned the golf cart over and tore up my clubs... it was upside down. Charlie would just go up and down the mountain with the golf cart and Barbara and I'd walk. We had a lot of good times...

And I'm sorry I can't play golf now. I still miss it at age 91.

Dr. Barbara Carlton: *I call Ninfa my accomplice in all kinds of crime. We got in more trouble... One time we were quail hunting out at the Strickland Place Bar Ā Ranch at New Zion and we had to pass by the church. There was always what we called a graveside covey of quail. So we'd see 'em out there in the cemetery and we'd look to see if the preacher was there and we'd slip out with our shotguns and crawl up as close as we could to 'em and shoot 'em on the ground, which is not "kosher," and about the time we'd start pickin' 'em up... here would come the preacher! He lived about two hundred yards from the church and he'd come running up. And I said, 'Uh-oh, Gram, we gotta share these quail with the preacher 'cause here he comes!' and he says, 'You know we have a rule to not shoot around the cemetery.'*

And I said, 'That's a good rule, Preacher, because you know a bullet could ricochet off that tombstone and hit somebody in the eye...'trying to get his mind off what we'd just done. So we'd give him half the quail and we'd load up and head back home. Then about half way back home one of the quail... you know when you shoot 'em on the ground they're just sorta stunned. So about half way back to the house which is about 15 minutes, one of the quail had come up under the seat of the Jeep and started fluttering and we started thinking there was a ground rattler snake up under the seat. And we'd have to stop, find the quail, ring his neck...

I remember one time we were shootin' doves and I had taken my husband's old gun, one that he used to use, and I didn't know how many shells you could put in a gun... I didn't know anything about what I was doing anyway. We were out there shootin' away and they came to check the field, Corvil Justesen, the Game Warden. He was checking ever'body and he came over to check me. The gun would hold five shells but you're only supposed to put in three. So he said, "Whatta you doin' with a gun with five shells?" I said, "Five shells? I didn't know it'd hold five shells... I've never put but three in there." He was trying to visit more than anything else, but he took my gun. That was a big deal that day 'cause I lost my gun. However, the next day he came to the door and brought it back to me.

Dr. Barbara Carlton: *And that was the year I was pregnant with Will. We were lying down in the ditch, trying to hide from the game warden but because I was so big, I was lying on my back and it looked like a watermelon there in the ditch and he saw us in there and he checked everybody's guns, took Gram's. I guess he felt sorry for me and didn't take my gun because I was so big lying there in a state of eminent pregnancy. William Albert Carlton, Jr. was delivered two weeks later. At that time I guess I had a legitimate excuse but since then there could be a question about my legitimacy.*

This one I had wasn't, but I didn't know it. Knowing Arnold (Dr. Miles Arnold Collier) as I did I should have known that he would have had a gun that was unplugged. I should have known... he lived "on the edge".

Dr. Barbara Carlton: *The story is told that when Dr. Collier played golf, he didn't play much but when he did if he hit one out in the rough he just went and got it and dropped it in the fairway. His partners would say, "Doc whatta you doing that for?" And he'd say, "I didn't come out here to hit the ball out in the woods in the rough... I'm gonna hit it off the fairway." His partner asked, "You gonna count it a stroke?" Dr. Collier said, "No! My time's too valuable."*

He did a lot of country practice, real rural country. I'd get up in the morning and go out to get in the car to go somewhere. He'd get a call from Lakeland or somewhere and whoever it was only had a wagon or a truck, and he'd say, "Come by my house and get my wife's car."

And he'd give 'em the key and he never told me. They'd just come by and get my car, go to Lakeland, Tampa, or wherever he was sending them and I'd go out and my car would be gone. So I'd call up and say, "Where is my car?" And he'd say, "Your car's in Tampa." He'd do everything for his practice... his patients. His patients were always first. We were second.

The old doctors were that way. Years ago a doctor was a friend, and a doctor and a preacher. They had to be everything. Today they look at you and write your number down for identification until the next time you come. It's not like it usta be...

"And you," Ninfa says to Dr. Barbara, "were very good to me."

Since Ninfa, like Barbara, came from Georgia, they've been state friends and were never inhibited in using their native Georgia accent.

BETTY ABBOTT
Dr. Carlton's Nurse

I came to Dr. Carlton's office for a physical. I had been through nursing school and I needed a physical to take the state board. We had graduated and I got all fixed up and took the state board and passed it. I had to come back to Dr. Carlton for blood work. It was then that she said, "Would you like to come to work for me?" And I said, "Well, right now I'm working at Lakeland Hospital and I would have to give them two weeks notice"

That was a long drive for me, 37 miles… but from home to her office it was much less… only about 14 miles. So I was thrilled, I said, "Yes, I would like to work for you. But let me give them two weeks notice and I'll come back." So that's what I did… finished my term at Lakeland Hospital and came here, met a new family, I didn't know, Albert at the time, didn't know any of them, but got to know a wonderful family… and they'll live with me in my memories as long as I live.

It was in the '70s that I was Dr. Carlton's nurse. I thoroughly enjoyed the 11 years I worked with her. She was like a sister, an adviser, just a wonderful person every day. She's not the type person to come in with… "I'm mad, don't speak to me." You know there are people who come to work with such an attitude. But she was the same every morning… we both were. Our personalities clicked for some reason.

I can tell a few things about the children, however, not with dates or their ages, and some of "our" patients. For instance, Mr. and Mrs. Joe Kersey of Myakka City. They were both diabetic, wonderful people. They would come with a urine specimen. We had asked them to fast without breakfast and we'd do a blood sugar then run the urine test. They would bring a little bag with two bottles, one

236

would be a Listerine bottle and one would be a Scope bottle. I'd say, "Mr. Joe, which one is yours?" He'd say, "I don't know." And his wife would not remember which bottle was hers. We'd do the tests and of course, we'd always have a high blood sugar. Weeks later Mr. Joe would come up, always came in the back door and he'd say, "Chile..." He always called her Chile, never did he call her Dr. He'd be shaking all over. We knew what was the problem... he was off his sugar pills, off his potassium, off his blood pressure medicine. Dr. Barbara would say, "Fix him a glass, Betty." I'd get the glass of water, put the potassium in it, get him comfortable in a room until he drank that glass of potassium water. In about 25 to 30 minutes he'd feel a lot better but she needed to talk to him to explain that you must keep taking it, you don't stop because the bottle is empty. You go get it refilled. But he'd forget about his medicine. That's understandable when we grow old.

One day a lady, very slender and tall, a black lady, knocked on the door and said, "I see the doctor... I see the doctor." I said come in and I sat her down and Dr. Carlton was sitting in her chair and she looked at her and asked, "What's your name?" She told us her name. "Well, how did you get here?" The lady answered, "I walked through some groves..." She was dirty where she'd walked through the groves. I did the vital signs and Dr. Carlton said, "Get a hemoglobin on her." So I did a hemoglobin and it was three.

The lady sat in that chair and she was so weak... how she made it through the groves to this house with a hemoglobin of three we never knew. It should have been at least 12.

Dr. Barbara Carlton: *It was a miracle. She probably had iron deficiency anemia, or pernicious anemia.*

That was one I never forgot. And then once in a while we'd get a little knock on the door... "Mommy, Mommy..." All Julie needed was just a few words and to see Mommy's face. They'd talk a little bit and then it was OK. We'd lock up again because we did pelvics, everything there… PAP smears, EKGS and we had to have privacy.

Another time, Julie came in and Pat had cut her hair… right in front in the center of her head. So when Pat came by, I said, "What happened to Julie's hair?"

He said, "I don't wanta talk about it."

Their ages were about three and five.

One day Dr. Carlton was suturing a laceration on a patient. Julie walked in… there was no need to keep the door locked that day, I guess it was "open door day." She said, "Mommy, I didn't know you could sew!"

Dr. Carlton and Albert took their vacation in 1965 and went to Europe.

While they were gone, Lynmama and I were here every morning. She was the children's grandmother, Dr. Barbara's mother. She was a sweet southern lady. She had a little southern drawl that most people don't have in Florida. And she had such a sweet smile; she was a wonderful, lovely lady.

Well, while they were gone, Julie learned to walk. I was so thrilled. I said, "She's walking! Wait'll they come back… wait'll they come back." We were in the office and that's where she learned to walk. It was pretty easy walking on that carpet instead of the bricks that are out here (in the dining room).

Often I would have to take papers to the hospital on patients who were admitted.

These were big sheets with answers "Yes" and "No," "Yes" and "No…" personal questions that I'd ask the patient. We were the only ones that used these forms; we bought them by the tablet. One of the questions was: (I remember one man in particular who was about 75) "Do you ever have hot flashes or just get hot?" He looked me straight in the eye and said, "Oh, no, my wife and I don't do that anymore."

That was a "Yes" or "No" question and I was so flustered by his reply that

I think I probably just put "No" and went on with the next question.

Someone brought a colored man in one day and he was real bad. We put him out in the guest house, put him in the bed with a tourniquet on both arms and both legs and I rotated him. I did this all day long… all day. I think we gave him some Lasix, and then someone came and took him to the hospital. What we did saved his life. The man was laying on that bed and I'd go out there every 10 minutes, come back in here, then it was time to go back… just rotated the tourniquets and leave one off.

This was just another day in the life of a country doctor. You take care of what is to be done right now. You don't say… go to the hospital, or I'll give you an appointment three weeks down the road. Dr. Barbara took care of the need right then.

Dr. Barbara Carlton: *There were some life and death situations presented on our porch and our waiting room. I'll never forget the Lambert boy who was playing in the barn and got into an insecticide. He had a seizure and became unconscious and they rolled him up here and the only thing I had was some atropine. Apparently he had gotten into an insecticide that cut off the acetylcholine chain. I pumped that into him, put him in a car, this was before ambulances, and sent him on to Lakeland. On the way*

Dr. Barbara Carlton's outside "waiting room."
Albert holding Charlie, Dr. Barbara, Will,
Pat and Julie, circa 1968

to Lakeland he waked up. They kept him and checked him out.

The boys had gone in the barn where there are always chemicals around and apparently he'd gotten one in him. We had to assume that was what happened...

She (Dr. Barbara) knew what was out there, we didn't need a laboratory and she knew what needed to be done.

Dr. Barbara Carlton: *Another time, Joe Kersey comes in, he's diabetic, he had extensive necrotic (rottening) lesion on his leg. Betty cleaned him up, we get him all fixed up, tetanus shot, antibiotics and dress it, and we give him gauze and tape to take with him, along with Neosporin to put on it. And he was told to change the dressing at least twice a day and to come back in a week.*

He comes back one week later with the same bandage on, it had not been changed a single time and it was black by then. So we debrided it again and I just had him come back every day until we got it cleaned up. I'm sure he would have lost his leg had we not kept after that wound.

And I never will forget... the hospital had just opened and his wife got real sick. And she was diabetic. They were so close, so devoted to each other, both diabetics. I don't know who gave who the insulin... one would go in shock and get a little glucose... anyway, they were always in and out of crises. At that time the hospital wasn't open and she went into heart failure, then kidney failure... and the end was pretty close. Telling old Joe that Miss Kate was not going to make it and seeing how he sat by her bed, holding her hand, weeping, not believing that she was not immortal. He would not accept the fact that she was going to die. I never will forget how that just ripped me because here was this couple who lived out in the boondocks, they had hogs and chickens, they lived off the land, made cane syrup and would always bring me a country ham and cane syrup, and sometimes a chicken, and we'd just wring its neck and pull the feathers off.

This was really my introduction to Wauchula and the practice of medicine... patients like Kate and Joe Kersey. I wouldn't have changed that experi-

ence for anything in the world.

I have to say this: People say... how do you feel about practicing medicine in those days? And I reply, I can say two things: I helped a few, and I helped to push a few along. And that's it, you can help a few and others you really need to let go... make their death dignified, easy as possible and Betty knows how many times we had to do that. I loved my old patients. The older they were the more I loved them because they were so thankful and so grateful. One day more that they could live... they were just so glad they could be here another day.

At this time there were three other fairly young physicians practicing at the same time. They were in Wauchula. I was the only one out here... the only country doctor.

There were two private hospitals when I came to Wauchula. Two of the physicians went to the same medical school that I did. I came to work here because of Dr. Collier, then he became very ill and he had a doctor wife and husband come in and they actually bought his practice. When they bought his practice they kept his hospital open. I referred all my patients out at that time, generally to Lakeland or wherever they wanted to go. The other two doctors, Dr. Sayre and Dr. Carmichael were with the Palmetto Medical Clinic, the other private hospital. It stayed active until the new hospital opened in 1970. That's when I built an office and moved my practice to town. I was on the original medical staff of Hardee Memorial Hospital.

I practiced there another seven years and then our kids got to be teenagers and I felt it more important to get a degree in home-making, and raise those kids than to practice medicine, and besides Albert's health was bad. It was ironic that I retired the same year that he had a major, major heart attack.

That's about the history of my practice. I came almost unannounced to this little town. There was a little article in the paper that I'd opened a practice and when I retired I don't think there was anything in the paper. I just faded away...

and that's the way I wanted it to be. I just wanted to be part of the community and I found right away that I didn't marry Albert Carlton, I married the community of Wauchula. It took a depression in my own life for me to realize that that's what I had done. That came about because of the crises we had at the hospital, the one in which the administrator and a member of the hospital board were at odds and the medical staff sided with the hospital administrator and it created a big, big splash in the newspaper. And I was pretty outspoken about my support for the adminis- trator. It impacted my own emotional stability in that I felt like the hospital board was trying to practice medicine. Anyway, it wound up that the hospital survived that, went on through the next 10 years doing well. And then the baby swapping scandal came along and the hospital eventually closed because of bad publicity and poor management. Later on it was leased or purchased by Florida Hospital. Since that time we've been on the upward path again.

Our hospital doors were closed for a period of time, about two years, but gradually it was reopened. So medical care in Hardee County has not been a piece of cake, it's been a hard fight and the average person in Hardee County does not realize the struggles that took place.

Betty Abbott continues: I remember one day when a lady came to the back door and she had a big bag in her hand and she said, "I was in the hospital and they gave me this but I don't think it belongs to me." We opened the bag and there was her catheter, her bed pan, water pitcher, and emesis basin plus a few other items that they give you at the hospital when you're discharged, because that's what you used. Dr. Carlton looked at those things and said, "I think you can take them home because they do belong to you." She really thought the hospital had made a mistake.

Dr. Barbara Carlton: *Can't you see somebody standing there washing and sterilizing all that stuff and taking all of it back?*

There is so much going on at the hospital that we're missing. I feel like saying, "Don't do it that way, do it this way." You know we made rounds together you and I, they don't up there and they miss so much that the nurse… I know because my husband has been in there a number of times and had the nurse made rounds with her doctor she'd know… Oh yes, he has dementia, he's gotta be put closer to the nurse's station. They put him way down at the end of the hall. Well, I went home with the assurance that he was going to be taken care of. They called me at one o'clock in the morning. "Mrs. Abbott, your husband has gotten out of the bed and he's got blood all over the floor…" I said, "Isn't he supposed to be taken care of? I'm not coming in." That was my problem, he was there because he needed to get some rest, have medication to make him sleep… I'm sure the orders were there but they had not paid enough attention to them. That has been at least four or five years ago… he passed away in July 2003. You know little things like that didn't happen back when we were there. A nurse making rounds with the patient's own doctor is really beneficial to the patient and the family.

**Albert and Barbara Carlton going to church on Mother's Day, circa 1981.
Photographed and produced by first son, Will Carlton.**

PART SIX
ALBERT'S RETIREMENT
and Death

Dr. Barbara C. Carlton: *If stories are designed to give insight into the turbulent and traumatic happenings to the child, Albert, as a child after his mother died, was surrounded with loving people, fair people, big houses along with eight uncles and one aunt (Ella), all who wanted him. However, with love and understanding he went to live with his half-sister, Matred Olliff, and her husband, Allen. He went to Hardee public schools, transferred to Bolles Military in Jacksonville, and then went in the Navy. After his discharge from the Navy, Albert enrolled at the University of Florida where he graduated with a degree in Agribusiness.*

At age 42, Albert had his first heart attack.

In 1965 we purchased a home at High Hampton in Cashiers, North Carolina. This was a vacation retreat for the family. And each May, Albert would have a 'men's only' golf outing.

I vividly recall the excitement a few days prior to a planned trip to North Carolina in that it would be a golf event plus he would be transporting coons from the ranch to North Carolina.

We had loaded the coons on top of the station wagon to be ready for early departure on May 1, 1968.

The day before at noon Albert told me that he had a discomfort in his chest.

Since I had my office in our home, I took an EKG while he was lying on the couch in our family room. It was evident he had an impending severe heart attack. I immediately loaded him in our car and took him to our cardiologist in Lakeland.

245

This was the beginning of a long and protracted journey in dealing with his indolent cardiac disease process.

Needless to say the coon transport and golf trip was postponed and Albert spent two weeks recuperating from this very serious heart attack.

He was advised to curtail all business endeavors, to stop smoking and was started on a cardiac rehabilitation regime that included jogging and diet restrictions.

At the time we had four children under foot and I, being a physician, was faced with the possibility of raising these children as a widow.

Post-coronary depression ensued and the attendant period of jogging, family and business, personal and private relations underwent daily rescheduling. I never knew any minute what I'd be able to do the next. Albert was the key in preventing and alleviating this stress load.

*As years went by we survived and I assumed a greater role in managing the family business and allowed him to do **his thing** – whether it was building, planting grass, or working cows. I was protecting him... enhancing his life by not making a cardiac cripple out of him.*

His children learned early to walk on eggs, not to disturb Daddy. No confrontations, no fits... yes sir, no sir. He wanted his three sons to have their hair cut, and in the event their shirt tails were out before going to Sunday School, he would take a large safety pin and pin the shirt tails between their legs!

Ten years passed of the utmost regimentation and in 1977 he had another major heart attack which really changed the way the family had to adjust. His cardiologist said in order for him to survive he had to become skinny and relaxed. These were the marching orders. He was freed up to pursue the interests that gave him pleasure and satisfaction. He looked the picture of health. He was not an invalid.

In fact, observing his passion for working in the yard, including growing roses, landscaping, even to working in the cow pens, playing some golf, (he allowed me to beat him... ho, ho, ho!), one would have thought that nothing was wrong with him. He was a picture of health... vibrant, engaging, inquiring and last of all, very opinionated.

This man lived his life to the fullest, and at age 64 died quietly in his sleep...

This nearly was mine...

It was in 1962 when we moved into our new house in the Oak Grove Community. At that time our friends were challenged to name our new home. That was in the 60s when JFK was president. At the time the Kennedys had a summer place called "Glenora" at Hyannis Port. In considering names for our new home, somehow, the word "Glenokra" was thrown out and it just happened to stick.

Thus, in 1992 at the time of Albert Carlton's death, it seemed natural and fitting to name the family burial plot "Glenokra."

Grave stone of William Albert Carlton 1927-1992

STAN PELHAM

I'm the business manager for Barbara and Albert...have been employed here at the home place for just over 30 years. My office is actually in the guest house of the home.

I came to know The Carltons back in 1976. I grew up in Bonifay, Florida, went in the Air Force and after the service went to Florida State University majoring in accounting. In my senior year there, I was interviewing with several accounting firms, one of which was Coopers and Lybrand, Tampa. At the interview, the partner that was interviewing asked if I would be interested in talking to one of their clients who they had done work for for many years. They said they were looking for someone with accounting background but also agricultural background. I had grown up on a small farm in Bonifay. I said sure. They were from Wauchula. I said I'd be glad to talk to them. So they set up the appointment but after I got back to Tallahassee I had to get out the road atlas to find out where Wauchula was! Because I'd never heard of Wauchula before.

That was in January of 1976 and so the appointment was set up and I came down, visited and they interviewed me.

I remember thinking that in most cases I'd be dressed in a coat and tie and when I got here they were dressed in jeans and work clothes. So I was a little over-dressed!

I remember coming out to the smoke house-guest house and sitting around the little table back in the little pub room and talking, which we did for quite a while. They learned about my background and they told me about their operation. Albert looked at me real straight and said, "I want to know one thing: do you mind getting cow manure on your boots?" I don't think he used the word "manure" when he asked that! I said, "Not at all... I grew up on a farm and had that happen many times." He said, "Well, I just wanted to make sure because you'll probably be getting some of that on you."

Dr. Barbara Carlton: *Stan, part of your job will be dove and quail hunting and especially you'll be assigned to clean the quail.*

Charlie Carlton, Stan Pelham and Dr. Barbara Carlton, 2 X 4 quail hunting

**Stan Pelham
and Brady Pfeil
cleaning
quail at the
2 X 4 RANCH**

Albert always liked working cows. If we were working cows he was right there in the cowpens with us.

We were down at the Rusty Pot Ranch, + or – 5300 acres near Myakka City -- one day working cows and it had rained two or three inches and the cowpens were full of mud... as sloppy as you could ever get. That afternoon we were covered from head to toe and I said, "Albert, you asked me if I minded getting manure on my boots. You didn't say I was gonna take a bath in it!"

He laughed... he was a wonderful person... I miss him dearly. It didn't matter what you were doing; he was going to be there... the groves, cowpens... and to have met him you wouldn't have ever known that he had anything. He was a down-to-earth person, most of the time dressed in blue jeans and work boots.

From the time I got here they had just sold their big ranch to Gardinier Phosphate but they were leasing it... still had their cows on that ranch but they were moving those. They had acquired the Rusty Pot Ranch at that time and they also had a ranch in Sumter County, Florida, + or – 8000 acres, the Half Moon Ranch, which they'd had for several years.

We moved the cows from the Strickland Bar $\overline{\wedge}$ Ranch to those two ranches and kept those for a considerable time. Of course, they also had property in Hardee County which they still own.

Then in 1978-79 we acquired the 2 X 4 RANCH, + or – 5700 acres, in Arcadia. So for a while we were quite spread out in Sumter, Manatee and DeSoto Counties.

Over the years they sold quite a bit of the property... a big portion to the state to preserve it from development. In Sumter County they sold half of that ranch to the Water Management District and the other half to DNR (Department of Natural Resources). It's now a state Wildlife Management Area (Carlton Half Moon). Several years later they owned property in DeSoto County with Ted Williams and Joe Davis Sr., which much later was sold to the Water Management District and is now a state park. Much later, the Carltons were able to protect from development over 10,000 acres as a result of these transactions.

In 1992 Albert died. I vividly remember the last time I saw him. It was Friday afternoon about five o'clock. I had finished the day's work, walked out of the office and he was in the driveway raking leaves.

They were building a new office and a place to put his antique cars. He was there sweeping up and raking the leaves and stuff from the building and we were joking, as he always did. I told him I'd see him Monday morning... have a good weekend.

Of course I didn't know at that time that I'd get a call about eleven o'clock that night from Barbara saying she needed me out here. When I got here, Albert had already passed away.

Barbara remembers that Stan stayed and assisted carrying Albert's body and placing him in the hearse as well as taking him to the funeral home. Carl Saunders joined Barbara and Stan, staying the night along with Bob and Gloria Gibson, Carl and Fran Simmons.

Big shock to everyone. Big loss, not only to us but to the entire community.

Going forward from there, we had started developing groves in DeSoto County and we continued that as Albert had hoped we would.

Then later on we sold part of the property in Myakka City, Rusty Pot Ranch, down-sizing some. We finally got to where all of our livestock basically was relocated to the 2 X 4 RANCH in Arcadia, DeSoto County. We had some here at the homeplace but the big operation for cattle was in DeSoto. We had groves here in Hardee County and a few head of cows but not a lot.

All of Albert and Barbara's children grew up, had interests other than agriculture so up to date in 2006, we've sold the 2 X 4 RANCH and basically have the operation in Hardee County and a small acreage in Manatee County.

One thing about Albert was that he was always so good-natured and always had a good sense of humor. We had an old hunchback colored guy named Warren Leonard, who had worked for Albert in the groves for years and years. Albert and Barbara also had a couple antique Rolls Royce vehicles. One of them is a chauffeur-driven 1949 that's black and white. One day, old Warren came up and told Mr. Albert he needed to go to town one day at lunch to get his social security straightened out. Albert said, "Well, at noon time when you take your lunch break we'll go into town."

Come noon, Albert put on his chauffeur's hat, got in the front seat of that Rolls Royce, put Warren in the back with his lunch, folded the table down and Warren was riding in the back seat heading to town with Albert chauffeuring to 'tend to Warren's social security.

Here's another story about Warren: After the Strickland Bar Ā Ranch was sold, Albert and Barbara became close friends with the Gardiniers who had bought the 9000-acre Strickland Bar Ā Ranch and they visited quite often. One day we were having a big luncheon and they came in their helicopter and landed right here at the back door. They were giving some people helicopter rides and Albert got Warren and said, "Let's take a ride..." Warren wasn't so sure about that, but he said,

"I'll ride wid you, Mr. Albert." So they loaded up and when they came back Albert said, "I don't hardly have any feeling in my leg because Warren was mashing it so!"

When the first people were walking on the moon. Barbara asked ol' Warren what he thought about people up there on the moon and he was quick to say, "Dey don't have no business up there!"

And Albert always loved

Warren Leonard, faithful yard man for the Carlton Family

roses. He always had a rose bed... garden. He just loved it. We sprayed roses and sprayed roses. At one time they had about died and he said he was going to start all over again. So he told Warren one day, "While I'm off getting the roses and stuff you go out and dig these holes." Albert told him how big to dig them, a foot by a foot by two feet because they were going to put cow manure in the bottom and do everything right. *Peace* and *Don Juan* were his favorite roses.

When Albert got back you could have almost used every one of the holes, 12 of them, for a grave!

Old Warren worked for years and years very steady. We'd pick him up and take him home. Later on he started slowing down, didn't work as much. But then one day he was missing. No one knew what had happened to him. It may have been a year later someone found some remains under an old cabbage tree out on the Fort Green Ona Road. It looked like he must have gotten up under it and died from over exposure to the cold. You couldn't tell if there was any foul play or not... nothing was ever suggested.

I never knew whether his name was Warren Leonard or Leonard Warren. He lived in a little two or three room house in Ona, south of the post plant across the railroad track. He lived there for years and years... until he died.

Photo: Luther W. Oehlbeck

Don Juan

Photo: Barbara Oehlbeck

Peace

BUDDY COLSON

Buddy Colson, native from Hardee County has faithfully served the Carlton Family for over 50 years. Even though semi-retired he maintains a close relationship with Albert and Barbara's family.

Buddy Colson

I was with Mr. Albert since January 1966. I was deliverin' fruit for Pepper Whidden, they run a pickin' crew for Van Adams. We was loadin' fruit and we were gettin' two and a half cents a box back then.

My cousin, James Colson, he went to work for Mr. Albert. He worked about two or three weeks and I was still loadin' fruit and he come by one night and said they was needin' somebody else so he asked me if I wanted to go to work for him. I told him yeah. So I went to work for Mr. Albert making $60 a week five and a half days. Back then in them days that was good money. Back then they was clearing a lot of new land at New Zion, what we call the Strickland Bar Ⓐ Ranch... palmeeter woods and all, cleaning a lot of it. A lot of farmers would farm and we'd come in behind 'em and plant grass. I worked with Mr. Bob Reddin' who was the foreman out there at that time. I worked with 'em and we planted the grass, worked the cattle. At that time, too, I worked the grove for 'em. Then I'd get through the grove and help 'em work the cattle.

I don't remember what year it was that Gardinier took over and

255

Mr. Albert wanted me to stay with Gardinier for a while. Mr. Albert wanted me to stay there and help them so I did for nearly a year I reckon. I left that and built fence for about a year. Every time Mr. Albert wanted to work cows he'd call me. I'm come back and hep him work cows and he'd have fence to build and I'd build his fences and all for him.

He was just a heck of a good person to work for.

We had a place at Myakka City and the boy that was down there they sent him to Sumter County to run that place up there. The boy that had the Brahma cattle here, they sent him to Myakka City so I went down there with him. Mr. Albert had called and wanted to know if I'd hep him to work cattle for two or three days. I told him yeah I'd drop the fence and go hep him. So after hepping him for three days, well, I've been there ever since.

In the last part of '78 or first part of '79 I come back to the grove... I was still living down at Myakka workin' with 'em down there. The boy(s) that was over the grove up here quit so I was living down there but wantin' to come back to Wauchula. I told Mr. Albert about it and said I could take over the groves and he told me, "I don't know if that'll work, Buddy, I don't know if you'll like that or not."

So I wound up coming back, I took over the groves and Mr. Albert told me he want those things cleaned and shaped up. So we went to work on that and he'd come out there and help.

The irrigation we had for citrus back then was the drip system. It was uh everyday job worrying with that stuff. So he wanted to put in all micro jets. We took out all the overhead, come back in and put in micro jets and all that stuff. We had a pretty good size crew at that time so we got it all done. Mr. Albert told us one day he wanted us to find where all the pipes and all were. We had an old feller that you couldn't joke with that old man a-tall, he took everything serious. So Mr. Albert said we'd have to dig 'em pipes again. I went down and told

Mr. Sessor, that was the old feller's name, that we wanted the pipes dug up again. They dug 'em up, found where they were, OK. Then Mr. Albert said cover 'em back up. They dug 'em out three times before it was all over with. Mr. Sessor told me, "You tell him that we ain't diggin' 'em out no more. This is the last time!"

Mr. Albert got a big kick out of it.

Russell Suggs left again and I took over the cows up here, too. Then I was doing the cows and the groves. Charlie put in that he wanted a horse, so Miss Barbara told me to find him a horse. We went and found him a horse. And we knew somethin' was wrong; we got down there and the old man had him tied to a concrete block. That old horse was real sweaty. So Charlie rode him and he seemed to be awright so we bought the horse and brought him back. Charlie was still going to school.

The next afternoon we was gonna move some cattle. We git in and Charlie saddles up his horse and we was waitin' on him. He went out through a horse pasture out here and I heard a sound and I looked back and Charlie was on the ground. The old horse had bucked him off. I hollered at him, "Git up and come on! You can't move cows layin down there." He got back on that old horse and he bucked him off again.

So finally we made the rounds that afternoon and finally got it done and we had to take the horse back to the man and git him another one. He finally got one he could ride.

Then Mr. Albert was gonna go to Carolina for the summer but Charlie wanted to stay down here and work with me. Mr. Albert called me and I come by the office. Mr. Albert says, "Charlie says he wants to stay down here and work with you..." And I said, "OK."

Then Mr. Albert says, "If he don't work, fire him and send him to me." Two weeks later he was headed to Carolina. So Charlie was sent to Carolina.

But backin' up a little bit, when they was in Myakka City they were workin' the cattle down there and we was workin' the cattle up here.

We had planted all this up here in rye grass. We had sold calves on Monday and we put ammonium nitrate out on Thursday. Then it rained and been nasty all weekend. So we sold calves on Monday, we was gonna go to New Zion and work the cattle out there but it was rainin' so we didn't go that day but they was workin' in Myakka City. We was workin' in the shop... had a Spanish boy workin' for us and I told him to go down there and feed the steer before he quit. He came back to the barn told me, "Mr. Buddy, there're dead cows down there." I said, "No, they can't be, they're just layin around waitin' on those calves."

He said, "No, Sir, I kicked one and she didn't move."

We took off and went down there and sure 'nuff they were. There was dead cattle layin' ever' where. We called the vet and they pulled all kinds of tests and they wound up being ammonium nitrate poisoning.

So I called Stan and 'em in Myakka City and told 'em what was happening but at that time we didn't know what the problem was.

So Mr. Albert and they all came on in... we'd lost 37 head of cattle.

So the next morning, me and Stan took off to the lab. That afternoon when we got through with everything I came up here to the house and told Mr. Albert. He met me out there and I told him, "I hate this." He told me, "It ain't your fault."

First he asked me, "You wanna drink?" I said, "Yes, Sir," and he had one. And he asked, "Whatta you want?" And I said, "Straight!"

And so we had a drink together and I said again, "I hate this." But it didn't upset him atall. I was the one that was upset but it didn't bother him. He told me, "Well, you was wantin' to downsize some up here but wouldn't there have been a better way to a-done it than this?"

So we had the cattle out there and he asked if I wasn't going to work that cattle today and I said, "Yes, Sir," he said, "Well, it's better for it to have happened here than to happen out there because there would have been many more dead cattle."

But that's what it wound up being... ammonium nitrate poisoning.

It didn't bother him, that's just the way he was. Most people woulda had a fit. It bothered me worse than it did him.

I've been with 'em a long time and I've enjoyed every bit of it. I still take care of Mrs. Barbara's feeders and everything here.

I'm gonna semi-retire in January but I'll still do her feeders and all this stuff for her.

One time we had an old truck, a little old Ford carrier and we started to rebuild the motor in it. I had it in the shop there. He (Mr. Albert) came down there and said, "I wanna help you."

I thought, "He ain't gonna wanna git up under here and git grease all over him, but he did." He helped me rebuild that motor and we was puttin' it back in. He didn't know what he was doin' but I'd tell him to do this or that or the other and he was right up under that thing with grease all over him just havin' a big time helpin' me put that motor back in that thing after we got it done. It didn't bother him atall.

When Charlie was born, Mr. Albert had two black men workin' here. One was named Warren and the other was named Charlie. Charlie's wife was Mr. Albert's housekeeper. So we got in the barn that morning, we all had to meet over here at the horse barn. So we both was here that morning and Mr. Albert he come out there and he was just tickled to death and told us he had a new son. So we asked "Whatcha name him?" He said, I named him, "Charlie."

I said, "Mr. Albert, I didn't know you thought so much of Charlie that you'd name your son after him." He didn't think too much of that.

A boy came back from lunch one day and parked his truck and came on down where we was working. We had to come back up there for something and there set Maurice's truck up against that oak tree. What had happened, I guess a silonoid had stuck or somethin' and the truck just come loping across and run right into that oak tree.

We asked Warren, he'd been settin there and saw the whole thing, "Were you drivin' that truck?" I can't tell you what he said, but he did say, "There wasn't nobody in that thing when it come crosst there."

Dr. Barbara Carlton: *There was a snake out there in the bushes, and I said, "Warren, there's a snake out there in the bushes. How about going out there and tell me what kind of snake that is." He said, "Well, if it's a snake and he's in the bushes... it's a bush snake, if it was on the ground it'd be a ground snake. When you see a turtle if he's on the land that's one of them go-fer turtles and if you see him in water it's a water turtle."*

A day or two before Mr. Albert passed away, I came by and was talking to him and he'd told me a few days before that they were gonna give him a surprise birthday party and he said, "They think I don't know what they're doing." I was standing out here talking to him and he just acted like nothing in the world was wrong with him.

Then they called me that night... and he was gone.

Bar A Brangus sign on the Carlton Homeplace barn

2 X 4 RANCH

Dr. Barbara Carlton: The ranch that later became the 2 X 4 was sold at auction in Tampa in bankruptcy court in 1978. It was the Jacobson Ranch that was sold at public auction at the Tampa Courthouse.

The day of the proceedings, Albert (Carlton) flew in from North Carolina. We met him at the Hillsborough County Court House, the site of the sale. On the way, Stan and I told him that Judge Paskay required coat and tie in his court room.

Photo: Joyce Hunter

The entrance to the 2X4 RANCH
Arcadia, Florida

We headed straight for Wolf Brothers Men's Clothing in Tampa and purchased appropriate attire for the court room. When we arrived, we were greeted by Gene Turner, a real estate broker from Arcadia and learned that he was representing a buyer for the ranch. Each of us submitted a sealed bid to the court. When the bids were opened we learned that we had been awarded the contract because ours was the high bid.

Mr. Turner was very, very upset that he could not continue bidding. So Judge Paskay elected to allow us, Carlton and Turner, to continue bidding in increments of $50,000 which ended up costing us several thousand dollars more. At the end of the bidding we were awarded the contract for the Jacobson Ranch, 5100 acres in DeSoto County about which we knew little or nothing except that there were two 85-foot silos on the land.

On the way home that day I thought about Albert's dogged persistence in bidding so aggressively to get that ranch. It reminded me of his bidding on a prize bull at the cattle auction.

When we first went to the ranch as new owners we enjoyed riding over that 5100-acre prairie. There was nothing there except those wide open spaces as far as you could see except for one little concrete shed and two huge Harvestore silos and a smaller one. There were approximately six sections in pangola grass, the remainder was Bahia… a ranch two miles wide and four miles long… all grass. And that's how our newly acquired ranch came by its name: 2 X 4 RANCH.

There were very few trees. Some straggly eucalyptus bordered the mile long road leading into the center of the prairie, and over the far reaches of the land there were several hammocks, mostly cabbage palms and oaks, and Deep Lake, the second deepest lake in Florida.

In 1970 we bought the Klein Place, 1000 acres on Horse Creek. In 1975 we purchased Rusty Pot Ranch at Myakka City, Florida then in 1977 - 1978 we bought the 2 X 4 RANCH.

The Homeplace, Glenokra, is 450 acres. Jack Kennedy was our president. The Kennedys had a place named Glenora at the Kennedy Compound. We had a contest in the '60s to name our place. A parody on the name Glenora is Glenokra, so that's what we named our homeplace, Glenokra Ranch in Hardee County. We moved in 1962 to our new home.

Prior to the auction resulting in our buying the 2 X 4 RANCH, a very close family friend who was in the fertilizer business mentioned a couple who was interested in ranch management. Well, after our friend, Wayne Jernigan had shown us the ranch, we visited the couple and were so impressed that Al said he wanted to hire them if we got the property. Thus Pat and Brady

Pfeil became our full-time managers. Early on Pat and Brady ascribed to our philosophy for the ranch.

So when our acquisition of the ranch became a reality, we all met in Al's office and talked in generalities of ideas, philosophies, etc. and I said, "We want to improve and build this property into a state of the art ranch, not necessarily to make any money… but." Brady had the same idea, calling it a Sea of Grass. This dry prairie, over-run with palmettos and native grass, was just that… a vast sea of grass. We were totally impressed with the grass growing ability of the land, a part of Florida's 90-mile prairie.

Brady embraced the project running! He planted all the trees that are here except the eucalyptus and a few oak hammocks. Since 1978 great heads of cypress have been planted in various wetlands. Now some are 30 to 40 feet tall, standing up against the sky as if they'd been "born" there.

We constantly upgraded. In 1978 we moved in a mobile home to use until Pat and Brady could build a house of their own.

In 1986 we added 244 acres, a section of citrus, plus road frontage on SR 31, which brought the total acreage of the ranch to 5867 acres. From the very beginning, Pat and Brady Pfeil ascribed to our philosophy.

$$\overline{A}\ \overline{A}\ \overline{A}$$

We want this book to evolve out of the soil, the passion for what we're doing. We have road frontage and we take no one else's water. The 2 X 4 RANCH is like an island, a prairie island, self-contained. Regarding sheet flow we are self-sufficient. The name of ranching is how to manage water and grass. Sometimes the land is covered with water six inches deep, however, in winter it can be a dust bowl. Extremes are constant. When you have an abundance of water, when you're flooded you build an ark, so you'll have the water to use during droughts.

You never know what you'll be faced with. You take what the Lord gives you, and seek the best advice you can find from the best sources you know. For us, these sources were the range cattle station, IFAS (Institute of Food and Agricultural Science), Ona Range Cattle Research Center, and from fellow cattlemen or citrus growers. We were constantly seeking the best advice and information on which to build the Carlton Crown Jewel.

The fruits of Brady and Pat's work are very evident... in all directions. We've been awarded two Stewardship Awards, State and Regional.

A̅ A̅ A̅

Albert and Dr. Barbara Carlton purchased the 2 X 4 RANCH (two sections wide and four sections long – hence the name – 2 X 4 RANCH), in 1977. Under the guidance and leadership of their managers, Pat and Brady Pfeil, they pursued a legacy of environmental stewardship and developed a model progressive agricultural operation. The Carlton family, for generations, has been proactive in conserving and protecting land throughout Florida. Through previous land acquisitions they have made possible for 8000 acres in Sumter County, Florida (Carlton Half-Moon Preserve) and 2000 acres in south DeSoto County (Deep Creek Preserve) to become part of the State's perpetually protected inventory. The sale of the Carlton 2 X 4 RANCH was the first transaction that may eventually become part of the development trend in Florida.

The legacy and love of the land by the Carltons has been well documented for over a century, and the passage of the baton to the state of Florida will insure perpetual enjoyment by generations to come.

BRADY AND PAT PFEIL

In most families there comes a time when decisions need to be made in order to perpetuate a traditional family enterprise.

The calling lies not only with the owners, Albert and Barbara Carlton, but also with the assembly of like-minded individuals.

The search began in the early '70s for a hands-on office manager who turned out to be Stan Pelham, and later Brady and Pat Pfeil became ranch managers.

These three individuals gave the Carltons a solid foundation for growth and development of a very successful ranch and grove operation.

These three also came with abilities that enabled the Carlton Family in their pursuit of not only prospering in cattle and citrus but also preserving the land and natural resources.

This common goal and calling was to continue for the next 30 years.

From its beginning in 1978 to 2006 when it was sold, Pat and Brady Pfeil were the managers of the Carlton 2 X 4 RANCH in DeSoto County, Florida. They gave their lives to building a state of the art cattle and citrus operation.

$$\overline{A}\ \overline{A}\ \overline{A}$$

Anticipating the purchase of another property, Albert and Barbara Carlton, blessed yet challenged (Albert was recovering from a heart attack), told their friends about the need for someone to oversee the next purchase. Wayne Jernigan, a Florida Favorite Fertilizer salesman and a lifelong Carlton friend, told them about a couple who might meet the need. Wayne showed Brady and Pat Pfeil the potential property and set up an interview with the Carltons. Brady, a South Texas native, was so impressed with the vast expanse of grass and plentiful water on the then J & J Ranch, he was willing to consider a move. At the meeting, Albert pointed out his desire to develop a state of the art ranch while Barbara expressed the need to have a profitable and sustainable cattle operation. Albert and

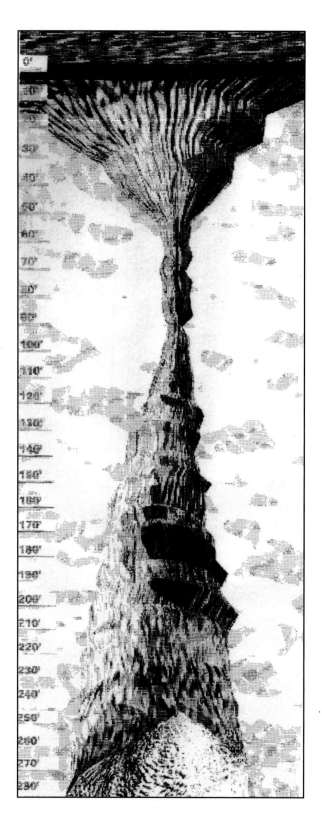

This is a sketch of the shaft of Deep Lake on the 2 X 4 RANCH, Arcadia, Florida. The shaft is in the center of the lake and starts at 60 ft. in depth. At 90 ft. the walls slope abruptly outward and continue to a width of about 200 ft. at the bottom. The floor is 240 ft. in depth in the center and 270 ft. to 300 ft. deep around the periphery. The mound in the center is typical of sinkholes. The width of the opening and the shape of the room were not determined.

Brady communicated well with each other and had similar values. The potential challenge of developing a ranch was intriguing to the Pfeils and Albert hired them contingent upon the purchase.

The fall of 1978 was the beginning of what became known as the 2 X 4 RANCH. (two sections wide, four sections long. A section is 640 acres or one mile square.)

Sunrise at the Carlton 2 X 4 RANCH, Arcadia, Florida

Sunrise at the Carlton 2 X 4 RANCH, Arcadia, Florida

BUILDING THE 2 X 4 RANCH

As the Pfeils preferred to live on the land, a singlewide mobile home was moved from the Carlton's "Rusty Pot Ranch" in Myakka City to "Dinner Hammock" that had been Jacobsen's (J & J) shade tree mechanic area.

The open flat landscape was deceitful. As you drove through, it seemed small but a hike or horseback ride put the distances in perspective. When you see two plus miles in every direction, it is hard to judge distance or size.

$$\overline{A}\ \overline{A}\ \overline{A}$$

Pat Pfeil: While we grazed cattle for other folks, we developed the facilities that were needed for a large cow/calf operation. Albert loved to develop land and build. Therefore he visited the property often. He would arrive at various times, mostly early, and help with whatever we were doing. He loved to plan and develop new enterprises on the land. One of our employees arrived at work before 7 A.M. and told us some man was picking up trash on the entry road side. Brady informed him it was the ranch owner. Albert never left litter where he went.

Albert had a way that inspired a person to do his best to please him. Being well-read, Albert enjoyed properly used language. He would correct me in a very polite way when I used words incorrectly. He critiqued my writing and encouraged me to improve my spelling skills. He and Dr. Barbara allowed us to manage our time and efforts to accomplish a task. They laid out their goals and we proceeded to try to make them happen.

Dr. Barbara Carlton had just retired from her medical practice in Wauchula when we started developing the 2 X 4. She was still living in the accelerated pace that good doctors develop as they balance patient care with family and personal time. She could speed read and was always working on a project. For about 10 years whenever we saw her she would hand us a pile of articles she had marked for us to read. Brady will tell you, trying to keep up with her reading assignments caused him to improve his reading skills.

As we expanded the cattle holdings on the 2 X 4 we traveled across Texas to purchase heifers. On one trip Albert and Carl Saunders joined us in Paris, Texas. They had been in an accident when someone had failed to stop at a light. We had to use the car as our truck was too small, so every time we stopped some where Carl had to climb out the window because the door would not open. As we traveled from one known ranch with heifers for sale to the next, Albert saw a hand painted sign on the side of the road that read "Heifers for Sale." He pulled in and we climbed out to see the veterinarian pregnancy-checking some young under-developed heifers. This was in 1980 when pregnant heifers in Texas cost $750 (about 800#). These little heifers were priced at $500 each (about 575#). Albert decided to buy them and we moved them with the others to the 2 X 4. Well, he was proud to see them grow to the point that by the next breeding season they all looked the same.

As the cow herd grew, Albert, Dr. Barbara, Brady and I worked cows together. This included Rusty Pot Ranch in Myakka City, Half Moon Ranch in Sumter County and, of course, the 2 X 4 RANCH in Arcadia, Florida. It took us six weeks each rotation. We traveled to each ranch staying in motels. The only time Brady recalls Albert getting angry was in Sumter County on the Half Moon Ranch. We were trying to load cattle and one cow ran over Brady. Albert climbed out of the pens, cut a palm frond, and climbed back into the pens. After about 3 laps around the pen with him "whooping" her with that frond, that cow finally loaded.

Albert would keep the records while Barbara would check the pastures and wildlife. During those years we learned what they liked and how they wanted everything done. Both of them were enablers allowing us to make decisions and handle the day to day business without their input. We all would lay out a plan and proceed with it till a different direction seemed necessary. The only change that took a "show me" for Albert was moving from 180-day to a 90-day breeding

COMMISSIONER'S *2001*
Ag-Environmental
LEADERSHIP *Awards*

WINNER

Carlton 2x4 Ranch
Arcadia, Florida

season. Well, the day we sorted those 90-day calving season calves into one pen, Albert walked through that uniform bunch of black calves and he told Brady, "Ok, change all the herds to a 90-day breeding season." As the years passed they entrusted all the ranches to our oversight. The Pfeils and the Carlton family had a true trust-relationship.

We were all rewarded in 2001 by receiving the 2001 Ag-Environmental LeadershipA Award given by the Commissioner of Agriculture Charles Bronson.

Posing after the award presentation are, front row, (from left) Joyce Hunter, Dr. Carlton and Pat Pfeil. In back, Brad Pfeil, Wendy Carlton, Will Carlton, Brady Pfeil, Stan Pelham, Pat Carlton and Commissioner Bronson.

BUILDING GHOST GROVE

After acquiring the ninth section of land on the north end of the 2 X 4 RANCH, Albert decided that this section would be a great place to plant a grove. A year later he enlisted Brady into dividing his time with developing a grove and running cattle on the ranch. Knowing Brady loved the cows he offered to get someone else to develop the grove. Brady said if it was on this ranch he would take care of it. When approached about whether to <u>permit</u> the grove development Albert said it was easier to do it up front than to have to correct it later.

Albert would bring a close family friend and accomplished citrus grower, Dudley Putnam, to inspect our progress. Then they would take Brady and look at South Florida groves. Albert loved the citrus industry and made a science of rootstock selection. He was interested in cutting edge technology from cloning trees to developing disease resistance to mechanical harvesting. He wanted this flatwoods soil conversion to citrus to use all technology available such as laser bedding, drain tiles, micro sprinkler irrigation with weekly injection of liquid fertilizer and close set trees.

This was a unique opportunity to check the environmental effects of flat woods conversion to citrus. Albert decided he wanted to know if the chemicals we used would cause problems. He knew that anything detected would be reported to DEP. It was a blessing to establish through 17 years of research that nothing was ever found. Even when Albert did not agree with you he would give you a chance to prove your ideas. Brady wanted to use tensiometers to monitor soil moisture and to determine when to irrigate. After much heated discussion, Albert told Brady to do what he thought best.

When Albert passed away Brady had a huge empty feeling. He had lived and worked to fulfill Albert's expectations for 16 years. But Dr. Barbara transitioned into the leadership role, and caring for the family land continued to be

Top: Representing the Carlton 2 X 4 RANCH at the annual convention held in 2003 in Phoenix, Ariz., are members of the Pfeil family on the left, son Orin (13), Brady and Pat and 16-year-old son Brad. Members of the Carlton family are pictured at right, with Dr. Barbara and daughter Julie McClelland in front and Pat and Wendy Carlton and Fletcher McCelland in back.

Left: 13th Annual Environmental Stewardship Award.
An old rancher points out to his grandchildren that conserving the land ensures future generations the ability to produce.

272

Brady's focus and a blessing. The ground work was being laid for one of the greatest achievements to the Carlton 2 X 4 RANCH. In 2004 the Carlton Family was presented with a National Ag Oscar - The 2003 National Environmental Stewardship Award.

We maintained a section of land in native vegetation. Dr. Carlton referred to it as the 2 X 4 Serengeti. Her love for bobwhite quail hunting motivated her to implement various management practices to enhance and sustain the bobwhite population. During the 2000s we participated with Tall Timbers Research Station and the University of Georgia in a bobwhite quail restoration project. Those management practices promoted wild turkey, producing a Tom Turkey during the last year we were on the ranch.

LAND RUSH 2005

After hurricanes swept over DeSoto County, all were busy with the clean up. Yet the effect was an increase in land prices. No one understood why but prices kept going up. By February 2005 there was an offer at twice the established value for the 2 X 4. The Carltons turned that offer down.

The escalating land values became a financial factor that could not be ignored. Beginning in April thru May several more substantial offers were made. By May 2005 a decision was made to sell the Carlton 2 X 4 RANCH and Groves. So the sale of the 2 X 4 RANCH and Groves came 10 years earlier than expected. Albert would have been proud of the deal that Dr. Barbara and the family made on this property.

True to form, Dr. Barbara insisted the family carry on the land ownership tradition by purchasing acreage in Georgia for the grandchildren to have for the future. So this family blessed us again by allowing us to develop the parcel for the next generation.

QUALITIES THAT MADE WORKING FOR THE

CARLTONS EXTRAORDINARY:

GENEROSITY

Albert and Barbara were willing to share all they had. Albert's attitude was… that is why we pay for insurance. Barbara didn't want something you could not enjoy. They allowed us to hire young folks so they could learn how to work, and the meaning of work. Over 150 youth (10 to 18 years old) learned how to work at the 2 X 4 RANCH. The ranch became a respite for numerous missionaries parking their campers at the cow pens or lodging in the round house and bunkroom.

INTEGRITY

Albert was a true Southern gentleman. He never spoke an ugly word about other people. His philosophy about business dealing was simple: pay cash for everything and treat folks the way you want to be treated. When an enterprise failed to net as much as anticipated Albert and Barbara didn't need a scapegoat, they just challenged us to move on and do better the next time. This trust and empowerment resulted in a strong desire to benefit them as much as possible.

SUPPORT

Albert and Dr. Barbara encouraged and supported the industries we worked with in addition to being active members of:
- Florida Cattlemen's Association
- Florida Cattlewomen's Association
- Peace River Valley Citrus Growers Association
- Florida Farm Bureau

They hosted numerous educational tours over the years. The Eagle Scouts,

Farm City Tour, Society for Range Management, Florida Brangus Association, DeSoto County Schools, University of Florida, University of Georgia, Tall Timbers Research, Rotary Clubs, Native Plant Societies, Ag. In the Classroom and many distinguished visitors from Australia, New Zealand, Kenya and Russia.

DEEP LAKE: (Located on the 2 X 4 RANCH)

- The second deepest sink hole in Florida
- 240' to the top of the mound
- 300' at the deepest point
- Classical hour glass shape
- Only natural lake in DeSoto County

Jack Carlton said he stopped a cattle stampede as a young teen. The cattle ran from Nocatee to Deep Lake where he held them up until the older men caught up with them. From that time on he was considered a cowman.

There was a platted development in 1915 that showed the lake as 500 ft. wide and 240 ft. known depth. Miss Edna (Cary) Carlton related how she went out on the palmetto covered prairie to Sunday afternoon picnics. The lake shore was a sandy beach hard enough to race Model Ts around the lake. Sitting under shade trees she watched World War I airmen use row boats to drop lines into the center area of the lake to measure its depth.

Gene Turner farmed around Deep Lake during a dry time. They pumped out of the lake until the pump had to be tied to a tree and let down into the cone of the sink hole. United States Geological Service (USGS) did "sounding" in the '60s and established that there was a shaft (now closed off) that went down 700 ft.

Sheck Exley, world renowned deep water diver, explored Deep Lake. Sheck measured and mapped Deep Lake and established that it was a closed off sink hole and the second deepest in the state. Unfortunately, Sheck Exley died in 1994 in an attempt to set a deep water dive record in a 1000-ft. deep lake in Mexico.

CARLSTROM FIELD

Carlstrom Field, Arcadia, Florida, 1942, Army Air Training Base using the "Jenny," a twin-seat (student in front of instructor) dual control biplane.

The entry road for the 2 X 4 RANCH was the Carlstrom Field entry. Carlstrom Field was an aviator training facility active in World War I and II. Many artifacts have been found on the ranch such as concrete targets, and dummy bombs. A narrow gage railroad ran from Carlstrom Field across the prairie to Dorr Field near SR 70.

THE PRAIRIE

Many, many years ago, the road to LaBelle-Arcadia went around Deep Lake. Goat Roan (deceased 2008) told us of the last lynching in DeSoto County that happened near Deep Lake. He also said a safe from the Mercer's Store robbery was left on the LaBelle-Arcadia road. We did find the remnants of a safe. Mr. Olliff of Wauchula told us about his father hauling freight in wagons on that road during the dry seasons. Mr. Harrison was on the survey crew that laid out the mosquito control ditches on this part of the prairie when it was covered with water. Hog Pen Hammock was fenced to raise hogs.

INTERESTING FACTS: Naming the Ranches

The Carlton Family has owned several different ranches in the last 80 years.

The Bar $\overline{A}$ Ranch (Strickland Place) – Hardee County – The Carl Carlton Ranch was inherited by Albert Carlton in 1948. The Bar $\overline{A}$ is the cattle and holding brand for William Albert Carlton and his successors.

Rusty Pot Ranch – Manatee County – purchased in 1975 from the Ruth Dirkes Konstantinou Estate. During the negotiations on the purchase of the new ranch there was a fabulous party house with a swimming pool that gave this particular ranch a real distinction. Inside the party house was a barbeque grill with a rusty pot hanging over the grill. Before the deal could be closed the rusty pot disappeared. This "crown jewel" of a rusty old pot was finally returned and the ranch was acclaimed the new Carlton Rusty Pot Ranch.

Half Moon Ranch – Sumter County - 1969 - Albert noticed when looking at the aerial maps the moon shape of the property as it lay east of the six mile frontage of the Withlacoochee River – thus the name.

2 X 4 RANCH – DeSoto County – 1977 - Two miles east to west and four miles north to south. Eight sections – rectangular in shape.

2 X 4 Serengeti – as the African Serengeti is an open grassland with an abundance of wildlife, Dr. Barbara dubbed the South East Quarter of the 2 X 4 RANCH as the 2 X 4 Serengeti.

Deep Creek Property – DeSoto County – 1966 - 2000 acres named after the Peace River's Deep channel that made part of it a 200-acre island.

Klein Place – Hardee County – purchased in 1970 from the Klein family. Horse Creek runs through the center of this huge native swamp and is the location of the new Hoss Creek Camp, the Lil' Ritz Carlton Cabin and Fort Carlton.

Photo: Joyce Hunter

**Hoss Creek Camp, the Lil' Ritz Carlton
and Fort Carlton, Hardee County, Florida**

Carlton Family Hunt 2008. Back row left to right: Pat, Caroline, Lilli, Dr. Barbara, Kate, Dan, Will, Seth, Jack, Abby, Watt tand kneeling in front is Charlie

JOYCE HUNTER
Girl Friday

My husband, Jerry and I got to know Mr. Albert and Dr. Barbara in early 1982. Over the next 10 years, we attended a lot of employee Bar-B-Qs and Christmas parties held at both the 2 X 4 RANCH and the Homeplace, The Little White House, in Wauchula.

I am considered a pretty good cook and my side dishes were always a hit at the parties. I was asked to cook for cow work, and I would take off from my ranch job at the Marsh Beef Master Ranch and plant nursery that bordered the 2 X 4 RANCH on the south side, to turn out two weeks of hearty meals and desserts for these hungry cowboys. My job at the Marsh Ranch required a lot of computer work and details for keeping horticulture plant records but that division was giving in to grove planting. This was freeing up some of my time and I started helping in the 2X4 office. I remember they had just experienced a computer crash and the data was so messed up we couldn't trust anything the computer printed, so we were about to start learning new programs. I guess that was the best and worst of times. We kept all citrus and cattle records on the computer. So one day turned into two days and before I knew it, I was at the 2X4 office four days a week.

I still work for the Marsh family on Mondays. Their ranch is all groves now and all computerized.

My most vivid memory will always be November 2, 1992. Mr. Albert was surely smiling down on us. On that cold Sunday morning Jerry and I were baptized in Deep Lake at the 2 X 4 RANCH. (This is the second deepest lake in Florida.) It had turned cold over night and the lake was up to the top step on the dock. The wind was blowing and the water seemed so dark; I am not a good swimmer so I was showing some anxiety. Jerry went first and I was next. I was hanging onto the preacher because I could not touch bottom and I said, "Don't you drop me 'cause I will pull you down with me." He started laughing as he was leaning me back in the water and as I came up for air he said, "Oops!" To which I replied, "What oops?" He said, "I have to dunk you again. I was laughing so hard I forgot to say the words!" The second time, coming up for air, the entire congregation was rolling with laughter. I could hear comments like... "We've never seen a do-over at a baptism before... she needed to be washed twice from sin."

We all had a good fellowship afterwards.

I worked at the 2 X 4 RANCH for 13 years and helped close it down when it was sold. That was a sad time for Jerry and me. We had lived on the ranch for eight years and raised our four kids. We had been full time employees for the Carltons for a total of 21 years.

But new opportunities present themselves. Dr. Barbara needed an assistant to help sort and search her archives for the historical family data for this book. She needed a better way to store and share the boxes of medical articles and family history and, of course, photos.

And there is always a Bar-B-Q or a Garden Party that needs Jerry and me to cook. He can fry turkey, quail, gator and deer better than anyone I know. And my cobblers, 'specially the peach, are always a hit.

When I look back on the fact that we worked, lived and played the best years of our lives for a Christian family who treated us like family and still does, I can truly say that God has blessed us.

He is truly ours.

JERRY HUNTER

I was first introduced to Carlton Country in 1982, when I was hired to work with the purebred Brangus and commercial cattle at The Carlton 2 X 4 RANCH in Arcadia. During cow work, which happened three times a year, Stan (Pelham) and Mr. Albert would come and help give the cattle shots and Mr. Albert would run the hydraulic chute. Sometimes he would just bring the newspaper and hang out with us cowboys. Now this wasn't the local newspaper. This paper was from the North Carolina mountains or Tampa Tribune. When he would run across a story that he thought us boys should know about, he would shut down the chute and read us the story. Mr. Albert was a personable man and a great conversationalist.

I remember when we were all working at putting the grove in and we were experiencing some trouble with the little trees dying. We figured out that there were air pockets under them and they would have to be remudded. The water wagon was acting up and we didn't have time to lose. The motor was running but it wasn't pumping any water. We weren't sure what the problem was. Mr. Albert said to me, "If you have to break it to fix it – let's break it!"

Mr. Albert named the grove "Ghost Grove" because it did not exist. He explained it like this:

Photo: Joyce Hunter

Orange trees in Florida

when Dr. Barbara was not at the 2 X 4 RANCH and Mr. Albert was, their conversations always included what they did that day. Mr. Albert would tell her that he was working on the grove. Now Dr. Barbara knew there was no grove at the 2 X 4 RANCH, at least not one she could see. There is a lot of planning on paper before it comes to planting. So after some time of Mr. Albert working on the grove that didn't exist, she replied, "Well, I'm just going to have to go and see this "Ghost Grove" of yours." And that's how it got its name.

I remember when I quit smoking (for the hundredth time). I was about three days quit. I asked Mr. Albert how long it would be before I wouldn't want a cigarette. I knew he had quit about 15 years ago. He looked at me and said, "I'll let you know."

During cow work we would always eat lunch as a group and Mr. Albert would always sit and eat and visit with all us cowboys.

I left the Carlton's full time employment in 1989 to start my own cowboy day-working business. I continued to work their cows and build fence and still work with Dr. Barbara to this day.

Photo: Joyce Hunter

Cow Work at the 2 X 4 RANCH

PART SEVEN
Introduction
HUNTING WITH BARBARA

Her passion for hunting was born with Barbara Cordeva Castleberry at age nine when her father first took her coon-hunting in Lumpkin, Georgia, where they lived.

"This, of course, was at night," she says. "We wouldn't shoot the coons, we'd just tree 'em. I loved everything about those night hunts. The sounds of the night creatures as we trudged through the woods, and the feel of carrying my first gun, a Winchester .410 pump shotgun, which I still have and use."

Those first experiences of hunting with her father are an integral part of Barbara's hunting life which has continued and grown through the years.

"While at Mercer and in med school there were few opportunities to do anything except study... study. Yet," Barbara continues, "every now and then there'd be an opportunity to go off in the woods with my Winchester and study the woods and watch the wildlife instead of books!"

And so the passion grew as did her remarkable ability in the art of hunting. There are more than a few who say – including Tom McEwen – that she is an earthly incarnation of Diana, the Roman Goddess of Hunting and the Goddess of Wild Animals.

Due to the tragedy in her husband's family when he was only five years old, Albert Carlton never owned a gun nor did he join Barbara in actual hunting, although he had great respect for her devotion to the sport. He went along with the hunting groups and was often kidded about being the host of the chuck wagon.

The hunting stories here cover the years between the time she began the practice of medicine in Wauchula and the present time.

283

HUNTING STORIES BY DR. B.
Learning to Hunt

I was raised in Georgia, in the gullies of Stewart County, Lumpkin, Georgia. As a child I was a tomboy, my Daddy's right hand person who worked with him in the fields whether it was sledding peanuts or driving the sled with two mules to take it to the peanut picker or helping him repair a peanut picker before harvest. I was always available to work for him particularly after school.

I can recall my early days when I was eight or nine, 10 years of age we would go on coon hunts. This was pretty much orchestrated by two to three people that my dad knew who loved coon hunting, who had coon dogs. We would go out at night with flashlights and pecans and sweet potatoes and we'd go coon hunting. We'd listen for the dogs to tree the coons then we'd go to that sound and we'd sit there around the tree, look up with the light and see the coons... sure 'nough they had a coon treed. We were delighted with that and we didn't kill the coon. We would sometimes build a campfire and sit there and roast pecans and sweet potatoes around the campfire and get the coon dogs away from that coon and have them start trailing another coon in the distance. We've have time to sit around the campfire and listen to that mournful sound of the coon hounds when they'd finally treed another coon. We would put our fire out and head to the next bay, or the next treed coon.

That was my introduction into hunting. I loved the outdoors, loved the dogs, the sounds of the night, it was one of the most memorable parts of my childhood.

Later on as I grew up and went to high school and then off to college, I had a brother-in-law, Brady Williamson, who introduced me into quail hunting. He had a friend who had a Jeep and good bird dogs and my dad had given me a Winchester pump .410 shotgun that he had won at a raffle, so that was the gun that I used as a child and into adulthood when I'd want to shoot something. Sometimes I'd stalk down a quail with a rifle, a .22 rifle. In fact I brought home two quail one day that I shot off a fence with a .22, shot one, it fell, loaded up and shot the other one and it fell. When I brought those two quail home my mother just couldn't get over how I could kill two quail with a rifle.

Anyway, the .410 became my gun and I would go quail hunting with Brady, my brother-in-law. Those were the days when we had lots of quail and we'd hunt on our 700-acre farm there in Lumpkin, Georgia. So I had that history of hunting when I located into Florida, a different terrain and different hunting victims like turkeys. So when I got married, since Albert, my husband, did not hunt at all, it was a challenge for me to figure out how I could have bird dogs, how I could go hunting and justify that when he didn't even hunt. He was pretty much sensitive to my needs, particularly when we first got married. You know the honeymoon isn't over 'til it's over, and so he had his foreman roost some turkeys out on our ranch. I'd never been turkey hunting and I can remember that morning, that was when it was legal to could shoot 'em off the roost. Bob Redding, his foreman, had told Albert where the turkeys were roosted and Albert led the hunting party to the turkeys. And here we go in the dark, four or five of us, with our guns, sneaking through the woods to get under the turkeys to shoot 'em off the roost. Well, Albert is leading the pack of hunters with his pipe and he'd light up his pipe and pack it and then he'd light it up again and we continued our trek looking for the turkeys. Finally, right before daylight he stopped us and pointed up and lighted his pipe again. How those turkeys stayed on that roost with all that firing up underneath them I'll never know, but we wound up banging away and actually bagged five turkeys and that was my introduction to real turkey hunting in Florida.

I have maintained that passion. It's not just a hobby, it's a passion with me, the turkey and the quail hunting. One of the first quail hunts that I experienced in Florida was very, very memorable in that Albert's cousin, Doyle Carlton, Jr., invited me to go to his place on Horse Creek. So we get down there and get off the Jeep, the dogs are pointed and I have my trusty Winchester .410 pump. The dogs point, the birds get up and I bang away with my .410 and knock two birds down. Doyle knocks one down, so he has a guy pick up my two birds and his one bird and when we got back on the Jeep ready to hunt the next covey, he said, "Now Barbara, we don't take but two birds out of each covey." In other words I had overshot that covey but what he really meant was that I had out shot him with a .410 pump and he's using a 12 gauge or 20 gauge, whatever gauge he had, and he was really pretty much put down. Well, the long story short is that was the last time I was ever invited to go quail hunting with Doyle, Jr. on Horse Creek or any other place.

Now and then I would go on dove hunts with Doyle, Jr. and Ted Williams, baseball player, but never quail hunting. So that's the end of that story but the beginning of my quail-hunting days in Florida.

Each November when turkey season opened I embarked on a pilgrimage to find out where the turkeys were. I learned to roost them myself, stayed in the woods a lot, going out early before dawn and then going back late in the afternoon, to diagnose the location of the turkeys so we would enhance our chances of success when we would have guests. Over the years, my two brothers-in-law, Brady Williamson and Dick Merrit would come down to hunt. They did this annually like a pilgrimage and we had a big cookout the night before and the next night which almost became a ritual for the family. I can recall that the morning of the hunt when we would bring the game in we had a contest. Each person would have to put up five dollars to enter the weight and the beard contest.

I wanted to always win if I could and so did Brady so we were in co-hoots with taking whatever turkey we got which could be a hen or a gobbler. If we had a hen we would fill it up with water to make it weigh a lot more and it would be the most broad-breasted turkey you'd ever seen. Then we would take hay string and tie on its neck to make the beard, (hens do not normally have beards), of course everybody knew that we had nothing but a little old hen turkey – we really tried to pull off a winner every year. Sometimes we won, sometimes we lost. We didn't win the money much but we sure did have a good time filling those turkeys up with everything from water to one year we dropped some heavy washers and bolts down the turkey to make it weigh more. We'd just do anything to win that contest!

It did not take long for Wauchula to discover that this woman-hunter could not only roost a turkey, shoot a turkey, but win the contest with the smallest turkey of all!

Dick and Brady at times would bring a guest and one time they brought this guy named Luke. Luke was a school bus driver up in Georgia and he would come down. He wore overalls and he'd go barefooted. They called him Uncle Luke. They really indicated that he was my mother's brother and that's the reason they called him Uncle Luke. They would put Uncle Luke out in the woods and he'd come back with two turkeys and he wouldn't go with us when we'd shoot 'em off the roost. He'd wait until we'd come in and have breakfast. Uncle Luke, you could strike a match on the bottom of his feet because he went barefooted even in the palmettos down through the swamps. He'd always come out about ten-thirty or eleven o'clock with two of the biggest turkeys you'd ever seen. It was just incredible what he could do. He was a woodsman who knew how to call 'em up and bag the turkeys and bring 'em in.

Albert would be the entertainer. He would provide all the spirits for the cookouts. He would procure the cooks. We never cooked, but we'd have somebody cooking and we would do that out at our place in New Zion for years and then we built our house in Oak Grove and continued that tradition at the house with the wild game cookout with 40 to 60 people attending. Bob Gibson became our chef and it was just grand old hunting days which I really cherish and will always remember. And the memories of those turkey hunts with my brother-in-law, and later on with my children, now with my grandchildren, embodies the true spirit of what our Creator has endowed us with. It's been a challenge to blend into this environment, this mind-set of taking and not giving back even though we'd take these turkeys we took care of them by feeding them, very careful attention as to how many we harvested every year and our turkey populations have continued to soar. So those who don't like the hunting but would love to be in the woods I'd love to share that with anybody who would like to be a part of this wonderful sport, the wonderful adventures just waiting in the woods.

Over the last seventeen years since Albert's death in 1992, there's been sort of a change in the way I pursue turkey hunting. There've been times when I've had the opportunity to have Governor Lawton Chiles down to turkey hunt and, of course, putting these guests with the turkeys, putting them in the area where the turkeys were, required some scouting and expertise but as time has gone on the challenge has been one of a different nature. It's not to take the game but to look at the turkeys, to figure out their habits and be enamored by their plumage and their wariness. The beauty is like having a unique and different experience every time I walk in the woods. The pursuit of the turkey has left an indelible print on my life; so much so that I have begun to name them, particularly the gobblers. There were High Pockets, King Kong, Mohammed Ali, Bin Laden, Mutt and Jeff, Three Stooges, Seven Dwarfs, Sadam, Godfather ad infinitum and on and on. It's like opening a book and reading a chapter, an unknown chapter because you never know what you will see or hear. So that has been the tone of turkey hunting in the last several years.

I can recall when Lawton Chiles, our governor and former U.S. Senator came to hunt on Horse Creek. He and I went into the swamp there on Horse Creek to see if he could call a turkey up to him. It was ironic that here he had spent years quote "turkey hunting" and I'd spent years "turkey hunting" and here we were together in a little pop blind, very intimate (I could hear his stomach grumbling). He would want to do the calling and I'd just do the sitting and looking and hearing. The gobbler would gobble but would not come, so I finally had to talk our governor into letting me do a little calling and free him up to do the shooting – hopefully... So he told me to go ahead and call. I just changed the tune a little bit which sounded more like a hen and sure enough here comes this big old gobbler. Lawton had a brand new gun with a scope on it, camouflaged, and I whispered...

here he comes, and sure enough a big gobbler stepped out and he banged away and dropped him. We lugged him out of the swamp and across a little foot bridge over Horse Creek.

We stood there at this little gate and we have a picture of me and Lawton, Governor Lawton Chiles at the gate and we named that Lawton's Gate because that's where we take a lot of the pictures as we come out of the swamp. It's just a very picturesque spot on Horse Creek.

There are two other people I've taken into what I call "Paradise," the place where Lawton

Dr. Barbara Carlton and Governor Lawton Chiles at Lawton's Gate on Hoss Creek, circa 1996

bagged his turkey. One was Billy Sasser, who was one of my very, very close hunting buddies (I call him Billy Bow-legs). He was just an avid, passionate old-timey turkey hunter. He made his own wishbone caller from a turkey breast bone, and he'd fix himself a little nest of palmettos and sit there all day calling up a turkey. He became ill later in life so I wanted to take him on his last turkey hunt. I took him into "Paradise" where I'd taken Lawton. The turkeys were roosted up in the trees, old gobblers, and we tried to call 'em but they wouldn't come. I said, "OK, Billy, come on." So we eased up, got under a big pine tree and I said, "All right, Billy, shoot 'em!" This was when you could not shoot turkeys quote "off the roost." But Billy shot that turkey and got him. It was the last turkey he ever killed.

I was so glad I could take him to "Paradise" before his last day. He really went to "Paradise."

It is a sanctuary. It is a place where the turkeys live and I dare not put foot there except on very, very special occasions. I have had one other person I've taken to "Paradise," a very close friend of mine named Barbara Curnutt. She had never turkey hunted so I took her into "Paradise." We had a little pop-up tent sitting there in the swamp, knee-deep in water, the turkey was gobbling, we sat up and put the decoy out. The turkey kept gobbling and gobbling and finally, here he comes. It just seems like an eternity when those big old gobblers come toward you.

As we sat there and I was doing the calling and the old gobbler would gobble every time I'd hit the caller. He was coming so I told Barbara to please be ready and all of a sudden I realized she didn't have any shells in her gun! So we had to get her loaded up and he was coming... it was pretty exciting. And all of a sudden he stepped out and I told Barbara to shoot! She shot and the old turkey fell down in the water and I told her to shoot again and so she shot again and she only had two shells in her gun so that was the end of her shooting.

The old turkey was still flopping so I jumped out of the blind to run it down. I had taken my gun and found out I didn't have any shells and I had to ask Barbara to find more shells so she was trying to give me shells and I was trying to run the turkey down in that knee-deep water. Finally, I put one shell in my gun... caught up with him and shot him again and we brought that turkey out of "Paradise." He was water-logged and we were water-soaked and we were... oh, it was an experience I will never, ever forget.

Just picture this little tent out in the middle of the swamp with mosquitoes, turkey gobbling and hens yelping and we're shootin' and turkeys thrashing in the water and here's this novice hunter who is always... I don't want to characterize her too much because she's a Baptist and I don't want her to think I've misrepresented anything but I can tell you one thing: that turkey was well baptized.

Even though my composure and my zest for turkey hunting was changing, there was one thing that never changed. That was the competitiveness of wanting to win a contest and we had a local gobbler trophy contest in the spring at the feed store here in Wauchula. I'd sign up every year, it cost $25 and whoever got the first prize got a new shotgun. So I plunked my

Barbara Curnutt at Lawton's Gate on Hoss Creek Paradise, 1998

$25 down and promptly started scouting trying to find the biggest gobbler. You were scored on the beard, weight and spurs. No hens allowed. Like in the old days, the brother-in-law days, I decided I was going to win that contest.

So I went down to Myakka City and bagged a three-bearded turkey, which was entered into the redneck "Turkey Open."

To my chagrin, a fellow turkey hunter opened the cooler and there lay a four-bearded turkey!

This <u>nearly</u> was mine!

Mounted three-bearded turkey

THE HONORABLE TURKEY

Precisely what is a turkey?

The cliché answer is: It probably depends upon who you talk to! Well, in days agone, a turkey was (and to some, still is) a large game bird of North America and Mexico. Turkeys are related to pheasants, and are traditionally associated with holiday feasts of Thanksgiving and Christmas.

However, for some time, in this latter part of the twentieth century, the word "turkey" has acquired a meaning a world away from the handsome bird that wanders the woodlands, adding distinctive sounds and movement to the nature of the forests, harming no one, nor any creatures of the wild.

To be called a "turkey" is ugly, even insulting, carrying a vulgar, uncouth connation. Yet, ask most anyone who has incorporated the use of the word to describe a person, and that person stumbles and stutters around without a clue as to what he or she is trying to say. There are a few other words that have surfaced in recent years that are equally inappropriate, which is another story…

Tom Gaskins sheds a little light on the subject: "I believe that this 'new' use of the word turkey, basically meaning that the turkey is not smart, even dumb, came not from the wild bird but from the tame turkey which has known nothing but living in captivity in a pen for the entire duration of his life. I'm told that a tame turkey will look up in a blinding rain and drown himself! Which may or may not be a true story. But don't tell me that a turkey living in the wild is not smart and wary! I know better. I can assure you that from personal experience an old wild turkey gobbler will outsmart you in a heartbeat! But that other one that's been raised behind a fence all his life, well "they" say that pen-raised turkey just ain't too smart! In other words, like dumb as a box of rocks."

For those who don't know just who Tom Gaskins is, he's the fellow who's famous far and wide for the classic Gaskins Turkey Call. Jokingly, he says, "I have the good fortune to have been raised on Fisheating Creek by an old mother hen. And that's reason enough to have more than a little knowledge of turkeys!"

Although Tom Gaskins has made turkey calls for years for hunters to use in calling up turkeys, he agrees that the swamps and flatlands, the prairies and woodlands of the region would never be the same without roving flocks of wild turkeys… and he adds, "I'm thrilled that in the last couple years, bird watchers, Audubon members and photographers are purchasing turkey calls not for hunting purposes but for calling turkeys to photograph!"

Photo: Barbara Oehlbeck

Osceola turkeys in the wild at sunrise

PARADISE

Dr. Barbara Carlton and Barbara Oehlbeck: A state of mind, a myth, even a passion, paradise is where you find it.

The prairie stretches east and west, as far as eye can see... even to the edge of the world. The land is dotted here and there with small islands of palmettos and bayberry and a silence of green that's almost overwhelming. A long trail cuts across the broad acres leading to a little pine cabin tucked in amongst giant oaks that have made their home at the edge of the woods for more years than the living can remember. A rustic porch stretches east and west with columns of lighter pine trunks, all left in their natural state, even with small limbs protruding here and there. The porch is unfurnished except for a rustic table with a checkered cloth and a few chairs.

No houses can be seen, no signs of commercialism. There is only the grass-covered earth, the great dome of blue and wayward mountains of snowy white clouds that keep coming and going.

She said, "This is my world. It's as if I have my arms around it, so that nothing can get away and nothing can intrude. It has seeped into my heart and soul, a poignant page in my life that I can never let go."

The sun began to seep through the trees casting long slender shadows onto this vast exposure of prairie green. The sounds of the sandhills floated in from their night stands. Then without a sound, their wide grey wings bring them in for a soft and perfect landing. This wide open space is their sanctuary, too, their paradise. Unlike many winged creatures, sandhill cranes seek uncovered open land with no growth to hide their enemies.

The last hoots of the barred owls are faint coming from afar in the swamp that separates the creek from the prairie.

"Suddenly there is the awareness of slight movements at the edge of the woods, hardly discernable. Deer! Five of them, two bucks, two does and a fawn, so young its spots are still prominent. They stand statue-still, apparently unaware of another presence, but not for long.

Like leaping ballerinas, they clear the ancient board fence, so old it appears to have grown there. The deer were heading for the creek. "Suddenly they stopped and I stopped breathing. It was as if they had become unafraid. They stretched their necks looking in all directions, raising their heads as if to see more of my – and their – world. Then they were gone, all together without a sound.''

Suddenly there were sounds, unmistakable sounds, coming from the edge of the ancient oak grove to the west. Turkeys! A dozen or more, gobblers, jakes and hens, strutting for what seemed to be, the simple love of life.

"I dare not think that this land, these giant trees, this green prairie will be uprooted... gouged and planted with buildings, covered over with concrete and asphalt. Even now the creek's water level is way down. No longer does it ripple with clear little bubbling waves that whisper sweet nothings to us who sit on her banks and watch.

"Paradise is slipping away, her sweet silence is becoming a plaintive memory, and there is nowhere to look for that which we are losing.

"Once paradise is lost, it is gone... forever."

HOSS CREEK
Lil' Ritz Carlton

In this chosen part of a southern world, just before the break of day, there is a hush soul deep. Not a leaf nor limb stirs, not even a little voice from the woods, not a sound from the ground.

Wrapped in stark silent stillness I am loath to move or even breathe. Staring at the eastern horizon, I cannot tell how far from light we are. Yet, having been here before in the same season, I know the first sound will come from a tiny, flitting bird that calls out a tiny, high-pitched cheep... cheep. There is no melody to his voice, but there is pure joy in his morning message... cheep-cheep... cheep-cheep, that's followed by a brief, slightly melodic trill. And I've yet to see where he comes from, but I know he heralds this fresh new day.

Every morning his greeting gift is the same, and I cannot think of the dawning of a new day without him.

A quietness and calmness envelopes this country, gentleness and kindness are all about and the solitude is a priceless gift.

Through the woods, across the swamps, there is a pride of place, a joy of being, not only for creatures of the land but for those men who lay claim to it.

As the morning dawn regresses, there is an abrupt interruption of this sacred silence of the woods. Suddenly a thundering gobble from "Old Tom" on the roost heralding this new day.

The sanctity of the woods is never the same after he opens his big mouth!

My day has begun... "This Nearly IS Mine."

TURKEY TALES

Those who don't care about turkeys may skip this chapter because you are "probably a turkey yourself!"

Just imagine that you have a grand opportunity to stalk, look, and/or shoot a Florida wild Osceola turkey. The hunter who ascribes to these two seasons will forge a relentless pursuit of a very wary Native American bird.

A passion for turkey-hunting borders on the edge of insanity. Getting up at five in the morning just to glimpse a tall, two-legged, bearded bird or in the spring just to hear a faint gobble in the deep of the springtime swamp.

Sometimes that gobble is a bit like a soft, throaty growl but there's no mistaking the sound coming from that long, limber neck of yours!

This experience is like no other in that you get to embrace God's natural beauty at sunrise and see the faint glowing glimmer of sunset at the close of day. The sounds of the natural birds as they awaken early in the morning give one a sense of wonder that infects the passages of the soul.

It becomes an addiction to Mother Nature and her bounty. This is the reason that I agree to lose sleep and wait in order to be fooled over and over by "my" big wonderful old Tom Turkey. May he rest in peace!

Today is the last day of this horrible odyssey. Glory hallelujah! It's been grand and exhilarating yet exhausting and fruitful – if you can count Mother Nature as the great benefactor.

TURKEYS!

It was three days before my birthday and Easter Sunday when I went to Cow Chip Camp to get my spring gobbler. Our family had tried two weeks earlier, but we were unsuccessful and the season is to close there on Easter Sunday.

The afternoon before, five jakes were roosted and one hen but no gobbler and no gobbling on the roost. Entering the same area just before dawn, I was hopeful to hear a gobble somewhere on the roost. The early morning was glorious! About 60 degrees and the woods were alive with the sounds and the joys of spring. About seven a.m. there was the sound of a gobbler to the east and one to the south. The jakes and one hen flew down about 60 yards away and I began to cluck to draw attention to the hen decoy near my blind. The jakes gradually worked their way to the decoy and again I heard the gobbler to the south some three hundred yards away in the swamp.

Completely entertained by the activity of the hen and jakes and I almost forgot about the gobbler. All of a sudden, a loud gobble some fifty yards away startled me because I was not ready for the showdown. There was no problem seeing the elusive bird strutting and looking at the decoy and it was time to put the box caller down and get my trusty 47-year-old Browning ready for a shot. The palm fronds in the blind shielded me from his wary eye, raising my gun, he lifted his head and was ready for a quick escape. Two shots were fired and the big 19-pound 11-inch beard, 1¼ inch spurs gobbler lay quiet at my feet. As I looked at "King Chip" there was a final strut when he raised his tail feathers and expanded both wings as his last benediction...

This truly was mine.

THE DEER

Pulling onto the main road heading west there was no sign of daybreak. Ground fog spread between the long rows of orange trees wandering off to the creek.

I wanted to get to the cabin before sunrise, to see the day awaken, to see the hawks stretch their grey-brown wings and go screaming across the prairie. It always seems as though they are the alarm clock for the swamp and the woods.

It's only a few miles to the cabin but this morning it seemed longer. Looking eastward over my shoulder, still no sign of daybreak. I kept driving through the low, dense fog. Suddenly, the Toyota Highlander shuddered and a loud crunching noise broke the morning's silence. I stomped on the brakes, jumped out and ran to the front of the vehicle. The bumper was crumpled and twisted, the hood and fender badly bent. And there on the asphalt, barely touching the wheel in a still-warm heap, lay a young four-point buck. Dead. The end had come instantly. His four points had not been marred by the impact. His soft, golden coat was smooth and sleek.

Since he was too heavy to lift, I pushed and pulled him off the road into the tall grass, heavy with dew. Saddened and bewildered, I drove on to the cabin.

There had been no sign of his presence, not the slightest movement that would have given any indication that he was there along the road. Yet I kept wondering how I could have avoided him, why I did not see him...

Approaching the last gate there was old Lijah trudging along the fence line, his worn, torn coat pulled up close under his chin. His bentwood cane steadied his steps. I stopped and spoke to him, telling him what had just happened.

He said, "I go git him fer ye..."

"No... no... not for me, for you. You'll have enough for you and your whole family for Thanksgiving and Christmas."

"You shore ye won't take him..." He wasn't quite smiling but almost, and I knew that he was thinking of having enough food on the table to feed his big, three generational family.

"No... no. He's for you, Lijah. I'll be glad knowing you have him. Come on, get in, we'll go back and get him... for you."

Lijah was bent and stooped but he was still strong and wiry. He deftly lifted the deer into the back of the car, handling him as carefully as he would have had he still been alive.

Not even 20 minutes had passed as I retraced my way across the prairie to the cabin and pulled up beside the surrounding lichen-covered plank fence. Unlocking the sagging gate, I unconsciously waited to hear the squeak-squeak that would follow.

Suddenly, a burst of light lit up the sky, the prairie and woods, the cabin. Turning toward the sun, there was a young deer, slim and swift, leaping over the fence in a grand golden arc. This was a "pinto painted" deer with the distinguished markings of an Appaloosa horse.

This nearly was mine.

A true story as experienced by Dr. Barbara Carlton...

Left: Dr. Barbara Carlton holding up the deer that ran out in front of her Toyota Highlander. Top: A "pinto painted" deer.

IAN'S THANKSGIVING HUNT

Passing the Turkey Torch to Grandson Ian

I had made myself stay snuggled down under a light blanket a few more minutes. It was going to be a long day, yet I was anxious for the start... not unlike waiting for the "clang of the bell" when the horses are all lined up ready to make a mad dash at the Kentucky Derby.

The alarm clock sounded off at four o'clock. I bounded out of bed, made a quick run for the kitchen to make a pot of coffee, waked up Ian and told him we'd have to be headed out in less than 30 minutes. He was so excited I knew he'd slept very little but it didn't matter. A nap would come easy for him in the afternoon, curled up on the floor in front of the cabin fireplace.

We pulled out of the driveway just before 4:30 headed west-southwest on SR 64. "Grandma, it's so dark black. I can't see anything except the headlights."

He was right. There was no moon and if there were stars I couldn't see them. I don't think he was uneasy because of the intensity of the darkness; for him it was simply a new experience. All by himself, he was going hunting with Grandma at Cow Chip Camp.

I knew we had a good hour before there'd be even a streak of light. I was anxious to get into the woods and get ourselves situated in a special blind called the sky box before any of the wild creatures knew we were there. On several previous occasions we would be there in the midst of turkeys on the roost and I was so hopeful that they would be there this morning for our big show.

We parked near the camp being careful not to slam any doors, pulled our hunting caps on hurriedly, took our shotguns and headed toward the blind. Almost like a stage whisper, he said, "Grandma, all I can hear is a little bitty wind..."

But there were other voices that would greet us at daylight. I put my arm around his skinny shoulders sayng... "Sh-h-h-h-h-h".

He never said another word as we headed deep into the woods toward the sky box. The farther we walked the more my eyes became accustomed to the darkness. We dropped Fletcher, Ian's father, at Sirman's Blind and we headed to the sky box. The trees were bigger here and the understory growth was heavy and thick so Ian edged closer and closer to me. I leaned over and softly whispered, "Just a little ways more and we'll be there." And sure enough, we had not walked another 50 feet until I recognized the tree I was looking for. I heard a faint sigh from him but still he didn't say a word.

I couldn't help but think how some of us who had hunted together through the years had kidded each other about "the stairway to the stars" referring to the ladder-like limbs and cross pieces we'd nailed to the trunk to get to our blinds. I had told Ian in detail how he'd have to feel his way up the ladder because there still was not a streak of daylight. I helped him up to the first step then positioned his small hand on the next step. He looked down at me whispering, "Do I go on up now?" I motioned yes and up he went almost as if he'd done such a thing every day of his 13 years.

I followed and we quickly eased ourselves into green plastic chairs. We had to sit close because that blind is quite little. I started looking around and he followed suit. I'm sure we had not been there 10 minutes when I suddenly realized that the roost, which is fairly close to the blind, was lined with turkeys! It was still too dark to tell one from another and it seemed as though they were as close to each other as Ian and I were in the blind watching for them to fly down and listening to them. We were on a great stage about to witness the chorus of the turkeys in the trees and then the great fly down.

All of a sudden he leaned over and whispered right in my ear, "Grandma, did you build this blind?" I shook my head and pointed eastward. I wanted him to see the day being born. In a short time through the tall trees there were faint pink streaks of daybreak, back lighted from the first light through the trees.

Then there was a strange muffled noise just below us. Leaning over and looking down carefully there was the biggest boar hog I'd seen in a long, long time. Ian was so fascinated he wanted to shoot him.

With the movement of the turkeys I knew the world in the deep of that forest would almost immediately awaken. And it did. And far off toward the swamp two owls began hooting to each other. I silently wondered if they were saying "goodnight" or "good morning." Then it was as if all the creatures of the woods awakened wanting to be heard at the same time. There were the trillers and the mockers and, of course, the cardinals with their wondrous repertoire. And suddenly, from the direction of the prairie that we'd crossed just a short time ago, the sandhills were in fine, loud voice. Yet we could not see them and knew that they, being open land creatures, would not come into the woods.

As the light of day intensified, the turkeys began flying into adjacent trees which was a precursor to their fly-down.

The stage was set for the grand experience as each turkey found its way to the ground. There was the putt sound of the turkeys on the roost with moving hens and a few bashful jakes, and we also heard a strange gurgle-gargle which definitely was a gobbler sounding off before the mating season.

And then it happened almost all at one time. It was as if they fell from the roost onto a giant moss and lichen-covered log on the forest floor almost directly below the roost. Their feathers were shining black, like they'd just been oiled, and there was an iridescence across their backs that spread slightly across their tail feathers. Their silhouettes were as sharp and realistic as if they were carved from ebony. These were young gobblers and in the light of day we could see beards on some of them.

Ian could not look in enough directions at one time. He was mesmerized but didn't utter a sound. And then he said, "Grandma, is it always like this?"

And I said, "Yes... and no. At least many times we have the good luck of seeing at least one gobbler! But this morning we are seeing 15 gobblers!"

As the turkeys flew down and we identified five huge gobblers that were charging the base of the sky box, I urged Ian to be patient because there were some 15 other turkeys in the same group and we wanted to pick out a large gobbler to shoot. Ian had agreed that we would let the turkey go to the feeder where his dad was in a blind and we would take a chance of bagging a turkey after his dad shot.

Ian had the .410 Winchester pump shotgun that I had as a child. He had it loaded and was ready to fire.

As we watched the turkeys file by, they began to turn away and were getting ready to exit so that we would not get a shot and neither would his dad.

All of a sudden, I told Ian that we had to shoot because the turkeys were leaving. I counted to three and we both fired! Two big gobblers fell and Ian wanted to celebrate but I told him to sit tight so his dad might get a shot.

A few minutes later, his dad shot and knocked down two turkeys.

Ian and I were ready to celebrate and as we unloaded our guns to get out of the blind, I discovered that his little trusty Winchester .410 had misfired.

(Grandma had bagged two big gobblers with one shot!)

It was time to go but I knew there'd be no time in my life when I'd forget Ian's first Thanksgiving hunt. Nor can I ever forget my red-headed grandson's expression when a squirrel suddenly appeared on the edge of the sky box and barked as if to say, "Go! I was here first!"

This truly was ours – two big tom turkeys with one shot!

Sometime later, Julie (Ian's mom) bagged a <u>bearded</u> lady turkey while Grandma and Ian each knocked down two trophy toms.

Three generations and three Osceola turkeys - Ian and Julie Carlton McClelland and Grandma, Dr. Barbara Carlton

LAST FLING AT THE 2X4 RANCH

The decision to sell the 2 X 4 RANCH prompted a desire on the part of the children to say goodbye. Will Carlton brought his family from Texas in April 2006 to have a last fling at gator hunting there on the ranch. We had obtained gator permits and Brady and Brad Pfeil had taken two trophy gators from the marshes.

Will and his family were anxious to hook a big gator and they were successful! Following the 2 X 4 hunt they went to Hoss Creek and bagged three large gobblers.

I never knew that Will was such a gator fan except for his love of the University of Florida Gators. He even had the head of one of the gators mounted which is in his home in Flower Mound, Texas. Kate, Will and Dan all joined in the fun.

Photos: Joyce Hunter

Top: Will Carlton had this gator stuffed afer his successful "final fling" at the 2 X 4 RANCH. Right: Brad, Orin & Brady Pfeil with the two gators taken at the "final fling." The gator on the left weighed 515 lbs at 12.5 ft. The one on left was 455 lbs at 13ft.

Following their successful gator hunt at the 2 X 4 RANCH, Kate, Will and Dan Carlton bagged three large gobblers at Hoss Creek. April 2006

ON WINGS OF THE WIND
Hoss Creek Camp
(Barbara Oehlbeck's Experience at the Cabin)

This was my first trip to Hoss Creek Camp and I had no idea what to expect. Dr. Barbara had mentioned various creatures that made their home there and she had described the land and the woods... and the wind. And, of course, she had told me about the little log cabin, the camp. But still I was having a hard time putting it all together, painting a picture in my mind.

It was still dark when we turned off Route 64. After going a few miles and skirting the edge of the vast prairie, I became aware that it was coming with the first splashes of daylight. The wind. At first, hardly more than a soft gentle breeze coming from the wide belt of woodland that borders the creek.

Then, almost as if the curtain is raised on a giant stage, it whips across the vast open prairie heavy with the fresh fragrance of new-green from the woods and animals – and every now and then passing whiffs of a smoldering campfire, a leftover from the night before.

Blowing in the wind are long strands of lace-like Spanish moss that never seems to lose its grip on limbs of live oaks... the epitome of an ageless grace. Who needs a windsock when Spanish moss is in sight?

She had told me that we'd likely see the sandhills and she was right. From the south, high over the ancient forest, came floating sounds of the sandhills. They won't light in trees nor understory growth. They must have wide open spaces where they can see and feel those that might lay in wait to do them harm. They even take their red-headed young, soon as they can walk on their long pencil-slim legs, into the open. Sandhills always know where they are going, almost never straying from their own chosen territory. After all, they mate for life, thus their wanderings are mostly the same throughout the seasons of their lives. At times they wander for hours, more or less in the same areas. At other times however, they gracefully touch down only to leap into flight the next minute. What it is that triggers their comings and goings? Only they know.

Dr. Barbara slowly stopped the hunting buggy, silently pointing to these elegant long legged birds, and then she said quietly, "These birds have an incredible ability to hear. The least unusual sound and they'll be up and away. For fear I might forget to tell you, thought I'd better do it right now."

Again she was absolutely silent for a few moments, then, "It seems that most people think the word 'Wauchula' is simply an Indian word. Right this minute you're looking at the meaning of the word 'Wauchula'... the call of Sandhill Cranes."

As we crept slowly across that vast prairie, the hawks were dipping and diving, streaking in from the cow pens on the prairie's east edge, and that not quietly. Highly protective of their young, they are loners in flight. By watching closely, one can be seen flying out, then before long, he's back over the cow pens to a stand of the ranch's tallest pines that he calls home... screaming all the way. His mate, not quite as large nor as colorful, takes to the air shortly after he comes home. She seems to fly closer to ground, swooping low to snatch a morsel for her young... a young snake or field mouse. Then with a running jump, she's up and away into the morning blue, banking almost full circle before returning home to the pines where their well hidden nest is safely situated.

Nearing the log cabin, a blue jay was making his presence known with a series of loud squawks, uniquely his song, even if it's not melodious.

And the cardinals, their brilliant flashes of red were flying close to the little log cabin, even in and out of the yet-to-be-screened sprawling east porch. With great ease and grace, they run up and down the porch columns that are made of native lighter wood from the swamp. They'll find a tanglewood of bayberry, or woodbine vines or a thicket of elder berries that are now in full bloom in which to make their nest. Cardinals are creatures of many songs, not unlike mockingbirds. At times they appear more or less at the same time. And then it's a challenge to tell their songs apart. However, it's the early morning time that red birds love the most. They'll come to the feeder even before the first streaks of daylight can be seen, while the mockers seem to prefer the hours nearer the close of day for their supper. And many times their songs are the most beautiful when a full moon has just appeared. This also seems to be the time when the mockers explore most of their repertoire which is extensive.

As we pull up beside the rustic fence that surrounds the cabin, little marsh rabbits, the color of dead grass and twigs appear. They don't seem to care if it's daylight or dusk. They come hopping, or tip-toeing from beneath palmetto islands or from under the weathered steps of the cabin but they don't venture far from their home cover. They seem to cherish the cozy "cave" under the big dead stump that hides the mechanics of the TV dish. The marshers are no match for bobcats that call the brush and wild grapevines by the creek their hallowed ground.

Dr. Barbara Carlton is in love with the land. The drama of the morning spreading out over the prairie is her joy. And she said, "I find myself wondering how it would feel to hold it all in my arms all day hoping for a repeat performance from all these native creatures that call this chosen land – and sky – home."

Looking around I'm suddenly aware of shadows flitting on the ground that I'd not noticed earlier. As a shadow or "for real," there is no more graceful a bird than the swallow-tailed kite. I could not take my eyes off the one that was headed straight for the tallest pines near the cow pens where their nest is. The one I was watching was undoubtedly a male because breakfast for his young could easily be seen sticking out his beak. The female kite stays with the young while the male captures small amphibians, reptiles and even other birds to take back to the nest. Swallow-tailed kites give every impression that they are ballet-dancing in air. Their stunning acrobatic flight patterns set this bird apart from all others.

This cloudless, pure blue sky is the perfect backdrop for countless birds. I find myself trying to look in all directions at one time. A huge gathering of ibis are gurgling around a shallow pond at the edge of the swamp along with several wood storks that look like praying monks. Sounding like a jackhammer, a pileated woodpecker makes himself known at the back of the cabin as he pounds the trunk of one of the biggest pines looking for insects.

Dr. Barbara checks her watch saying, "All this here at the earliest beginning of day and I'm suddenly realizing if we don't hurry along to the woods and swamp back of the cabin we'll miss the turkeys!

"If the other Barbara[1] were here, she'd already be late for finding her prey, the Osceola wild turkey."

And then she adds, "The joy of turkey hunting is merely an introduction to Mother Nature's bounty at her finest. Learning to live and enjoy this ever repetitive exhilarating experience could never be diminished. This truly is a legacy that awaits each person who is willing to stop, listen, and enjoy the parting of the curtains on this grand natural stage."

"There is no bottom line here, only a Line In The Sky – This Nearly Is Mine."

1. Barbara Curnutt - Georgia hunting friend from Texas.

THE PREACHER HUNTING

It seems that the reputation of this woman to hunt has been broadcast far and wide.

All of a sudden there is this preacher from St. Petersburg who almost arrives in a restored MG convertible roadster. About two miles from his destination, his gas gives out.

I had to rescue him, put him in my African Queen (my '79 Ford Bronco, my first hunting buggy) to take him to the selected site on Horse Creek in South Wauchula.

As the preacher and I sat there together, the old gobbler started his gobbling from the roost and eventually flew down but would not come to our call. He would gobble with every call, so I told the preacher to circle around behind the gobbler and bushwhack him. It took 30 minutes for him to carefully cut through the bushes and not spook the old guy. Of course, sitting there calling, I was a little

The African Queen

fearful that the preacher might get lost and by mistake, shoot me instead of the gobbler!

After an eternity in that swamp, the mosquitoes chewing me up, the old blabber-mouth gobbling with every call, I finally heard a loud bang, the gobbling ceased and the triumphant preacher comes out with a beautiful 20-pound gobbler!

It just goes to prove that you can give out of gas and still get a turkey!

PS: Successor to the old worn out "African Queen" is the "Silver Queen," beautiful, buxom, bright with enough room for six and dogs and eleven grandchildren. Long live the queen!

Photo: Joyce Hunter

**Dr. Barbara Carlton standing beside the "Silver Queen"
a true upgrade from the African Queen**

Godfather Gobbler presented by Dr. Barbara Carlton to Governor Lawton Chiles with Jerry Chicone looking on, circa 1997.

HUNTING THE GODFATHER
Governor Chiles and Dr. Barbara Carlton

Dr. Barbara Carlton: Serving on the Florida Citizens Hall of Fame Selection Committee, I was frequently asked about getting Governor Chiles to be our guest speaker at our annual luncheon.

I quickly found that the "best bait" was to ask the governor to come turkey hunting the morning after the luncheon. He accepted the invitation to both being the speaker and, of course, to go turkey hunting. And it was my duty to find him a large gobbler that he could bag.

This became more of a challenge than anyone could realize in that we failed on two ocasions to call in the wary Godfather Gobbler.

The end of the story was there was no turkey bagged by our famous turkey-hunting governor!

The next week I pursued the same old Godfather Gobbler and bushwhacked him because of his special status of eluding our famous governor twice. I had him mounted in full strut, his vitals an 11-inch beard, 18½ pounds with 1¼ inch spurs.

One year later Governor Chiles attended our next luncheon as the guest speaker and I awarded him a lame duck Godfather Turkey award.

Ironically, this was one of his last hunts as Governor Chiles. He died unexpectedly in 1998 while in office.

**Dr. Barbara Carlton, son Pat, and Governor Lawton Chiles
at the Carlton Homeplace Ranch.**

Pat Carlton, Dr. Barbara Carlton and Governor Lawton Chiles at Hoss Creek.

QUAIL

Quail hunting was my first love when moving into the Florida pines and palmettos back in 1959.

At that time most quail hunters had their bevy of bird dogs moving pointers, and quail were abundant everywhere – the great northern bobwhite quail.

Photo: Wes Marston

Native bobwhite quail

As time progressed it became incumbent on me to try to join the crowd of bird hunters which required dogs, a Jeep and a hunting partner. Since Albert did not hunt, his friends would always be ready to go with me on our ranch. In the good "ole" days we could find 20 – 25 coveys a day and would bag 40 to 60 quail in one day!

Then in the '80s it became evident that quail numbers were decreasing. In 1979, we owned, and were managing the land for quail at the 2 X 4 RANCH. Quail numbers were still at their peak. However, beginning in the mid 1980s quail numbers became scarce even on our Carlton 2 X 4 RANCH.

Much research has been done and scientific data gathered to document the reasons for the quail demise including loss of habitat, protection of quail predators, including endless numbers of fire ants and cattle egrets.

In 1990 and early in 2000, a concerted effort by our family to reverse the quail depletion was met with failure. So Tall Timbers Research and Environmental Center in Tallahassee became instrumental in developing a research program on the Carlton 2 X 4 RANCH.

In retrospect, had we known about the dramatic decline there may have been a chance for reversal but since numbers have dropped so drastically, quail are on borderline extinction... this nearly was mine.

Brady Pfeil, Dr. Barbara Carlton and Stan Pelham at the Becker Plantation in 2002. The Beckers are actively pursuing establishing native bobwhite on their Georgia Plantation near Buena Vista, Georgia

GRAND FINAL OF OSCEOLA
Look and Let Live

Over the years turkey hunting has changed my life. I have 11 grandchildren to train in this fading sport. Safety is always Number One, fun is Number Two, teaching how to appreciate Mother Nature is Number Three, Number Four is knowing the 10 rules of turkey hunting!

One through 10: DON'T MOVE! The great anticipatory joy of that opening day when after a hundred hours of scouting I can place each hunter in a place where they will see or hear something, but... it may not be a turkey!

After all, this is more of a learning experience and less of a shooting experience.

I can truly say that I have received more joy over missing a turkey – "the big one always gets away" -- so you'll wait for the next time. It's almost like a recycling of the turkey. You look and you let live.

The grand finale comes in unexpected ways. There is always an urge to be able to bag a turkey during the season. The last day without a turkey is like a day lost in Paradise.

Photo: Wes Marston

Big Boss and girlfriend

PART EIGHT
SUNSET

Dr. Barbara Carlton: As the sun sinks in a scarlet sea, I sit on the little rustic porch holding sunbeams in my arms, and reliving this day.

I refuse to think that this land will ever be anything but what it is now with grass growing coarse and thick, solid and heavy. Meandering trails of native inhabitants weaving in and out and around palmetto islands and ancient oak hammocks.

Early this morning, the sun had just started coming up as I was walking toward the turkey blind. Settling myself quickly, I started looking down and around and there in a line were eight gobblers strutting beneath me! As the sun hit their feathers the reflection made them appear as colorful as peacocks. They all hopped up on a log so covered with moss it looked as if it were upholstered in that plush, green growth. At that moment it did not occur to me to even reach for my gun. I knew I'd rather watch them than shoot 'em, and then the quick thought... ***if only these thoughts and this appreciation can be passed on to my grandchildren...***

Another time, as day started to break and again as I had just settled myself in the blind, there were 26 hens and two jakes and no show of gobblers... not even one. But there was a show of something else! A huge boar came crashing through the underbrush scattering the turkeys, making straight for the creek!

And yet another morning, actually it was Thanksgiving; from the sky box I suddenly became aware of 10 gobblers on the roost! Quickly spotting the one with the longest beard, I took a deep breath and pulled the trigger, only to find out that my gun had malfunctioned!

Twilight was fast coming on, but in the far off distance I could see great stands of cypress poking holes in low gathering clouds. And here and there, all the way to the edge of this green world, towering lone pines reached high in the twilight sky, their brown bark arms outstretched, laden with gleaming needles, heavy with seeded cones.

Time was, in the early part of the twentieth century, the land was covered with giant stands of virgin timber. The trees were so tall and massive, when walking beneath them even at midday, it was like a teal twilight, the sun being obscured by the leaf canopies that overlapped each other. And the massive oaks with their outstretched arms growing parallel to the ground, enveloped with miles and miles of resurrection ferns hugging the rough bark from their trunks to the tip end of the limbs. Some of the ferns reach out so far they hang like Christmas garlands. In times of drought, these ferns turn brown and brittle, as if they were dead. Yet the minute rain begins to fall, all the hugging fronds resurrect themselves in gleaming green.

Here the loudest sounds are of silence. Yet now and then, the long lonely cries of sand hills are heard over the vast openness, their moving shadows a dancing choreography of grace while hawks dip and dive, screaming with ecstasy or agony, the backlight through their wings a silent golden glow. And on the wing in the immense deep blue, a regal bald eagle soars and dips, proclaiming in loud voice, his rightful place amongst all the other creatures. And then, seemingly, from the other side of "my world" there are three specks against the sky... specks that quickly became swallow-tailed kites, their ballet dancing in air the epitome of grace and elegance.

As I sit here looking and thinking, I am frightened for the land and all its native creatures, fearing that even now there is no turning back. The vast destruction has already gone too far... too deep.

CONCLUSION
Learning To Love The Land

"The land," she says, "will only give you so much. Unless you tend to it – unless you understand the economics and the balancing act that come with ownership—the land will exhaust your means."

Barbara Carlton knows those lessons all too well.

For nearly 50 years, Dr. Barbara has lived off the land, though her profession was in medicine. She has doctored the people of Wauchula and Hardee County but she has also maintained the Carlton Homeplace where she and her late husband, Albert, raised four children. The Carlton roots run six generations deep in Hardee County.

Barbara Castleberry Carlton may have been born and raised one state north but this Georgia Cracker has been transformed into the Florida Cracker whose heart lives in the rolling green pastures, scrub oak stands and piney woods of "The Heartland."

She has authored two books, this one entitled *This Nearly Was Mine: A Journey Through Carlton Country*, and an earlier one titled *Our Beginnings: At The End Of The Road, Memoirs of the Castleberrys.*

And when she's not stalking a wild turkey or grandmothering one or more of her eleven little ones who come to visit often, she's involved in various community work as well as her church. Or maybe even helping produce a movie which she did most recently.

The movie, "Cracker: The Last Cowboys of Florida," was released in 2008 at the Palm Beach Film Festival and several Florida cities, featuring the life and history of Florida cattle people in these parts. Her role as co-producer came about quite by coincidence, as a keeper of the flame and preservationist of the cowboy culture. Director Victor Milt, who has done numerous national TV commercials

CRACKER - The Last Cowboys of Florida, a film by Victor Milt

and documentaries, lives in Boca Raton with his wife, an Arcadian lady. He had become deeply interested in the Florida land boom – and how it was chewing up so much of the natural beauty and serenity of the Land of Flowers – so he began interviewing "the real people" who revered the land.

Keeping the story going, Dr. Barbara says, "I was in Clearwater when a guy called and said, "Dr. Barbara, could you come to Arcadia? We have someone here who's doing a movie and he wants to interview some real Florida cattle people. He's making a documentary and he's been told he must talk to you."

"Well, I went to Arcadia in October," Barbara said. "It was hot – I mean hot! They made a roaring fire anyway and sat me down next to it and started asking a bunch of questions and telling about the land being gobbled up."

Dr. Barbara Carlton is anything but a cowgirl, yet she's worked ranches, she can ride and she can brand cattle.

But then she adds, "Most of my riding has been in a Ford Bronco."

The Carltons are large landowners, having held property in Manatee, Hardee, DeSoto and Sumter Counties. They sold their 2 X 4 RANCH in DeSoto and turned the Sumter property into "Carlton Half Moon Management" to be preserved in its natural state.

The second Carlton son, Pat, is the owner and operator of Chinquapin, a "green" community still being developed near the Cashiers-Highlands area of North Carolina.

As much as a preservationist, Barbara Carlton is also a realist and a capitalist. And she writes about her feelings in this new book.

"It's about the land," she says simply. "How to manage the land. Use the land. Farm the land. Protect the land. Enjoy the land.

"It's hard to make a living off the land unless you do something with it. It doesn't just give you a living because you own it. You have to figure out what to do with it.

"These people who paid $10,000 an acre for pasture, they can't eat that. They've got to produce something. They've got to have a return on it. They've got to pay taxes on it, protect it. They've got to mow it. There is an attendant cost to owning the land that these people don't realize.

"Pastoral living comes with a price.

"The first thing people want to do is get a place out in the country... 10 acres. They put horses and cows on it, and then it doesn't have any grass on it. They've overgrazed it. They ate it all up. So there is a balancing act that must not be overlooked."

"The land," Dr. Barbara says, "allows you to eke out a living. Have a wonderful lifestyle. I call it 'genteel poverty.' Never have any money. The way you make money with the land is you sell it. That's so sad, unless you can see your way to keep it."

Which brings into question *what will happen to the 400-acre Carlton Homeplace after Barbara is gone?*

She doesn't see it being taken over by any of her four children, all of whom are involved in entrepreneurial or philanthropic projects out of the area.

"I faced that about 10 years ago," she said.

And so the question: What would she like to have happen?

"I would want one of the grandchildren to come in and work the land, love it, and live it," she said with a measure of passion in her voice usually reserved for turkey hunting. "So much history. It's not only a good place to live; they have a legacy they have not dreamed about."

She wants her grandchildren to have the grand adventure of discovering her legacy. "I could tell one of them, but I'd like them to say, 'Gosh, that grandma, she was standing there talking to those turkeys, branding the calves out there, taking care of that creek...'"

Only three grandchildren had been born when her husband, Albert, passed away.

"Maybe one of them will become fired up enough to come back and see what Grandma and Grandpa did," she said, with the sparkle of a dream in her eyes.

What they would find out is that Grandmother still has plenty to do as well as the tireless energy and drive to do it, from the constant tracking of wild turkeys to unfailingly supporting her community including major projects like the widening of U. S. 17.

And, they'd find, too, that Grandma Carlton has been – and is – an excellent steward of the land.

The sparkle is still in her eyes as she quietly says, "Who knows...one of these 11 just might see the *light of the land* one of these days..."

We should all be so believing and dedicated.

--Adapted from an article by Buddy Martin/

Wauchula – the *Hardee Sun*, Florida

Photo: Joyce Hunter

The land - a view from the home at the Carlton Homeplace

BENEDICTION
The Last Day

Dr. Barbara Carlton: It is never easy saying goodbye... even though we've only been "seeing" each other for these past three months.

You have fed my passion so many times and opened so many doors to me in our domain, and allowed me to listen – with such joy! – to your unique language and voice across your native green land.

By the time we meet again there'll be a new generation of baby turkey poults in your world and we'll start all over!

You may or may not have known that you've been dubbed "The Godfather" and you won't be forgotten. But for now we have no choice. We must say goodbye for at least these next six months... woe and misery.

So in summary: This year was **not** nearly mine!

Photo: Barbara Oehlbeck

Baby turkey poults

PART NINE
EPILOGUE
Generations - Eighth and Ninth

Beginning the eighth generation of Carltons, William Albert Carlton, Jr. was born December 3, 1960, to Barbara and Albert Carlton in Wauchula, Florida, where he attended public schools, graduating from Hardee High School. Will attended the University of Florida, graduating with a degree in Agriculture Education.

In March 1987 Will

Seth, Carol, Will, Dan and Kate Carlton

married Carol Thomas of Texas, a graduate of Baylor University where she earned a Bachelor of Arts degree. She is also a graduate of the University of Texas at Arlington (Texas), an MSW, (Masters of Social Work), and a graduate of Southeastern Baptist Theological Seminary where she earned an MACSS, (Masters of Art and Church Social Services).

Will and Carol have three children: Seth, Kate and Dan which begins the ninth generation of Carltons.

The family lives in Flower Mound, Texas, where Will is employed as an Information Technology Consultant.

Pat, Wendy, Jack, Wyatt and Lilli Carlton

Patrick Edwards Carlton, second son of Barbara and Albert Carlton, was born March 5, 1962. He, too, attended public schools, graduating from Hardee High School. Patrick attended the University of Florida and graduated with a degree in Agriculture Science. Later, in 1991, he graduated from Rollins College Crummer Graduate School, Orlando, Florida, with an MBA.

In 1996 Patrick married Wendeline Gay Furen of Gainesville, Lakeland, and Sarasota. She attended the University of Florida, the Laboratory Institute of Merchandising in New York, and graduated from USF with a Bachelor of Science degree in Marketing.

Patrick and Wendy are parents of three children of the ninth generation: the oldest, Lillian Grace, and twin sons, Albert Jackson and Michael Wyatt.

The family now lives in Cashiers, North Carolina, where Patrick works with the family real estate development.

Ā Ā Ā

The first and only daughter of the eighth generation of Carltons is Julie Barbara Carlton McClelland, born August 1964. Like her brothers, Julie attended public schools and graduated from Hardee High School, after which she attended Clemson and the University of Florida where she earned her masters degree in Architecture with a specialty

Ian, Sam, Julie, Fletcher, and Zack McClelland

in Historic Preservation. In May 1990, Julie married Fletcher Kirk McClelland who earned his masters degree in Counseling and Psychological studies at Georgia State University with under graduate work at Gordon College in Massachusetts.

He is a licensed professional Christian Counselor in private practice in Athens, Georgia. Julie and Fletcher have added three children to the ninth generation of Carltons: Sam, Zack, and Ian.

The McClellands live in Watkinsville, Georgia, where Julie continues to take on architectural work.

Ā Ā Ā

Abby, Michelle, Caroline and Charlie Carlton

The third son of the eighth generation of Carltons is Charles Stewart Carlton, born April 1967. Like his brothers and sister, Charlie attended Florida public schools and graduated from Hardee High School. He attended the University of Florida earning a degree in Agriculture Economics.

In 1995, Charlie married Michelle Chira, who graduated with a double major in Political Science and Communications Bachelor of Arts, H. Sophie Newcomb College, Tulane University.

Charlie and Michelle are parents of two children: Caroline and Abby. With the addition of these two, the ninth Carlton generation now numbers eleven.

The family resides in Orlando, Florida, where Charlie is a partner in Lee Chira and Associates.

A̅ A̅ A̅

A LASTING TRIBUTE

Lynmama
Evelyn Dowd Castleberry O'Brien
1909-2000

No book about the Carlton Family could or should be written without tribute to Lynmama, who incidentally was my mother.

She was a mountain of strength and vigor, having raised five children of her own and five other children that were abandoned by their own father.

The mark she left on the Carlton Family was deep and indelible and so intimate to my four children because she was the only grandparent they ever knew or ever had. She made up that void of grandparenthood that is truly reflected in all their lives. She was not only grandmother of my children; she was their Nanny from the moment they were born until she got them out of diapers and their baby beds.

She went to the field to pick strawberries, fishing on Troublesome Creek, cooked breakfast in the woods while we turkey-hunted... all out of pure love and devotion and never complained except when she found out I was pregnant again!

You see, all of my pregnancies occurred in a span of seven years, giving Lynmama a PhD in Grand-Nannying!

She was an integral and vibrant part of this family. She did it all... made jelly, chicken pot pie, hot rolls and biscuits...

Albert never had a mother 'til Lynmama came along.

Her epitaph could well be from the old song, "We loved her and she loved us. We thought she walked on water... "

GRANDAUGHTER JULIE'S LYNMAMA

Julie McClelland: Oh Lynmama...

My clearest and most endearing memory of my Lynmama is of her laughing. When she laughed her entire body was involved in seismic movement. She laughed with her whole self and she literally shook like a bowl full of jelly. She had a way of expressing herself that was so full of life and joy and honesty. You could usually tell what she was thinking because of the expression on her face, but if she didn't think you were getting the message, she had no problem filling you in on her opinion.

It was easy to tell she loved children. She always had Lifesavers in her pocket when she came to visit. She liked to tease us by threatening to take our appendix out as she tossed us up onto the chopping block. She used to cut up oranges for an after-school snack and leave them in the refrigerator for us. She made the best rolls. She was thoughtful and no-nonsense all wrapped up in one delightful grandmotherly package. We had fun-times when we would wear her bra on our heads and she would stick out her false teeth at us to make us squeal. When we misbehaved she was on the job. I had to go cut my own switch several times so she could tan my hide.

Once I thought I had killed her. Charlie was chasing me for some unknown reason and I was running hard and fast to escape. I ran to the back door, opened it fast, ran through it and then slammed it to slow Charlie down. I was still running down the hall looking back over my shoulder when I took Lynmama down! She hit the floor and lay silent. I yelled "Lynmama!" but she didn't answer. I ran out to get help and by the time I came back in, she was sitting up, trying to catch her breath. She forgave me that day and I can't tell you how thankful I am I didn't kill Lynmama.

Later when I graduated from high school, I decided it would be a wonderful adventure for my Lynmama and me to go on a cruise together. My parents graciously arranged it and we set sail for a week long cruise to the Caribbean and Mexico.

Before we got out of port, she was missing in action. I found her a little while later hunched over a slot machine trying to hit the jackpot. What a woman!

She lived many more years and watched as her grandchildren had children of their own. She continued to share her sage advice, but mostly her unbridled opinions about anything from what you named your children to how you looked without lipstick. She was honest and authentic. She touched my life in ways I'll never be able to express or measure.

She certainly was a gift. She was my Lynmama.

Granddaughter Julie and Lynmama

POLAND

What does a widow do with her time?

Real opportunities for service are manifest in almost supernatural ways.

In the fall of 1993, I was invited by General Ollie Peacock to go on a fact-finding mission to Poland under the auspices of The Order of St. Stanislaus regarding a humanitarian assistance program for excess property of the U.S. Government.

Our group was comprised of several doctors and military staff who attended meetings of the consulate in Warsaw, Poland. As a medical doctor I had the privilege of touring a children's hospital in Warsaw.

The medical care of those children was equivalent to the 1950 era of the United States. One of the most striking examples was how the families were involved with the hospital care of their own children, even sleeping in their rooms and tending to them post op. The only thing they lacked was the modern technology of United State medicine. But the deficiency was well complimented by the extraordinary commitment and education of the medical

Dame Dr. Barbara Carlton is knighted by H.S.H. Prince the Count Prince Juliusz Nowina Sokolnicki. (1993)

doctors and their personnel. Most oftern the physicians were educated in London, Paris, and in some U. S. medical schools.

We met with the consulate and the Polish Ministry of Health.

Our visit to Poland resulted in the U. S. Army delivering medical supplies which made a significant difference in this timely humanitarian initiative.

Following this outreach effort, some members were ordained by the exiled prince in Poland as Ladies and Lords of the Sovereign Order of St. Stanislaus (1030-1079), the patron Saint of Poland.

He was named bishop of Krakow by Pope Alexander II, and became a saint of the Roman Catholic Church in 1253. His outspoken attacks against sin in both low and high places led to his death by Poland's King Boleslaw.

The order of St. Stanislaus continues in its mission of outreach to the poor and deprived, and compliments the medical needs of the people of Poland.

This ended an international medical tour of duty and helped fill a void in my life following the death of my husband, Albert.

Dame Dr. Barbara Carlton (1993)

CASHIERS

Hurricanes bring adversity and opportunity.

In September of 1960, Hurricane Donna dealt an almost lethal blow to Wauchula, Florida and a lot of the residents had to leave because of the severe damage done to their homes - no electricity or water.

Albert and Barbara Carlton where victims of this disaster and sought refuge in the mountains of North Carolina where they found the wonderful village of Cashiers and stayed at the High Hampton Inn.

Following the initial visit the Carlton's bought their first mountain home located on No. 3 Green of High Hampton. This became a retreat for the family in summer and winter.

Summertime in Cashiers, N.C. at the Carlton Golf House at High Hampton

Winter in Cashiers, N.C. at the Carlton Golf House at High Hampton

Carlton Log Cabin, High Hemlock, Cashiers, N.C.

In 1976, after the sale of one of the ranches, Albert and Barbara Carlton sought to replace that property and in 1977 made a tax free exchange for 2,000 acres of beautiful native mountain land near Cashiers, N. C. A log cabin was constructed on the property and became the primary residence of the Carlton Family while in Cashiers. The Carltons had become engaged in growing Christmas trees and the four Carlton children spent their summers working in the Christmas tree fields, horseback riding, fishing and golfing.

The log cabin was constructed from authentic 1800's hand hewed hard pine logs from Old Fort, N. C. It symbolizes the true pioneer spirit of those brave early settlers in the world known as Appalachia.

The ax marks truly display the blood, sweat and tears of those brave pioneers.

Barbara and Albert Carlton with their family in Cashiers, N.C. circa 1970

Albert Carlton
CASHIERS COMMUNITY LIBRARY

1992 became a pivotal year in my post-mortem Albert life.

Shortly after Albert's death in 1992, I received a call from Ervin Baumrucker who wanted our family to purchase a site for a new library in Cashiers, North Carolina.

I was thrilled with the idea and told Ervin that I would speak with the family. However, I would need a site plan as to where the library would be located and also a rendering of the proposed building. He sent both to us and we all agreed that such a project would be a wonderful tribute to Albert.

Ervin was a close family friend and continued to nurture that friendship by naming the new proposed library after my husband – The Albert Carlton Cashiers

HEREIN THE FIRST BOOK
✦ ALBERT CARLTON'S BIBLE ✦
A CORNERSTONE
OF SPIRITUAL STRENGTH
AND SOLACE
TO MARK THE BEGINNING
OF A LIBRARY
TO ENRICH OUR HEARTS
SOULS AND MINDS

"BLESSED ARE THOSE
WHO DREAM DREAMS
AND HAVE COURAGE
TO MAKE THEM COME TRUE"

JULY 22, 1994

Photo: Victor Milt

Community Library.

The fund-raising for the new library construction began in June 1992 and was completed by October of the same year.

Our community had raised funds to start the community library and ground-breaking occurred in June 1993.

The library was dedicated in June 1994 as the Albert Carlton Cashiers Community Library. The cornerstone was Albert's own personal Bible.

Even though this was a state of the art new library, it soon became apparent that it was not big enough.

Therefore in 2004, a needs assessment was made for an expansion. These plans included an expanded small performing arts room, new conference room, intimate personal reading lounge, and a children's area with outside reading garden. All this was finally dedicated in 2007.

The Friendship Garden is in honor of Deen Day Smith Sanders and Dr. Barbara Castleberry Carlton. The Garden was dedicated in 2008.

The interior of the Albert Carlton Cashiers Community Library

Dr. Barbara, Dan, Zack, Kate, Seth and Sam at the 1994 dedication of the Albert Carlton Cashiers Community Library.

This portrait of Albert Carlton hangs in the library.

Sandy Bayley, Deen Sanders, Dr. Barbara Carlton and Rev. Virgina Monroe at the dedication of Friendship Garden at the Albert Carlton Cashiers Community Library 2008.

Dr. Barbara Carlton and daughter Julie Carlton McClelland in the Friendship Garden 2008.

CHINQUAPIN

Albert and Barbara Carlton purchased a 2000 acre mountain parcel of land in 1977 in Cashiers, North Carolina. In 1980, the family moved into the first home (a log cabin) at High Hemlock (a 150 acre parcel which has 28 lots and now 15 homes.) The large mountain tract (2000 acres) was managed for recreation, boating, hiking, camping, and fishing for the family and High Hemlock owners.

Photo: Phillip Merritt

Any of several species of deciduous trees of the genus Castanea and evergreen trees and shrubs of the genus Castanopsis, both in the beech family. These porcupine looking clusters house a small black nut - Chinquapin.

In 2005, the family was approached by Trillium Land Company about developing the large tract into 200 home sites. In an effort to carry on the Carlton Legacy of environmental and land stewardship, the family elected to place 700 acres in a conservation easement. This easement will protect the North American Appalachian brook trout as well as the pristine creeks of Robinson, Packs, and Cow Mountain. The waterfalls including Julie, Charlie, Will and Pitty Pat, will be forever protected and enjoyed by generations to come.

The development is named Chinquapin after a small porcupine-looking cluster housing a small black nut – Chinquapin. The Chinquapin tree is a cousin to the American Chestnut that was decimated in a blight back in the early 1930s.

The journey thru Carlton Country that started in Duplin, North Carolina has found its way back from Florida to Cashiers, North Carolina and those descendants emerge as the new pioneers in the Carlton legacy.

First row left to right: Seth, Katie, Dan. Second row left to right: Carol, Will, Wendy, Pat, Michelle, Charlie, Sam, Wyatt, Dr. Barbara, Caroline, Abby, Jack, Lilli, Julie, Fletcher, standing in the back are Ian and Zack.

THE VERY END
Going Home

Those who have loved reading this book must conclude there is an ending.

For nine generations the long and sometimes fragile blood-line has been passed on. The Carlton roots have been totally exposed and the authentic transparent legacy has given the author new insights into the very <u>soul</u> of this family.

The history of the Carlton Family is a rich tapestry embracing the true virtues centered around a strong faith, stewardship, charity and love. In the end those things placed in their hands were lost, but those placed in God's hands endure forever.

A sense of forever pressing mortality now looms over the end of this journey. There is a great reward as the bearers of the Carlton legacy. Eleven grandchildren seek to perpetuate their own imprint into future generations.

It is my hope and prayer that Grandma has been an inspiration in carrying the family toward new heights - may their wings spread like eagles as they embark on life's journey.

As the time to live becomes the time to die, there is a special place at Glenokra at Albert's side where Grandma will revel at the sound of the trumpets.

This nearly was mine.

Your Grandchildren
are the only
earthly
possession
you can take
to Heaven.

Anon

GRANDMA'S LEGACY 2009

**Left to right: Abby, Lilli, Caroline Carlton, Ian McClelland, Kate, Dan
and Seth Carlton, Sam and Zack McClelland, Dr. Barbara Carlton.
In front are twins Wyatt and Jackson Carlton.**

AWARDS

On the same day, Sept. 14th, Dr. Barbara Carlton of Wauchula, Hardee County, was honored with two prestigious recognitions.

The North Carolina Public Library Directors Association selected Dr. Carlton to receive their Benefactor's Award for 2007. This award is presented to an individual who has made significant contributions toward the development of public library services in their community.

Dr. Carlton was nominated for this award by Karen Wallace, Director of the Fontana Regional Library System, for Dr. Carlton's extraordinary contributions to the Albert Carlton Cashiers Community Library.

The North Carolina Public Library Directors Association recognized Dr. Carlton at their annual awards banquet on Thursday, November 29, 2008, at 7 P.M. at the Grandover Resort and Conference Center in Greensboro, North Carolina.

The Foundation of the Georgia Academy of Family Physicians invited Dr. Carlton to be one of their keynote speakers at its inaugural Legacy Club Meeting and Luncheon on November 8, 2008, at high noon at the Cobb Galleria Centre in Atlanta, Georgia. She was asked to speak on her lifelong legacy of giving back to her community. Dr. Ferrol and Dr. Helen Sams were recognized for their lifelong practice of medicine in Fayetteville, Georgia. Dr. Sams is also a well known author of several books and is currently planning his retirement.

The North Carolina Patrons Award, the Albert Carlton-Cashiers Memorial Library, 2007.

Georgia Family Practice Award, 2007.

Since Dr. Carlton's retirement in 1977 she has been deeply involved in community affairs in both Florida and North Carolina. She embarked in helping the Main Street project in Wauchula and spearheaded a fund-raising campaign to establish a new library in Cashiers, North Carolina.

Dr. Carlton makes her home at the Bar A Ranch at Glenokra in the Oak Grove Community, west of Wauchula, Florida.

Ā Ā Ā

CARLTON RANCH AWARDS

Florida Farm Bureau Environmental Stewardship Award, Carlton 2 X 4 Ranch 2001.

National Cattlemen's Beef Association Environmental Stewardship Award, 2003.

Ā Ā Ā

Florida is fortunate to have three Barbara Carltons: Dr. Barbara Carlton whose medical career was spent in Hardee County. Barbara Blanton Carlton of Sarasota County, Florida, was named Florida Woman of the Year in Agriculture 2001. And, Barbara Oxford Carlton, of Arcadia, Florida, is the Executive Director Peace River Valley Citrus Association.

Index

353

Whidden, Mary 87, 133
Whidden, Mary Vashti 32
Whidden, Melt 87
Whidden, Pepper 255
Whitehurst, Dr. James 226, 231, 232
Wiggins, Red 114
Wildlife Management Area 251
Wilkerson, Thomas G. 26
Williams, George 52, 53
Williams, Ted 190, 251, 286
Williams, Zeb 115
Williamson, Brady 284, 286
Willoughby Tillis battle 21
Willoughby Tillis family 15
Wilmington 21
Wilson, Beth Saunders 35
Wilsons XIII
Wilson, Daniel 8
Wilson, Nana 3
Winter Haven 173, 175, 197, 198
Withlacoochee River 277
Wolf Brothers Men's Clothing 261
Wood, Polly 61
Woodruff, George and June 214
Woodruff, Jane 213, 214
World War I 68, 275, 276
World War II 60, 67, 147, 180, 276
WPA 69
Wyatt, Michael 330

Y

Yankee 157, 199

Z

Zanesville 68
Zolfo Springs 62, 119, 141, 170, 175

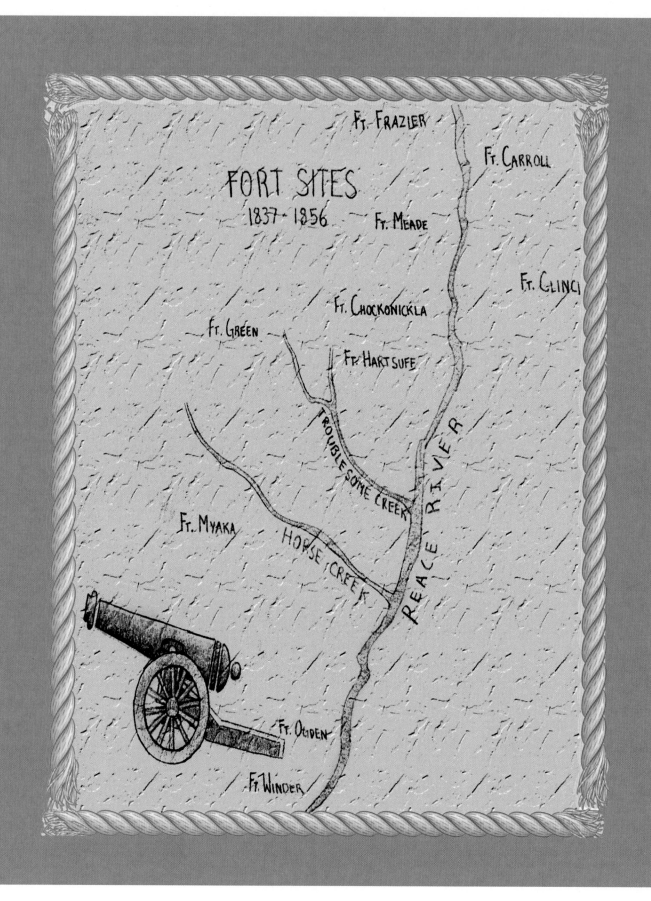